Sunflower
Salvia, Blue
Scabiosa
Clarkia
Chinese
Forget
Cockscomb
Coleus
Peach bell
Catnip
Columbine
Petunia
Carnation
Painted
Daisy
Parsley
Pansy
Cape
Marigold
Zinnia
Coral
Bells
Coreopsis
Canterbury
Bells
Coriander
Candytuft
Vinca
California
Poppy
Wallflower
Calliopsis
Calendula
Lace
Flower
Bells of
Ireland
Virginia
Stock
Borage
Salpiglossis
Begonia
Wax
Sage
Primrose
Pinks
Basil
African
Daisy
Phlox
Balsam
Ageratum
Aster
Balloon
Flower
Snapdragon
Baby's Breath
Bachelor's
Button
Strawflower
Summer
Savory

Seedlings

Seedlings

The ABCs of Gardening

OUTDOOR AND INDOOR

The ABCs of Gardening

OUTDOOR AND INDOOR

Marjorie J. Dietz

Illustrations by Jack Crane

DOUBLEDAY & COMPANY, INC.
GARDEN CITY, NEW YORK

Library of Congress Cataloging in Publication Data

Dietz, Marjorie J.
The ABCs of gardening—outdoor and indoor.

Bibliography: p. 230
Includes index.
1. Gardening. I. Title. II. Title: ABCs of
gardening—outdoor and indoor.
SB453.D593 1985   635   84–13819
ISBN 0-385-18544-8

"Plant a Nosegay Garden" is to be published
in *Family Circle* magazine.

Contents

THREE
BOOKS FOR MORE INFORMATION   230

FOUR
SOURCES FOR SEEDS, PLANTS, AND SUPPLIES   232

INDEX   239

SPECIAL PROJECTS
Additional projects to enjoy as your gardening skills develop

The ABCs of Gardening

OUTDOOR AND INDOOR

ONE

Getting Started in Gardening

Of all the ways and means for making a start in gardening, what could be more logical than beginning with the basics, that is, the ABCs. These basics are as diverse as might be expected from the many-faceted pursuit that gardening surely is. They range from annuals and bulbs to cut flowers, indoor gardening, soil, vegetables, and many, many more.

TAKING THE FIRST STEP

Becoming a new home owner is the introduction to gardening for many people. Although it is an entrance through the back gate, so to speak, a step taken because you want to improve the look of your property, that first step leads to another and before you know it, you are a full-fledged gardener.

But if you're a new home owner, where do you begin? You might turn to *L* for Landscaping in the ABCs section. Make a rough plan of your property, giving careful thought to the sort of layout that will fit the wishes and needs of your family. Probably you will want a terrace and outdoor living area and perhaps hedges for screening and privacy. The entries for these topics, Terraces and Hedges, will help make your property comfortable and attractive.

Making or renovating a lawn may be the next project, and this involves soil. Here again, you can get off to a good start by reading through the sections Lawns and Soil before you begin.

TOOLS AND EQUIPMENT

But nothing can be done without tools and equipment. Upon reading the section on that subject, as a new gardener you will be glad to know that it is unnecessary to acquire a lot of tools at the beginning. A small flower or vegetable garden can be planted with as few tools as a spade or fork, a rake, a trowel, and a watering can.

WHAT'S IN A NAME?

Quite a bit. Before embarking on a plant-buying spree, you should have some knowledge of the correct names of the plants you want. Many plants have several common names and often the same names are applied to quite different plants. However, each plant has only one botanical name, and this is used internationally. No chance of your choosing the wrong plant if you have its botanical name. No one can reel off botanical names at the first venture into gardening, but knowing why they are important and so much more reliable than their often parochial names is a big step toward making their use as easy as rolling off a log. Check the section on Nomenclature—Names of Plants for a fuller explanation of this.

FLOWERS FLOWERS FLOWERS

The great English gardener Gertrude Jekyll, whose name has long been associated with flower gardens, was particularly fond of perennials, especially in long borders. Perennials are once more in vogue (see the entries for Perennials and Borders), although few of the new gardeners they attract probably have anywhere near the space—five acres or so—Jekyll considered necessary for the gardens she envisioned.

And much can be done for more modest space. Small gardens and pots can be filled with masses of color by annuals. Bulbs supply a succession of color, beginning in early spring and continuing into fall. In addition to the entries for Annuals and Bulbs, see those for Evergreens, Shrubs, and Trees. You may soon become a collector of a particular group in any one of these major plant categories.

HERBS AND OTHER SPECIAL GARDEN PLANTS

Then there is the entry for Herbs. Growing them, indoors or outdoors, can soon lead to an almost manic interest in other herbs, including those that were once medicinal but are now mainly ornamental.

The perfection of the rose flower and its often powerful scent lures many into gardening. The entry on Roses tells how to grow and use this ever-popular plant.

A wooded property provides a ready-made setting for growing wild flowers, one of the most enjoyable of gardening specializations and also one requiring the least time in maintenance. Also low in maintenance and for those with larger properties and country places, there is the sunny wild flower meadow. The Wild Flower entry gives all the particulars on this.

INDOOR GARDENING

Indoor gardening gives apartment dwellers the chance to become involved with plants and allows others to continue gardening interests all year. If window exposures are unfavorable, fluorescent lights provide a reliable substitute for sunshine. Creating a bottle or terrarium garden (see the entry Terrariums) is an intriguing experience and in the case of the bottle, also challenging.

FOOD GARDENS

Planting that packet of radish seeds has sent many down the path toward total gardening commitment. Such commitment begins in spring with the arrival of seed catalogues and finally ebbs in temporary dormancy with the harvesting of the last broccoli in late fall. Some edibles can even be grown indoors all year. (See Winter Salads to Grow Indoors in the Vegetables section.)

There are so many good reasons for growing vegetables and

fruits. Flavor and freshness of the home-grown products certainly count, but so do the personal satisfaction of getting so close to the earth and being involved with the coming and passing of various seasons.

THE TECHNIQUES—HOW TO DO IT ALL

The urge to reproduce a neighbor's favorite plant introduces many to the techniques of propagation—rooting plants from cuttings, sowing seeds, and dividing old plants to obtain a number of new ones from each. The entry Propagation tells all about this.

Involvement in one aspect of gardening soon ensnares the new gardener in other related and equally engrossing procedures. Making a flower, vegetable, and shrub garden can lead to the building of compost, an important source of organic matter and, eventually, humus for improving the soil. Mulching can help suppress weeds and reduce the need for frequent watering. Compost, Mulches, Weeds, and Watering in the ABCs section will give you the basic information.

And finally, if you can't find specific information on a particular question in *The ABCs of Gardening,* call the Cooperative Extension Service, which will be listed in the telephone book under the county government. Many problems are of regional concern, and there is no better source for dealing with them than these helpful, friendly people.

By now you have probably caught on to the importance of the basics in getting off to the right start in gardening. All of the elements mentioned here—and many more—can be found in alphabetical order in the text. There is also an Index.

Gardening is meant to be a pleasant pastime. There are almost as many ways to practice it—and enjoy it—as there are gardeners. Do not be afraid to experiment and exercise your own common sense in raising your plants. The roads to gardening success are many, and they lead to much satisfaction and pleasure.

TWO

The ABCs of Gardening

A

ANNUALS. These flowering plants fill an important niche in gardening's ABCs. Annuals tend to bloom and bloom, and with a little assistance from the gardener last all summer.

Annuals have a short—though decidedly merry—life. Their seeds are sown in spring; their delightful flowers appear 6 to 8 weeks later. The plants die at the end of summer or when killed by frosts.

THE MANY ASSETS OF ANNUALS—Their very temporariness makes annuals so useful. You can throw caution to the winds and plant them all over the place. If you make mistakes, no matter, you can easily correct them the next year.

Annuals are especially useful around the brand-new house and its often bare property. Relying on them gives you a chance to become acquainted with new surroundings before investing in permanent plantings. Annuals, because of their temporary nature and comparatively quick methods of propagation, are more reasonable in price than permanent plants. For the same reasons, they are good choices for vacation houses, where quick color effects are needed. With the versatility of annuals, you can change your selections or color combinations each year. But if you discover that a particular annual, for instance impatiens, is carefree and truly everblooming, then by all means, stay with it every summer thereafter.

Annuals fit well into space-restricted situations, including small suburban and city gardens, apartment balconies, and terraces. There is never any need to worry about their outgrowing their limited space in a few years, as can be the case with a shrub or tree. At the other extreme in space, the large country property, annuals can be a special joy. Here there is room to grow many different kinds in large groups and to experiment each spring with new varieties.

The versatility of annuals extends to their source of color: not all comes from flowers. There are several annuals whose leaf colors are as bright as flowers, the best-known example being coleus. Others include snow-on-the-mountain, whose leaves are a cool green and white, while Joseph's coat has leaves in torrid red and yellow. Then there are ornamental peppers. Their shiny red, cream, or yellow miniature fruits stud the low, bushy plants like Christmas ornaments. These little peppers are edible—but hot!

For those who enjoy bringing garden color indoors, annual flowers will supply a summerlong source of bouquet materials. In fact, cutting flowers for indoor arrangements actually benefits the plants by forcing bushy new growth and encouraging flower production. (See also Cut Flowers.) Annuals remain the major source of flowers for dried arrangements. Everlastings is a term for these special annuals that include strawflowers, various ornamental grasses, and several other kinds. (See also Dried Flowers.)

WAYS TO SHOW OFF ANNUALS—Most annuals are sun lovers, but see the Sampler later in the section for some shade-tolerant possibilities. Beyond that main requirement, they are probably the least temperamental of all flowering plants and grow well in a variety of soils (no swamps, though, please) and situations. Most are fine in sea- and lakeside gardens, where they bask in the sun and reflected sparkle from the water.

Perhaps annuals are most colorful when massed in circular or free-form beds, usually on lawns. This use is and has always been common in public gardens and parks, and is where the term "bedding plants" originated. Many home gardeners who have the space are adapting this traditional use for annuals to their own place. An advantage to massed plantings is that little maintenance is required, especially if varieties of low-growing annuals like impatiens, coleus, wax begonia, or geranium are selected. The plants grow together, leaving no space for weeds.

On the other hand, such plantings can be monotonous, and less formal annual gardens are certainly desirable. Place groups of annuals in the bays formed by shrubs; plant narrow borders or beds around terraces and outdoor living areas or along walks and drives. Plan a practical cutting garden adjacent to the vegetable plot that will have the charm of an old-fashioned garden. To accomplish this, study catalogue descriptions, especially heights, and group several of the same kinds of annuals together to get the best color impact. Keep tall annuals to the rear, those of medium height in front of them, and the lower kinds toward the foreground.

If you have a new perennial garden (see Perennials) that has not filled out, add annuals to help carry on a succession of color from midsummer into fall. Most perennial gardens planned today leave permanent space for the addition of annuals.

ANNUALS IN CONTAINERS—Annuals increasingly are being used in containers—pots, tubs, planters, and hanging baskets. Although almost any annual is suitable, those that are not too tall are usually chosen. (However, I recently saw a modern concrete planter filled with three or four plants of a 2- to 3-foot scarlet cockscomb—the effect was striking.)

Container-grown annuals require more attention than do those grown in the open garden. (See Pots and Other Containers.)

A few annuals can be grown as house plants indoors all year round. What is needed is a bright window, preferably one that receives 4 to 5 hours of sun. During the winter months, better

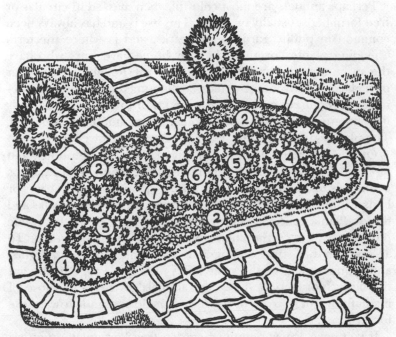

PLAN FOR A WALKAROUND MULTICOLORED GARDEN

This garden, approximately 5 feet wide and nearly 15 feet long and slightly kidney-shaped, can be adapted to any shape or size by increasing or decreasing the space occupied by each plant group. The suggested varieties or similar ones should be available as ready-to-plant seedlings in most garden centers in midspring. Or grow your own seedlings. KEY: **1** Sweet-alyssum (white), 4 to 6 inches high. **2** Ageratum 'Blue Blazer,' 'Blue Angel,' or 'Blue Daniel,' 6 inches. **3** French Marigold 'Yellow Boy,' 'Yellow Janie,' or similar variety, 8 to 10 inches. **4** Zinnia 'Thumbelina,' mixed colors, 6 inches. **5** Zinnia 'Peter Pan Gold,' 10 to 12 inches. **6** Zinnia 'Old Mexico' or 'Persian Carpet,' 12 inches. **7** Zinnia 'Peter Pan Pink,' 10 to 12 inches.

Becoming familiar with the shapes of flowers and growth habits of annuals aids in their uses and arrangement in the garden. Top, left to right: marigold, snapdragon, zinnia. Center: gloriosa daisies and petunias. Bottom: sweet-alyssum.

---

plant growth and blooming result when the plants are grown under fluorescent lights. (See Indoor Gardening.)

The annuals most often grown as house plants include wax begonia (this is really a tender perennial rather than a true annual), coleus, geranium, and impatiens. I had success one spring sowing seeds of sweet-alyssum in eggshell containers (as suggested by Montague Free in *All About House Plants*). The objective was to have seedlings in bloom by Easter, and with the help of fluorescent lights, success was achieved. Some of the following should also make passable house plants. Don't be afraid to experiment!

SOME ANNUALS FOR CONTAINERS

AGERATUM	KOCHIA
BEGONIA, WAX	LOBELIA
BLACK-EYED SUSAN VINE	MARIGOLD
BROWALLIA	NASTURTIUM
COLEUS	PEPPER, ORNAMENTAL
DUSTY MILLER	PETUNIA
FUCHSIA	SWEET-ALYSSUM
GERANIUM	TORENIA
IMPATIENS	VINCA (Madagascar Periwinkle)

GETTING STARTED WITH ANNUALS—There are several options. By far the easiest is to buy seedling plants from local garden centers. These started annuals, often called transplants or bedding plants, are offered in small flats or individual pots for larger plants, and are ready for immediate setting in your own garden. You can have an instant garden in a jiffy (almost). The method is more expensive, though, for the grower has done most of the work.

When buying annual plants, try to catch them at the beginning of the season when they are fresh and before they have begun to outgrow their containers. Choose those that have healthy green leaves. Some plants may be blooming. This is not necessarily an asset, although it does give you the look and color of the bloom. It is usually a good idea to snip off these early blooms when setting out the plants. New flowers will quickly appear.

For more fun and the satisfaction of growing annuals from their seeds and for greater economy, start annuals from seed yourself. As a first step, send for mail-order seed catalogues (see Sources for Seeds, Plants, and Supplies at the end of the book), which are usually ready about the first of the year. Some seed catalogues are prone to exaggeration, but the good ones are packed with nuggets of information. The color photographs, besides being inspirational, allow you to become acquainted with the plants before you grow them.

A second source for seeds is the local hardware store or garden center. Here some of the better-known mail-order seed companies and others that never sell by mail set up display racks that contain a wide offering of flower and vegetable seeds.

ANNUALS TO SOW INDOORS—Before sowing one seed, indoors or outdoors, it pays to read the seed packet. All sorts of growing and sowing information is listed, such as when to sow, how deep to plant the seeds, and how far apart to space them in the seedling stage.

Some annuals, such as petunia, snapdragon, and impatiens, need a longer growing time before they are mature enough to flower. They are the ones it pays to sow indoors in early spring—a good 6 to 8 weeks before it is safe to set them outdoors. (But they are also the ones you can buy as bedding plants at garden centers.)

The plain facts on indoor seed sowing are that it is not as simple a procedure as rolling off a log! The environment of many a house is often too warm and dry and lacking in sufficient light. Yet indoor seed sowing can be successful if you are willing to follow a few common-sense guidelines (see Propagation for details). Using fluorescent tubes to augment your weak window light is almost a necessity.

Many eager gardeners, who desire the earliest possible bloom outdoors, often sow faster-maturing annuals indoors—in addition to the slowpoke petunia. These faster-growing annuals can be sown indoors a little later—usually 4 to 5 weeks before it is safe to plant them outside.

ANNUALS TO SOW INDOORS IN EARLY SPRING

AGERATUM	LOBELIA
BEGONIA, WAX	PEPPER, ORNAMENTAL
COLEUS	PETUNIA
DUSTY MILLER	SALVIA (Sage)
GERANIUM	SNAPDRAGON
HOLLYHOCK (annual types)	VERBENA
IMPATIENS	VINCA (Madagascar Periwinkle)

ANNUALS TO SOW OUTDOORS—The first seeds to sow outdoors are those classified as cold-hardy annuals. In fact, they germinate better in cool soil and are not too successful if you wait until the soil has warmed. Sweet peas and larkspur (annual delphinium) are two prime examples and you have to be the early-bird in the garden to get them off to the right start.

If you have doubts about the proper time to start seed sowing outdoors, check with your friendly extension agent, who is usually listed in the telephone directory under the county government. (See also Cooperative Extension Agents or Specialists.)

COLD-TOLERANT ANNUALS TO SOW OUTDOORS IN EARLY SPRING

BACHELOR-BUTTON (Cornflower)	LARKSPUR
CALENDULA	LOVE-IN-A-MIST (Nigella)
CALIFORNIA-POPPY	STOCKS
CLEOME (Spider Flower)	SWEET-ALYSSUM
GLORIOSA DAISY	SWEET PEA

There is yet another group of annuals, rather tender ones, whose seeds germinate best in a warm soil and after heavy frosts have ceased. Many old favorites, such as marigolds and zinnias, belong here.

Outdoors, you have the choice of sowing seeds in a special seed bed (see Propagation), from which they are transplanted to their permanent blooming sites, or sowing the seeds where they are to bloom. Seeds of sweet-alyssum, one of the quickest annuals to reach blooming size and an ideal edging plant, can simply be scattered over lightly scratched soil where they are to flower. Seeds of larkspur, California-poppy, and portulaca can also be handled in this easy fashion.

ANNUALS TO SOW OUTDOORS AFTER THE SOIL HAS WARMED

CHINA-ASTER	MORNING GLORY
COSMOS	NASTURTIUM
DAHLIA	PHLOX (Annual)
FLOWERING TOBACCO (Nicotiana)	PORTULACA
MARIGOLD	SUNFLOWER
MOONFLOWER	ZINNIA

SETTING OUT ANNUAL PLANTS—This is a simple procedure, whether the plants are home-grown from seeds or purchased at a garden center. The plants are small and have a limited root system compared to many perennials and shrubs.

The annuals you buy as bedding plants are often in divided flats, like eggs in their cartons. The annuals are easily popped out by pushing up the bottom of each compartment. Sometimes the flats are not divided. To avoid mangling the roots and plant tops when removing them, first take a sharp knife and cut around each plant—as though you were dividing a pan of baked brownies.

Still other purchased annuals are sometimes sold in peat pots. In this case, set out plant and pot together, as the peat will gradually disintegrate. You will notice that the roots are probably already growing through the peat walls.

Before cultivating the soil prior to planting, spread about 2 to 3 pounds per 100 square feet of an all-purpose fertilizer such as 5-10-5 over the area (see also Fertilizers) and fork it into the soil to a depth of 4 to 5 inches or so. (See also Digging and Soil.) Rake over the soil to level it and remove any surface stones.

Annuals that you have grown from seeds indoors must undergo a gradual adjustment to the outdoor environment before being permanently planted. This process is known as "hardening off." (See also Propagation.)

Annual seedlings grown outdoors are readily transplanted, preferably with a narrow-bladed trowel, and should then be thoroughly watered. Avoid transplanting or setting out purchased plants on a windy day. Keep seedlings shaded with sheets of newspaper while they are out of the ground. Check seed packages for planting distances. In general, most annuals should be set from 6 to 10 inches apart. One caution when setting out plants in peat pots: dig a hole deep enough to fit the entire pot and be sure the pot's rim is beneath the surface. Water thoroughly after firming the soil over and around the pot.

MAINTENANCE TIPS—Annuals are truly labor-saving plants. Some kinds, such as impatiens and wax begonias, require no follow-up attention except the enjoyment of their nonstop flower display.

Attack weeds when they are small. I am an advocate of close spacing of most annuals to crowd out weeds—even if the plants themselves are a bit overcrowded. Better that than a weed patch! (See also Weeds.)

Snip off fading flowers and developing seed heads, cutting just above a set of healthy leaves. Annuals can become obsessive about forming seeds and race to accomplish this before the fall-winter deadline, when frost ends their existence. Once seeds form, the plant's main reason for flowering ends, and it is downhill thereafter as the plant declines in vigor.

Cut off fading flowers of zinnias, marigolds, and other annuals before seeds have formed. Make the cut just above healthy foliage.

Do not overfertilize annuals. That early application may be adequate if your soil is reasonably fertile. If plants appear lean and yellowish, apply a quick-acting liquid fertilizer, mixed according to instructions on the container. Do not fertilize in bone-dry soil.

Annuals growing in containers may require daily watering. The soil around annuals in the garden should be well soaked when droughts occur. (See also Watering.)

⬚⬚⬚⬚ A SAMPLER OF ANNUALS ⬚⬚⬚⬚

Ageratum or Floss Flower *(Ageratum houstonianum)*. Sun or light shade. Fluffy flower heads in lavender-blue shades and white. Height 5 to 10 inches. Space about 6 inches apart. Fine for massing or edging. Buy plants or start seeds indoors.

China-aster *(Callistephus chinensis)*. Sun. Flowers in wide color range resemble chrysanthemums. Height 6 to 24 inches. Space 6 to 15 inches apart according to variety. Buy plants or sow seeds indoors or outdoors when soil warms.

Coleus *(Coleus* x *hybrida)*. Sun to part shade. Brilliant foliage colors and varying leaf shapes. Height 8 to 15 inches. Space 8 to 12 inches apart. Prefers humus-rich soil—mix in peat moss before planting. Versatile annual—use in pots or as border or background for other annuals. Can be massed in formal beds. Buy plants or start seeds indoors.

Cosmos *(Cosmos* species). Sun. Two types: The early-flowering, 3-foot Klondike varieties in gold and yellow to fiery red; space 8 to 10 inches apart. Sensation varieties in white, pink, rose, on 4-foot bushy plants useful for background and cutting: space 10 to 12 inches apart. Sow seeds indoors, or outside after soil warms.

Impatiens *(Impatiens wallerana)*. Sun to shade. Perhaps the most widely grown annual today. Too popular? It has crowded its old-fashioned relative, the garden balsam, right out of the garden. Many other favorites may be in danger of the same fate. Yet there is no annual so floriferous, so accommodating, so versatile. Prefers humus-rich soil—add peat moss to planting holes—that never dries out. Many varieties, varying in color, habit, and height, from 6 to 15 inches. Start seeds indoors in early spring or buy plants. Easy to grow from cuttings (see Propagation), and scattered seeds from last year's plants often germinate as the soil warms. Plant from 8 to 12 inches apart according to variety. This is one plant that keeps up its flower production while forming seeds.

Lobelia *(Lobelia erinus)*. Sun or light shade. Dainty violet-blue to white flowers. Height about 4 inches. Space 4 inches apart. For containers and edging. Buy plants or sow seeds indoors in early spring.

Marigold (*Tagetes* species). Sun. Yellow, orange, and rich red colors recently joined by the once-elusive whites. Bushy, profuse bloomers from low-growing French to 3-foot African types. Space 6 to 10 inches apart according to variety. Marigolds are marvelous, long-lasting cut flowers. Versatile—use in containers, as edging, for mass effects, and for variety in flower gardens.

Morning Glory (*Ipomoea* species). Sun. Fast-growing twining vine with true blue, white, rose, or red flowers. Height 8 feet. Space 12 inches apart. With support, plants make thick screen. Sow seeds where they are to flower, as seedlings resent transplanting. Before sowing, you can soak hard-coated seeds overnight in a glass of water.

Petunia (*Petunia* x *hybrida*). Sun or light shade. Fragrant flowers in wide color range. Height 12 to 15 inches. Space 10 inches apart. For foreground, massing, and containers, especially hanging ones. Plants tend to peter out in hot, humid weather. When plants become straggly and vinelike, cut back about halfway and fertilize. In a few weeks they should show renewed vigor, but alas, sometimes they don't respond. Buy plants or start seeds indoors in early spring.

Snapdragon (*Antirrhinum majus*). Sun. Fragrant flowers in spikes in wide color range. Height 7 inches to 3 feet, according to variety. Space from 12 to 18 inches apart. Long-blooming stately plants for background in flower gardens. Popular cut flower. Sow seeds indoors in early spring or buy plants.

Sweet-alyssum (*Lobularia maritima*). Sun. Small, dainty flowers, fragrant, from white to rose, cover creeping plants. Space 3 to 4 inches apart. For edging, also containers and hanging baskets. Sow seeds where they are to flower, then transplant as necessary to fill in empty spaces. Self-sows. Use scissors to trim off fading flowers and seed heads about midsummer.

Wax Begonia (*Begonia semperflorens*). Sun and part shade. Rose, pink, red, white flowers above waxy foliage in green, bronze, and maroon tints. Height 8 to 12 inches. Space 8 to 12 inches apart. Breeders have made this old-fashioned house plant into a mod-

Give sweet-alyssum plants a haircut when flower production seems to lag in summer by trimming off seeds and fading flower heads with garden shears or scissors. Do not cut the plants off at ground level. In the fall, allow seeds to develop. They will germinate the following spring.

ern everblooming wonder for borders and massed effects. Slow from seed: start in winter indoors. Or buy as bedding plants.

Zinnia (*Zinnia* species). Sun. Single and double flower heads in wide color range, including chartreuse 'Envy' variety. Heights 6 to 26 inches. Space from 8 to 12 inches apart, according to variety. 'Peter Pan' zinnias, 12 inches tall, are outstanding bedding plants for mass color effects. Easy from seeds when ground warms. Or sow a few weeks earlier indoors or in a cold frame. (See also Cold Frames.)

☒☒☒☒ A SPECIAL PROJECT ☒☒☒☒
ANNUALS FOR AN ALL-WHITE GARDEN

The more familiar you become with annuals, the more apparent is their versatility. Trying something different each year can add some zing to the seed selection process and of course carry over into the garden design. Planning a flower garden of different flowers—but specializing in the same color throughout—can provide a challenge and a bit of that zing. Relying on annuals makes it possible to change the chosen color each spring.

The all-white garden is a restful switch from the vibrant, nervous colors that seem to be the rage today in so many popular annuals. The logical place for it, with its white flowers showing so clearly at night, is just off a patio or close to any outdoor living area used in the evening. Most people use their swimming pools at night, making the garden around the pool another possibility.

It pays to plan this garden well ahead of planting time, as you may want to order some of the seeds from mail-order firms. You can also buy seeds from racks in garden centers. Or you can wait until garden centers and nurseries offer bedding plants, which is usually about the right time to set the plants in the ground. However, you may have to do some searching to find white varieties of the annuals you decide to use in your design. This is all part of the challenge of planting a one-color garden.

Here is a list of suggested white annuals. Most should have the stamina to survive summer and continue into fall if their fading flowers are cut off before seeds form. If you decide on some petunias—and their fragrance can be so pervasive in the evening that they are almost essential—more drastic pruning back may be required when blooming slows. (The annuals are listed according to their heights, starting with the lowest.)

ANNUALS FOR A WHITE GARDEN

Sweet-alyssum 'Carpet of Snow.' 4 inches. Sow seeds.

Ageratum 'Summer Snow' or any white. 5 inches. Buy plants.

Impatiens 'Imp White,' 1 to 2 feet, 'Elfin White,' 6 to 12 inches. Buy plants or start seeds indoors in early spring.

Dusty Miller. Silvery white leaves. 9 to 10 inches. Buy plants or sow seeds indoors early.

Petunia Multiflora 'White Joy' or other white. 12 inches. Buy plants or sow seeds indoors in early spring. The class of Multiflora petunias, which has slightly smaller flowers than some other varieties, seems to be more weather-resistant.

Snow on the Mountain *(Euphorbia marginata)*. Green and white leaves. 12 to 18 inches. Sow seeds after soil warms.

Flowering Tobacco *(Nicotiana)*. 'White Bedder' or 'Nicki White.' 15 to 18 inches. Sow seeds after soil warms. Plants may be available.

Marigold 'Snowbird.' 18 inches. Sow outdoors after soil warms, but for earlier bloom of this particular variety, Burpee suggests sowing seeds indoors 6 weeks before last frost in your region.

Zinna 'Big Snowman' or any white you can find. 2½ feet. Sow seeds after soil warms.

Snapdragon 'Topper White' or any white variety. 3 feet. Buy plants or sow seeds indoors in early spring.

Cleome or **Spider Flower** 'Helen Campbell' or 'White Queen.' 3½ feet. Sow seeds after soil warms.

▨▨▨▨ A SPECIAL PROJECT ▨▨▨▨
PLANT A NOSEGAY GARDEN

The old-fashioned nosegay, a bouquet of tightly arranged flowers enclosed in a lace doily, can be the inspiration for a circular garden bed of carefree annuals with a center accent of miniature roses. Unlike the nosegay, which can give pleasure only for a few days, this little garden will be decorative all summer. If possible, it should be located off a raised terrace or other outdoor living area where you can enjoy its plant pattern and mingling flower fragrances. By midsummer, there should be enough flowers to supply cutting material so you can design your own nosegays, nestled in paper-lace doilies and tied with ribbon. (First wrap the stems in foil to keep them in place and to retain freshness.)

DESIGNING THE GARDEN—Start with a circular bed about 6 feet in diameter located in full sun. Choose plants for their suitability to the subject (for instance, sweet-alyssum 'Carpet of Snow' plants for a white edging that simulates the lacy doily of the bouquet), their durability, and ability to bloom abundantly all summer (with a little help from you), and near uniformity of growth.

You may not agree with the plant choices that follow and may wish to conduct a treasure hunt of your own for appropriate plants. While you pore over seed catalogues, remember that you need low-growing, especially floriferous, plants that may possess a bit of the nostalgic charm of the traditional nosegay.

Some fragrance is essential if the garden is to be a replica of a nosegay, one of its definitions being "a pretty bouquet for the nose." Besides the lacy effect of its multitude of tiny white flowers, sweet-alyssum gives a delicate honey scent.

Although ageratum 'Blue Blazer,' the annuals that follow
sweet-alyssum in my nosegay plan, are barely fragrant, their fluffy
lavender-mauve flower clusters on mounded 6-inch plants are
just right for a living nosegay. They contrast well with the
rounded dwarf zinnia flowers that come next. Even today's newest hybrid zinnias have an unpretentious, cheerful mien that is
reminiscent of yesterday's gardens. The fairly new dwarf 'Short
Stuff' zinnias grow about 8 inches tall, but their flowers are 2½ to
3 inches in diameter, which can result in a well-delineated color
pattern. Zinnia 'Short Stuff Pink' seems a good choice, but the
series contains the usual good clear zinnia colors.

Another good dwarf zinnia is 'Thumbelina.' Its plants reach
about 6 inches and are covered all summer with dainty 1½- to 2-
inch flowers, available in a mixture or separately as 'Mini Pink' or
'Mini Salmon.'

Traditionally, the center of a nosegay bouquet is a fragrant
rose, often a partially opened bud. The solution for the center
spot in the nosegay garden is a miniature rose bush. Actually,
there should be space for three to six, depending on variety. Just
be sure to choose fragrant miniatures that are generous with their
blooms.

In fact, miniature roses have such endearing qualities that they
deserve even more use in the living nosegay and could be substituted for the ring of zinnias suggested above. In this case, the
center position could be occupied by a single large plant of lavender *(Lavandula)* or three small ones. The long-lasting spikes of
lavender's flowers repeat the pleasing lilac-blue shades of ageratum. Even more welcome is the familiar and powerful fragrance
emitted by every part of the plant. (See Herbs.)

Other choices for the center of the nosegay garden are the old-
fashioned purple-flowered heliotrope, white or lavender-blue petunias, or snapdragons—all of which offer delightful summer
scents.

As with the All-White Annual Garden that precedes this, you
have the choice of growing the plants for the nosegay garden
from seed or obtaining transplants from local garden centers.
You can even sow sweet-alyssum and zinnia seeds in place, once

you have outlined your circular garden bed (ground limestone makes a good marking material).

Space the plants from 4 to 6 inches apart, even closer for the sweet-alyssum. It's better to err on the side of crowding in the nosegay garden, where the aim is to quickly obtain a definite color pattern.

A LITTLE MAINTENANCE—To keep the nosegay garden looking like a nosegay, follow the various suggestions in the section on Annuals. That is, remove fading flowers and renew the sweet-alyssum plants with an occasional haircut.

You must spray or dust the miniature roses every 10 days or so to prevent unsightly mildew and especially black spot disease and to discourage such pests as aphids. (See also Roses and Pests and Diseases.)

B

BIENNIALS. In between short-lived annuals and more permanent perennials are biennials, which usually have a 2-year lifespan. During the first growing season, a biennial develops a root system and above-ground stems and leaves. The second year it produces flowers and seeds, then dies.

The pansy is a well-known biennial. Its seeds are sown in early to late summer, with the young plants spending the winter in the open ground (or in a cold frame's protection in very cold climates), then begin to flower in early spring. By the time hot weather arrives, the pansy plant begins to peter out. Other biennials with a similar life cycle are Canterbury bells, foxglove, hollyhock, and sweet William.

Since most biennials bloom from late spring to early summer, they should be displayed in a flower garden planned for that period. When set out in groups of three to five or more plants, the tapering spikes of foxgloves contribute impressive architectural elements to the background of the garden. Canterbury bells and sweet William have more brightly colored flowers.

GETTING STARTED WITH BIENNIALS—An easy way to make their acquaintance is to buy them as bedding plants in spring. The plants, if not in bloom, soon will be, giving you opportunity to enjoy their flowers and decide whether you want to grow your own from seed.

The seeds of most kinds are sown in the open ground or in a special seed bed (see Propagation) from late spring to summer. Then in midsummer, the young plants are transplanted to about 6 to 12 inches apart, where they can remain until being placed in their final blooming positions in the garden. If this sounds like too much bother, you can skip one transplanting operation by moving the seedlings to their final place in the garden—if there is space. The English used to have what they called "a reserve garden," where young plants were set out in rows until needed in the garden proper. Such a nursery area works very well with biennials, as they can be moved even when in bud and flower. When they have finished their blooming, they can be yanked out, and their empty spots filled with annuals or perhaps chrysanthemums.

Not to add additional confusion to an already arcane classification, it should be pointed out that not all biennials behave as they should. Hollyhocks sometimes act like perennials, living longer than 2 years. And sometimes biennials do not bloom the second year, as they are supposed to, usually because the seeds were sown too late the previous year. Such plants often survive and bloom the third year. Most biennials, especially the foxglove and hollyhock, when allowed to form seeds, happily scatter them all over the garden, giving the impression that the same plants are living on year after year.

▨▨▨▨ A SAMPLER ▨▨▨▨
OF BIENNIAL PLANTS

Canterbury Bells *(Campanula medium)*. Spikes of beautiful, large pink, white, lavender-blue bells on bushy 2- to 3-foot plants. Sun, but young plants develop well in filtered sun to light shade the first summer. In cold regions, carry plants over winter in a cold frame.

Foxglove *(Digitalis purpurea).* Drooping bell-shaped flowers, white, pink, on tall 4- to 5-foot stalks from rather massive foliage clumps. Does well in part shade. Plants left on their own in informal setting or shaded wild flower garden will self-sow, making a striking display in early summer each year.

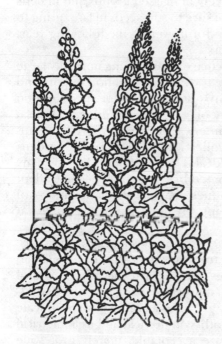

Three popular biennials are the stately foxglove, often-towering hollyhock, and cheerful pansy.

Hollyhock *(Alcea rosea).* A background plant, as the round single or double flowers, pink, rose, dark red, yellow, appear on 6-foot stalks. Sun. Tolerant of dryish soils.

Pansy *(Viola* x *wittrockiana).* In spring, everyone's favorite. Plants are widely available, but the best ones are those you grow yourself from seeds. They can be sown as late as early August in most of the North. Seedlings develop quickly during the cool autumn days. Transplant once, allowing about 6 to 8 inches between plants. In very cold regions, protect over winter in a cold frame, otherwise they are hardy enough to survive in the open ground with light mulching. (See Mulches and Mulching.) In spring, the plants, already in bloom, can be moved to their display area in sun or light shade.

Sweet William *(Dianthus barbatus)*. Tightly packed flower clusters, sweetly fragrant, in salmon, deep velvety red, pink, white, on bushy 24-inch plants. Sun. Lovely in massed groups and in beds adjoining a terrace. Caution: be sure to sow seeds in late spring to give the plants time to develop for flowering the following year.

BONE MEAL. See Fertilizers

BONSAI. The Japanese practice of maintaining normally large trees and shrubs in a permanent dwarfed condition in pots and trays is an example of the many opportunities for specialization that exist in the varied world of gardening. Authentic bonsai (pronounced bone-sigh) specimens that can be viewed and appreciated like works of art in collections of many public gardens may be hundreds of years old and are priceless. Yet so many Americans have become fascinated by this art and become adept at the special cultural techniques that excellent imitations of these aged specimens are being created—if not overnight, at least in relatively quick time.

Bonsai combines both aesthetic principles and growing skills. The object is to duplicate a tree or shrub that has remained comparatively dwarfed as it ages over the years because of natural yet difficult conditions, such as a precarious existence on a windblown mountain ledge. A plant grown as a bonsai must be in scale with its container and while both symmetrical and asymmetrical shapes, as found in nature, are acceptable, merely grotesque forms are to be avoided.

SUITABLE PLANTS—Almost any hardy young woody plant, except one with very large leaves, which would spoil the balance that must exist between trunk and foliage or between the plant and its container. A quick way to start a bonsai is to dig a seedling from the wild—perhaps a juniper—that already shows a promising shape. Or collect any tree or shrub seedlings from your place or along the road and start training them. A third way is to visit a garden center or nursery and choose a young but well-developed evergreen with needlelike foliage that is in a container and ready for the necessary pruning and training. Small-leaved evergreen azaleas are other possibilities. However, bonsai is not confined to evergreen plants, although these are usually easier for beginners. Various kinds of small-leaved maples, including Japanese varieties, birches, and other plants that drop their leaves in winter are often used.

GROWING SKILLS INVOLVED IN BONSAI—Meticulous pruning of roots to maintain the dwarf stature of the plant usually starts at the first potting and continues thereafter—usually yearly for young plants, less often for older ones. Also necessary is pruning of the branches and twigs as needed to obtain and maintain a chosen shape and to keep the plant in scale with its container and roots.

Some shaping is often reached by means of soft wire wound around stems or branches to force them to bend in a desired direction. The wire is usually kept in place for a year or less.

Careful attention must be paid to watering, especially critical because the roots are confined in small containers with little soil.

In cold climates, overwintering bonsai subjects can be a problem. Because most plants are hardy, they cannot endure the dry, hot rooms of most houses. And even though hardy to winter cold when growing in the open ground, these container-bound plants cannot survive long freezing periods or the alternate freezing and thawing temperatures of many northern regions. Possible solutions to these problems are protected but mostly frost-free rooms and breezeways, cool greenhouses, and cold frames. Some specialists remove the plants from their containers, set them rather deeply in trenches, then cover with leaves.

INDOOR BONSAI—Although frowned upon by some purists, a recent twist to the ancient art of bonsai has evolved that eliminates the overwintering problem in cold climates. Indoor bonsai, which uses tender plant material normally grown as house plants, not only solves the overwintering problem, it also considerably speeds the whole procedure of training a bonsai. It has become a very popular hobby in Florida and other mild climates too warm for most of the usual hardy bonsai subjects.

Indoor bonsai is a good introduction to the more complicated and longer process of creating a bonsai from hardy plants.

Some house plants that adapt to bonsai include forms of English ivy, grape-ivy, Otaheite orange and other kinds of citrus, figs, such as the weeping and mistletoe, gardenia, jade plant, Singapore-holly, pittosporum, podocarpus, dwarf pomegranate, tender evergreen azaleas (the kind available from florists during the winter), and the herbs rosemary and myrtle.

For detailed instructions, you must consult some of the excellent books on bonsai. Many are filled with inspiring and useful illustrations.

BORDER. A garden that is considerably longer than it is wide. A term once familiar to gardeners and nongardeners alike was "herbaceous border," a long, graceful garden, perhaps 60 feet long by 5 feet wide, of perennial flowering plants arranged in informal drifts with the tallest plants in the background, medium-height ones in the center, and the lowest in the foreground. Although still seen on large properties to some extent and in public gardens, the herbaceous border is somewhat in eclipse today because of smaller properties and concern for maintenance-free gardening. More modern, modest borders usually contain a mixture of annuals, some bulbs, and perennials to extend the blooming season as long as possible with less effort.

In addition to herbaceous or mixed flower borders, there are shrub borders. In today's landscapes, these are most often planted along the boundaries of properties. The bays between the shrubs can be filled with groups of annuals and perennials.

The term "bed" is often used to designate a round, square, rectangular, triangular, or any formal geometrical or free-form garden that is the opposite in shape to a border. (See also Annuals, Bulbs, Perennials, and Shrubs.)

BOTTLE GARDEN. See Terrariums and Bottle Gardens.

BULBS. The contribution in beauty that bulbous plants make to our flower gardens and landscapes is enormous. There are kinds of bulbs for each season, even bulbs for indoor bloom as house plants.

Perhaps the best-known bulb of all is the edible onion. Favorite garden bulbs include the tulip, daffodil or narcissus, hyacinth, and lily. These are all considered "true" bulbs—a bulb being defined as an underground storage organ of the plant, actually a sort of stem, that contains an embryo flower while dormant.

Not technically bulbs, but often similar in appearance and in growing requirements, are corms and tubers. The beloved crocus and the summer-flowering gladiolus both grow from corms. The caladium, popular in summer for its highly colored foliage, the dahlia, tuberous begonia, and essential potato and sweet-potato are tubers.

As well as there being bulbs for every season, there are bulbs for every purpose and every kind of garden. But before making any choices for your garden, you should have at least a nodding acquaintance with the various kinds and when they bloom.

BULBS FOR SPRING

DEPENDABLE DAFFODILS—Daffodils or narcissus (botanically *Narcissus*) might as well be named *the* spring flower. Some have large, bold, trumpet-shaped flowers while others have more shallow cup-shaped centers or crowns. Some daffodils are dainty and miniature in scale, others stately and dramatic.

On small properties, groupings of daffodils—from five to twenty or so of the same variety—can be planted in shrub borders, under high-branched trees where they receive good light in the spring, or in gardens around a patio. This last use can be very uplifting in early spring when the flowers can be viewed from indoor comfort while the outside weather is blustery.

Daffodils are rugged enough to endure in nearly wild situations that are typical of larger properties. In bulb catalogues, you will notice mixtures of daffodils sold for "naturalizing." Naturalized plantings are the gardener's way of imitating nature's landscaping methods. (See also Naturalizing.) In the case of daffodils and other spring bulbs, the bulbs are usually scattered over the ground—a lawn area, meadow, or sections of a woodland, beside a drive or informal path, on a slope—and then planted where they have fallen. They remain in the ground for years, the cheering display improving each season as the bulbs multiply.

All spring-blooming bulbs must be planted in the fall, the earlier the better. Daffodils, in common with other bulbs, are not especially fussy about soil, as long as it is not perennially soggy.

It's a good idea to apply fertilizers before planting the bulbs (unless the soil has been recently fertilized). To encourage sturdy root development, use fertilizers like superphosphate or bone meal, which are high in phosphorus. (See also Fertilizers.) Either one of these can be spread over the ground (bone meal at rate of 5 pounds per 100 square feet and superphosphate at rate of 3 to 4 pounds per 100 square feet) and forked into the soil to a depth of about 8 to 9 inches. (See Digging.) Or for larger areas, use a rotary tiller. When few bulbs are being planted, a scant handful of fertilizer can be well mixed into the planting hole for each bulb.

New gardeners often fuss unnecessarily about planting bulbs. For a start, it helps to plant them right side up! Most bulbs are roughly cone-shaped, with the point being the top from which stem, leaves, and flowers will emerge. (If you plant the bulbs upside down, they will eventually come up.) Planting depths for daffodils are about 4 inches deep for the small bulbs to 7 to 8 inches deep for the largest. These depths are from the bottoms, not the tips of the bulbs. Space smaller varieties about 4 to 5 inches apart, the large trumpets from 6 to 8 inches.

Not all daffodils bloom at the same time in spring. Some are very early and others do not flower until spring seems on the wane. You can enjoy several weeks of daffodils by choosing varieties according to their blooming times.

10 TIME-TESTED DAFFODILS

Name	Bloom Time	Color	Height
BEERSHEBA	early	white	18 inches
DUKE OF WINDSOR	midseason	orange cup, white petals	18 inches
ICE FOLLIES	midseason	yellow cup fades to white	16 inches

KILWORTH	late	orange-red crown, white petals	19 inches
LOUISE DE COLIGNY	very late	pink crown, fragrant	16 inches
PINK RIM	late	pink crown, white petals	16 inches
PEEPING TOM	very early	yellow	14 inches
SPELLBINDER	midseason	inner yellow of trumpet fades to white	20 inches
TÊTE-À-TÊTE	early	yellow	5 inches
THALIA	late	white	16 inches

TULIPS FOR A RAINBOW IN THE GARDEN—Tulips continue the spring show started by daffodils, with some of the earliest tulips blooming with the daffodils. If you were to plant a sampler of tulip varieties from the early, midseason, and late classifications, you could enjoy 8 weeks of tulip color.

And what a rainbow of color it is. There is special elegance in the sculptured beauty of the tulip flower and its dark green crisp foliage.

Tulips are superb in a flower border, where they combine and contrast so well with all the early-flowering perennials. The bulbs can be planted close together in graceful drifts of a dozen or more of the same variety. Or in small gardens, place five to six bulbs in clumps or circles at intervals.

As with all spring bulbs, the foliage must be retained after flowering is over (but cut off the fading flower) to feed the bulbs for next year's blooming. By summer, this ripening process ends and the foliage dries up. Fill the spaces left with annuals, either as seedlings or scattered seeds.

Tulips look good in front of shrubs, in terrace plantings, or in double or triple rows along paths or drives. (Single rows never look right.) Although most tulips seem too formal for the natural-istic settings that suit daffodils so well, the early low-growing waterlily tulip (Kauffmanniana types), the Greigii hybrids, and

Fosteriana hybrids do not look out of place in drifts in open woodlands or in a meadow.

Tulip bulbs must be planted in the fall. The suggestions for fertilizing and soil preparation recommended for daffodils apply as well to tulips. However, the largest tulip bulbs can be planted quite deep, 8 to 12 inches. Supposedly, this places the bulbs below the runs of mice, may prevent the bulbs from being accidentally chopped up while dormant (which can easily happen in a flower garden), and slows the splitting of the bulbs that can result in smaller flowers the next year.

10 TIME-TESTED TULIPS

Name	Bloom Time	Color	Height
APRICOT BEAUTY	midseason	apricot-rose	16 inches
BLUE PARROT	late	lilac	24 inches
BURGUNDY LACE	midseason	wine-red	20 inches
PALESTRINA	midseason	salmon-pink	20 inches
QUEEN OF BARTIGONS	midseason	light pink	24 inches
RED EMPEROR	early	bright red	15 inches
RED RIDING HOOD	early	scarlet	8 inches
THE BISHOP	midseason	deep violet	30 inches
WHITE HAWK	early	white	14 inches
WHITE TRIUMPHATOR	midseason	white	26 inches

HYACINTHS—FRILLY AND FRAGRANT—Hyacinths are very pretty with their bell-shaped flowers so tightly packed along the fleshy stems. Only a few bulbs are needed to fill the spring air with intoxicating fragrance.

Hyacinths can be used in situations similar to those recommended for tulips. The bulbs are often planted in formal geometric or round beds in public parks, a use that can be adapted to the home garden. For instance, you would need about twenty-five bulbs for a round bed 3 feet in diameter. After the foliage has ripened, plant annuals for summer flowers.

A caution: don't plant hyacinth bulbs in too windy a location, as the heavy spikes are bound to be blown over. A mud-spattered hyacinth wallowing on the ground is indeed a fallen beauty. Plant the bulbs from 6 to 8 inches deep and about 8 inches apart. Remember, as with all spring bulbs, the foliage must be allowed to ripen (turn brown) before you remove it if you want flowers the following year.

5 TIME-TESTED HYACINTHS

Name	Bloom Time	Color	Height
CARNEGIE	late	white	9–14 inches
DELFT BLUE	early	light blue	9–14 inches
ORANGE BOVEN	midseason	salmon	9–14 inches
PINK PEARL	early	deep pink	9–14 inches
YELLOW HAMMER	early	yellow-orange	9–14 inches

SPRING'S SMALLEST BULBS—One of the major assets of these little bulbs is that several have lovely blue flowers, a shade mostly missing from the larger bulbs. They are all easy to plant, about 2 to 4 inches apart and 3 to 4 inches deep (measured from tips of bulbs, not bottoms), which helps keep them below mice tunnels and makes it harder for chipmunks to dig them.

These bulbs fit into any number of situations; even on small properties you will want to plant them by the hundreds. They all do well in lawns—but then you can't mow the grass until the foliage has ripened. Scatter them freely at the base of trees, in front of shrubs, between steppingstones in a walk or between flagstones of a terrace, in rock gardens and retaining walls, and as a carpeting among daffodils or tulips for color contrast.

The sky-blue glory-of-the-snow (*Chionodoxa luciliae*) is especially lovely interplanted among early-flowering yellow daffodils. (First plant the daffodils that require deeper planting, lightly rake or smooth over the soil, scatter the glory-of-the-snow bulbs, and plant them 3 inches deep.)

Snowdrops (*Galanthus nivalis*), with white drooping flowers above grassy foliage, are the first to flower, usually right through the snow in my Long Island garden. The snow crocus (*Crocus chrysanthus*) is another early bird. It can appear in late February in many northern areas if the bulbs are in protected, sun-drenched sites. The last crocuses to flower are the large Dutch hybrids.

Overlapping their blooming periods are all the various blue-flowered little bulbs. In addition to glory-of-the-snow, there are Siberian scilla or squill *(Scilla siberica)*, puschkinia *(Puschkinia scilloides)*, which has white and pale-blue striped flowers, and the always perky short spikes of the grape-hyacinth *(Muscari* species) in various shades of blue. Most of these bulbs scatter their seeds about freely, the happy result being that flowers turn up in all sorts of unexpected places. Yet they never become a nuisance.

Crocuses can be brought into early bloom indoors by planting the bulbs, very close together with their tips at the soil surface, in pots. Water, then place the pots in a cold, dark cellar or wherever they receive temperatures of around 40° F for 10 to 12 weeks. Then bring indoors to a sunny window.

BULBS FOR THE SUMMER SEASON

BALLOONS OVER THE GARDEN—As spring gives way to summer, one of the most spectacular of all bulbs begins to flower. It is the giant allium *(Allium giganteum)*, whose perfectly round heads of small violet-purple flowers on sturdy 5-foot stems look like floating balloons above the garden. There are other alliums you may want to grow, but surely this is the most outstanding. The large bulbs are available in the fall and should be planted deep—about 5 to 6 inches to the tip of the bulb. After blooming, the foliage clump soon disappears, so you will want to mark the bulbs' location to prevent accidental injury.

CALADIUMS FOR SHADE—The triangular leaves of the caladium with their splashy or stenciled color combinations are most dramatic. The plants will light up shaded terraces and are often combined with tuberous begonias (see subsequent section).

The dormant tubers are available in early spring from garden centers or mail-order firms and are usually started into growth indoors. Fill a carton or wooden flat with damp peat moss (see Peat Moss) and bury the rather knobby tubers, covering them with about 2 inches of the peat moss. Keep in a warm place (from 70° to 85° F) or the tubers will not grow and may simply rot. When leaf growth shows, move to good light, but not outdoors until weather has warmed and frost dangers have passed.

Caladiums are superb pot subjects, but will require a large container (about 8 inches in diameter). They can also be set out in open garden beds in part shade in humus-rich soil (incorporate generous amounts of peat moss). In the fall, you can save the tubers for another year by storing them in plastic bags—after digging the tubers and letting the foliage dry up—in a frost-free area.

DAHLIAS FOR FLOWERS IN ABUNDANCE—The dahlia endures because it is a superb cut flower, but the lower-growing kinds so popular today are in perfect scale for flower gardens among annuals and perennials. The lowest varieties grow about 10 to 15 inches high and have single daisy flowers. Others with single and double flowers range from 20 to 30 inches tall.

Dahlia tubers are available in spring and can be planted in the garden about the time you set out tomato seedlings. They need full sun and a humus-rich soil (see Peat Moss and Compost) that retains moisture.

The tubers, which resemble sweet potatoes, should be planted horizontally in a hole about 6 inches deep. Cover with a few inches of soil, filling in the hole as growth appears. (Giant dahlias, the ones grown by hobbyists, should be set 10 to 12 inches deep, and a stout stake, 6 feet high, should be placed next to the tuber at planting time.)

Cut off fading flowers, and in drought, water dahlia plants generously. After the first frost blackens the foliage, the tubers can be dug up and allowed to dry off in the sun for a week. Then cut back the stems and store the tubers in a cool but frost-free place. Keeping the tubers in some dry peat moss in plastic bags is a good idea. Or treat them as annuals and start over the following spring.

GLADIOLUS—The gladiolus is another bulblike plant, most famous as a cut flower. Its bulbs—technically corms—are usually planted in rows adjacent to the vegetable garden or as part of a cutting garden. Yet there is no reason why five or six corms of the same variety can't be set out at intervals in flower borders. (White varieties of gladiolus would do very well in the all-white annual garden, for instance.)

Plant the corms in midspring, about 4 inches deep and 3 to 5 inches apart, making successive plantings every few weeks, up to July 1 in most of the North. As with dahlias, you can handle gladiolus as transients, or after a hardy frost, dig the corms, let the foliage dry, and store.

GRACEFUL LILIES—Lilies are outstanding in the summer flower border. They tolerate light to partial shade, too, and make attractive groupings at the edge of a woodland and in front of shrubs. Study catalogue descriptions of the many kinds available, which also vary in height.

The lily is a true bulb and very hardy. Its bulbs are available in the fall for immediate planting but are increasingly being offered in spring as well. Most bulbs should be set in the soil so their tops are covered with 4 to 6 inches of soil, but some kinds should be set as deep as 12 inches. Follow the planting instructions sent with your bulbs. Do not remove the roots that should be attached to the bulbs! Since the bulbs will be in their places permanently, mix superphosphate or bone meal in their planting holes (see Daffodils).

If you plant lily bulbs and they fail to appear, the culprits could be mice. Sometimes the mice chew away at the bulbs, but leave remnants (scales or bulb divisions) that eventually put in an appearance and may flower.

TUBEROUS BEGONIAS—Their beautifully formed flowers resemble those of roses and camellias. They make decorative pot subjects for patios and any paved area. The cascade varieties, so-labeled in catalogues and garden centers, are offered for hanging containers.

Tuberous begonias, well along in growth, are always available from garden centers in late spring, but you will save money if you buy the dormant tubers in late winter or early spring and start them into growth indoors in a west or east window or under fluorescent tubes.

Fill flats or cartons with damp peat moss, as recommended for caladiums, then bury the tubers 2 to 3 inches apart so the tops (the concave side with small pink buds just emerging) are covered by about an inch of peat moss. When top growth has reached about 3 to 5 inches, remove each rooted tuber and plant in a 6- to 8-inch pot or put several tubers in a window box or planter. Choose a humus-rich soil or you can mix about half your garden soil with half of one of the synthetic soils, such as Jiffy Mix or Redi-Earth. (See Soil.)

Tuberous begonias grow well in light to partial (but not dense) shade. A few hours of sunshine daily is beneficial and keeps the plants sturdy. You should place bamboo stakes, about three to four, around the plants in pots, and tie as much soft green twine to them as needed to keep the flower-heavy stems from falling or breaking off.

Tuberous begonias also do very well in the open ground. Add peat moss to the soil and water the area during drought.

It definitely pays to save tuberous begonia tubers from year to year. Dig them in the fall—before the arrival of heavy frosts—and try to retain the brittle stems and foliage. Place the tubers with adhering soil in a flat or shallow box and allow to dry for a few weeks in a frost-free area safe from rainfall. Eventually the stems will fall off or can easily be removed. Then the tubers, with most of the dry soil shaken off, can be stored in plastic bags in a frost-free area, perhaps with a little dry peat moss, until it is time to begin the growing process again the following spring.

For bulbs such as amaryllis, which are grown as house plants, see Indoor Gardening.

C

CLIMATE. See Zones, Climate.

COLD FRAMES. A special protected environment in the garden for plants. The cold frame, a bottomless boxlike shelter with a glass or plastic cover, has probably been around as long as the wheelbarrow. Although not essential equipment for every kind of gardener, it can be useful in several ways: it can acclimatize indoor-grown seedlings to the outdoors, serve as a seedbed for starting tender annuals and vegetables, such as tomatoes, be used as winter storage for biennials, and become a propagating place for rooting cuttings of perennials and shrubs. Over the winter, cold frames are increasingly being used as salad gardens.

A cold frame's source of heat is the sun, but when electric heating cables are laid in sand at the bottom of the frame, or a layer of fresh animal manure is laid to generate heat as it ferments, the cold frame is called a hotbed.

A cold frame should face south and be in a practical location, such as near a vegetable garden and a hose outlet. Avoid windswept locations so heat can be retained.

The size of the frame has traditionally been 6 feet by 3 feet, and the removable glass top, called a sash, is sold in that size. However, you can improvise a frame of any size that suits your purpose and use plastic fastened to a wooden frame or a sheet of fiberglass in place of the sash. A frame can be built to fit a discarded glass window. The back wall of the frame should be about 15 to 16 inches high, with the side walls sloping to the lower front wall, which can be about 8 to 12 inches high. This is to trap as much sun warmth as possible.

A cold frame's interior can heat up surprisingly fast when the sash is closed, with the unhappy result that the trapped plants become "cooked." On warm spring days, the sash must be partially open to avoid this condition, but then must be closed at the end of the day as the temperature drops. Knowing how to manage a cold frame's ventilation can be difficult at first as well as inconvenient.

However, there is a solution to this problem now. It is the same solar thermostatic device that has revolutionized greenhouse management by automatically opening and closing vents. The solar devices for cold frames open the sash when the inner temperature reaches 75° F and close it when the temperature drops to 68° F. You can buy these openers from mail-order houses, together with plans for building your own frame. Or you can splurge and buy a complete solar-operated frame that is quite easy to assemble.

Another problem in cold frame management is watering the plants, which may be necessary daily if the plants are in small pots or flats. Plants growing in the soil directly can also become dry as the temperature warms and of course any time when the frame is closed so that natural rainfall is excluded. Using generous amounts of peat moss in the frame's soil mixture helps retain moisture.

COMPOST. As plant residues start to decay, they are known as compost. In its ultimate stage of decomposition, when it is a dark, crumbly mass of organic matter, compost becomes humus. Humus is an essential ingredient of good gardening soil. It retains soil moisture, aids in the release of soil nutrients, and itself slowly releases nitrogen over long periods. Humus helps break up stiff clay soils and adds body to sandy ones, thus preventing loss of moisture and plant nutrients.

A readily available source of humus is peat moss, sold in bags and bales at garden centers and nurseries. (See also Peat Moss.) Yet there are free sources of organic materials available on most home properties and in surrounding neighborhoods. Fallen leaves, including the needle leaves of pine trees, straw, hay, grass clippings, discarded plants and weeds, including their roots, kitchen wastes, sawdust and wood chips, seaweeds, and animal manures are all examples of organic materials that can be combined in a compost pile to decay before being incorporated in the garden soil.

Fallen leaves too often are raked off a property, then carted off to a disposal area or town dump. Rather they should be added to the compost pile or composted separately in chicken-wire or snow-fence enclosures to decay into leaf mold, a potential source of humus. Enclosing the leaves prevents them from blowing away and also keeps them compacted, thus hastening decomposition.

Small properties do not always have space for compost or leaf piles, but there should be out-of-the-way areas for them on large suburban and country places.

There are probably many recipes for making compost. A compost pile is often described as a club sandwich, with 6-inch layers of the various organic materials just mentioned alternated with a thin layer of fresh animal manure or about a quart of 5-10-5 fertilizer. (See Fertilizers.) The purpose of the fertilizers high in nitrogen is to hasten decay. Adding layers of soil was once recommended for compost piles, but the thinking today is that soil is unnecessary and may in fact impede the decaying process by restricting aeration and drainage. The compost pile should be moist but never soggy. As the layers are built up, usually in a square or rectangular shape to a final height of about 3 to 5 feet, the necessary air movement can be maintained by inserting a pole into the pile to make several holes.

The bottom part of the pile decays faster than the top. Removing this section from the side shakes up the pile and in the process the less-decayed layers can be dropped to the bottom. Compost is usually ready to use in a year or so, the time depending on the materials used, the consistent addition of fertilizers, temperature, and rainfall. Most gardeners add compost to their gardens in various stages of decay rather than waiting for the entire pile to become decayed. (See also Mulches and Mulching.)

CONTAINERS. See Pots and Other Containers.

COOPERATIVE EXTENSION AGENTS OR SPECIALISTS. University-trained men and women who are employed by the Cooperative Extension Service offices located in nearly every county of the country. The Service is funded by federal, state, and county governments and has connections with the U.S. Department of Agriculture and each state's land grant universities.

The extension agents assist farmers and professional and home gardeners in any aspect of gardening, especially concerns that may be of regional importance. Extension agents can answer questions on insects and diseases, test soils or tell you where to obtain such tests, advise you on soil improvement, and give you the latest findings on pruning. They can tell you about bulletins and leaflets that may be available. The Service can be especially helpful to those who move into a climate zone different from the one to which they have long been accustomed.

You can reach the Service by telephone. The number is usually listed in the telephone book under the county government.

CUT FLOWERS. One of the rewards of having a flower garden is the supply of cut flowers it supplies, not only for your enjoyment but for bouquets to give to friends. Annuals, especially, are favorite flowers for cutting. The more they are cut, the bushier their growth and production of flowers.

Experiments have shown that late afternoon and early evening are the best times to gather cut flowers, with the next best time being early morning. Use a sharp knife or pruning shears whose edges are not dull. Make the cut just above a leaf node or joint. When cutting flowers from annuals and perennials, leave enough foliage so the plant can go on living—and producing more flowers.

The sooner the stems of cut material are placed in water, the better. Make a slanted cut rather than a flat one at the far end of the stem. Woody or hard stems should have their ends crushed with a hammer or mallet. If you are unable to put cut flowers into water immediately, make fresh cuts at the ends of the stems before you plunge them into water. Always strip off lower foliage that would rot in the water.

Woody branches are especially thirsty and the water supply in their vases should be checked often and replenished as necessary. To prolong the life of cut materials, change the water daily. If this seems like too much of a chore, at least add fresh water to replace that which has evaporated.

CUTTINGS. See Propagation.

D

DIGGING. Much of this down-to-earth procedure, which is sometimes more nobly referred to as soil preparation, has been eased by the rotary tiller, a machine powered by a gasoline engine that churns up the soil. Still, much digging can only be done by hand. There are holes to be dug for large shrubs and trees (although a tiller can even accomplish much of this labor) and medium-size holes for perennials. Or there may be a small garden area in which it is more convenient to prepare the soil by digging it with a fork or spade. A long-handled spade is easier on back muscles. If the soil is difficult to penetrate, use a fork instead of a spade. Drive the spade or fork into the soil to the full depth of the blade and at a nearly upright angle by stepping on the shoulder of the tool's blade. Lift the spade or fork and dump the soil upside down in the hole—or to the side if you are preparing a planting hole for a shrub or other plant. (See Planting and Transplanting.)

DISEASES. See Pests and Diseases.

DIVIDING. See Propagation.

DRAINAGE. While some plants can exist in a constantly waterlogged soil, the roots of the majority of garden plants—annuals, perennials, vegetables, fruits, roses, trees, and shrubs—will rot if planted in such a site because they are deprived of essential oxygen.

Poor drainage may be caused by excessively clayey soil, an impenetrable subsoil, or simply very low land into which water runs from a higher level. Remedies for improving poor drainage include adding large amounts of coarse sand and compost to clay soils, adding fill to raise the soil level, constructing individual

When preparing soil for a garden, insert the spade to the full depth of the blade before lifting and turning over the soil.

raised beds, or installing a network of agricultural drain pipes about 2½ feet deep.

If you are faced with bogs or swamps, the sensible solution is to leave them as they are and enjoy them as a unique environment that supports many unusual native plants.

DRIED FLOWERS. The urge to retain summer's flower colors and forms for winter's dry bouquets has a long history and in this country goes back to colonial times. One group of annuals, known as everlastings, is usually specifically grown for dried arrangements, but many other garden flowers as well as ornamental and wild grasses, weeds with interesting seed heads, and even some trees and shrubs (hydrangea flowers dry themselves right on the bush) can be preserved by drying.

METHODS OF PRESERVATION—The easiest is to lay the material on newspapers, but even better is to air-dry by suspending the flowers upside down in a dry place out of direct sun, such as your garage or attic. Tie the stems together in loose bunches and fasten to a coat hanger or wire or cord stretched between rafters. Air-drying can take 3 or more weeks. An old drying method is to place the cut materials on a layer of sand in a carton, then carefully cover with additional sand. It can be hard on fragile blos-

soms and of course must be very dry. Borax, alone or mixed with
corn meal, is quicker and less likely than sand to injure the flowers. The newest method is to use silica gel, which can be obtained
in many garden centers or from some mail-order seed companies. Serious practitioners of the art of dried flower arrangement
often substitute florist wire for the original stems of flowers,
making them easier to arrange and less liable to breakage. The
wires should be inserted in the flowers before they are dried.

An attic is a good place in which to dry annuals and other flowers
for later arrangements.

In the following list of flowers for drying, A = Annual, B =
Biennial, and P = Perennial.

FLOWERS TO PRESERVE BY AIR DRYING

BABY'S-BREATH (P)	GLOBE-THISTLE (P)
BEEBALM (P)	GRASSES (A and P)

BELLS OF IRELAND (A)	HONESTY (B)
BUTTERFLY WEED (P)	LARKSPUR (A)
CALENDULA (A)	LAVENDER (P)
CELOSIA (A)	LOVE-IN-A-MIST (A)
CHINESE LANTERN (P)	OKRA PODS (A)
CHIVES (P)	SALVIA (A and P)
EVERLASTINGS (A)	SEA-LAVENDER (P)
GAILLARDIA (P)	STATICE (A)
GLOBE-AMARANTH (A)	STRAWFLOWER (A)

E

EQUIPMENT. See Tools and Equipment.

EVERGREENS. The balsam fir *(Abies balsamea)*, widely used as a Christmas tree, is the typical evergreen, but there are many more trees and shrubs, of all sizes and shapes, native as well as introduced, to grow in our gardens. Some evergreens are very low-growing, while others, like the giant redwood, are awe-inspiring and seem to grow out of sight. The term "evergreen" is somewhat of an exaggeration as sooner or later all evergreen plants drop some of their leaves. However, they are never bare of foliage, as are deciduous trees and shrubs.

Evergreens can be divided into two major groups. It soon becomes easy to determine at a glance to which group each evergreen belongs.

NARROW- OR NEEDLE-LEAVED EVERGREENS—Pines, hemlocks, redwoods, firs, spruces, junipers, yews, cypresses, and cedars belong here. They are known as conifers because of their seed-bearing cones, which can be so handsome in fall and winter. There are coniferous evergreens for mild and cold climates. Many are long-lived, often giant trees more suited to large properties, fields, and forests than the average backyard. Fortunately, there are exceptions, and even the large conifers can be planted on limited properties to be enjoyed until they outgrow

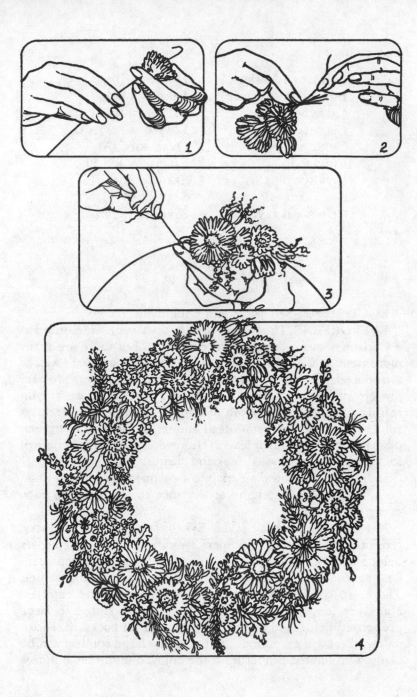

their space. When that time comes, cut down the tree and give it a glorious ending as a Christmas tree.

Among the many landscape uses for these evergreens are as ground covers (many junipers and yews), as hedges and windbreaks (hemlocks, yews, arborvitae, pines, spruces), as accents for open lawns and around large buildings (arborvitae, Italian cypress, and certain forms of junipers and yews). On larger properties, evergreens can be mixed among such leaf-losing trees as oaks, dogwoods, and birches to add life to the winter landscape. Hemlocks will grow in light to part shade and even white pines and spruces do quite well in not too dense woodlands.

DWARF CONIFERS—These slow-growing evergreens are becoming very popular because they use far less space than the standard conifers. Dwarf conifers are planted among rocks and in rock gardens, on sunny slopes, and in other special garden areas.

Some dwarf conifers are creeping in habit, others, drooping or rounded, and some are upright like regular conifers. Some others might be considered freaks—they are derived from abnormal growths called sports or witches' brooms that appeared on standard-size conifers in the wild or under cultivation. These discoveries have been propagated by cuttings or grafts and given their own names. Because of their size and often bizarre shapes, dwarf conifers make fit and sometimes dramatic subjects for tubs and containers and also bonsai training. The less exotic-appearing dwarfs can be used around a house's foundation; unlike many

---

Making a dried flower wreath: **1** Insert wire through flower head, hooking each wire at the top as shown to prevent flower from slipping off the wire. The wires serve as pliable stems. **2** Combine various flowers in loose bundles, twisting their wire stems together. **3** Fasten them to a wire frame (easier to work with if it has been first wrapped in tape), or use a straw wreath, often available around the holidays, or a grapevine wreath. **4** Finished wreath can be hung or laid flat as a table centerpiece.

standard conifers, are unlikely to outgrow their location for many years.

BROAD-LEAVED EVERGREENS—This second group of evergreens includes many of our most popular and useful shrubs and trees for landscaping on both a grand scale and for limited spaces. Only regions with the harshest winters are deprived of the beauty of these evergreens. Their outstanding flowers and berries are displayed to great advantage against the handsome evergreen leaves that are considerably broader than those of needle-leaved evergreens.

Favorites include rhododendrons and azaleas, camellia, mountain-laurel, pieris, gardenia, drooping leucothoe, and hollies. In addition to hollies, other evergreens known for their berry displays include the ground-covering bearberry, whose bright red berries gleam above glossy, evergreen foliage; Japanese skimmia, with persistent red berries on the female plants; several kinds of barberry, mostly with black or dark blue berries; many evergreen viburnums, with orange, red, and dark berries.

Boxwood is one broad-leaved evergreen that is grown for its billowy, often irregularly graceful shape assumed when it is not sheared into geometric forms. Heaths and heathers are mostly low-growing evergreens with pretty bell-shaped flowers and needlelike leaves, although they are not at all related to the conifers.

There is such diversity among the broad-leaved evergreens—in flowers and berries, foliage types, heights and shapes, and adaptability to varying climates and sites—that there is hardly a landscaping situation for which there is not a wide choice. Unlike conifers, which generally prefer sunny exposures, the majority of broad-leaved evergreens do better in partially shaded locations, and a few kinds grow well in deep shade. They do need a humus-rich soil that retains moisture. (See also Landscaping, Shrubs, Trees, Ground Covers, and Planting and Transplanting.)

F

FERTILIZERS. The major nutrients that are essential for plant growth are nitrogen, phosphorus, and potassium. These elements are usually the chief components—in varying amounts —of most fertilizers because they tend to be deficient in many soils or are used quickly by the plants grown. Other elements, such as calcium, magnesium, and sulphur, are also important, but they are more likely to be present in sufficient quantities in most soils. Still other elements, such as iron, manganese, and boron, are known as trace elements because they are needed in such small amounts by plants.

Fertilizers are available as liquids, which must be diluted in water before using, in granular or pulverized forms, as animal manures and other derivatives from animals, and as products from plant wastes, such as cottonseed meal. The last two groups are often referred to as "organic" or "natural" fertilizers, and are the staples of the organic gardening movement. (See also Manures and Organic Gardening.)

In addition to animal manures, organic fertilizers include dried blood, which is very high in nitrogen; bone meal, high in phosphorus and some nitrogen; seaweed; cottonseed meal; fish emulsion (a liquid); wood ashes; and rock phosphate. Organic fertilizers tend to become available to plants more slowly and, with the exception of fresh animal manures, are generally less likely to injure plant roots.

Chemical or inorganic fertilizers, also called commercial fertilizers, include superphosphate, muriate of potash, nitrate of soda, and the commonly used 5-10-5 formula.

Whether you use an organic or inorganic fertilizer, it may contain one element such as superphosphate, or, more likely, the major elements—nitrogen, phosphorus, and potash—will be the main ingredients. They will be present in varying amounts, with the percentages indicated on the label, as 5-10-5, 12-4-8, or other combinations. The first number refers to the percentage of nitrogen, the second, to phosphorus, and the third, to potash. The order of elements is always the same, even though the amounts may differ.

How do you decide which fertilizers to apply? First of all, the point of applying fertilizers is to maintain and improve plant growth. When plants appear to be growing well, flowering nearly as promised in seed catalogues, and performing their functions as food sources to your satisfaction, it can be a waste of money to pour fertilizers on them.

Few gardens won't benefit from some fertilizer applications at some point, however. A soil test (see Soil) is one way to find out what your soil contains or lacks. Seek the advice of local authorities (see Cooperative Extension Agents or Specialists) and follow fertilizer recommendations for various kinds of plants given in books and articles. For instance, bulbs and flowering plants need fertilizers high in phosphorus to encourage root development and flower production, so superphosphate or the slower-acting bone meal can be mixed in the soil at planting time or as soil tests indicate the need. Vegetables vary in their requirements, with leafy vegetables responding well to nitrogen. A general purpose inorganic formula, such as 5-10-5, is the usual recommendation for vegetable and flower gardens, at the rate of 3 to 5 pounds per 100 square feet.

The times to apply fertilizers vary across the nation, but generally most applications can be made in spring as plants begin active growth, during soil preparation for flower and vegetable gardens, and in spot applications throughout the growing season as recommended for certain plants.

Fertilizers high in nitrogen are usually not given to plants in late summer, as the resulting soft growth can be injured later by freezing. Most fertilizers can be toxic to plants when applied with reckless abandon. When in doubt, use less and pay attention to recommendations on the container. Keep dry fertilizers off the leaves of plants and away from their stems. (See also Watering.)

FRUITS. Most suburban and country places can support some kinds of fruits, although the majority of properties may not have space for the well-rounded fruit gardens of yesterday.

Before taking the plunge into becoming a home orchardist, consider the following needs of fruits in relation to your region and property and the amount of time you can give, as many fruits require more effort than growing tomatoes or most shrubs.

SITE AND SOIL—An open, sunny location that is not shaded by surrounding trees or buildings. The soil should be well drained and have a higher percentage of sand than clay. (See also Soil.)

INSECT AND DISEASE CONTROL—Most fruit trees must be sprayed from seven to twelve times (depending on type of fruit) a season and at the right time if the spray is to accomplish its purpose of controlling specific pests. Study spray schedules distributed by county agents (see Cooperative Extension Agents or Specialists) and decide whether you want to undertake this responsibility. There are now multipurpose sprays that somewhat simplify home orchard spraying. (See Pests and Diseases.) Blueberries, raspberries, and strawberries are generally bothered by fewer pests than apples, peaches, and other fruit trees.

SPACE REQUIREMENTS—Standard-size apple and sweet cherry trees become very large and spreading and can soon swallow up the average backyard. But there are dwarf fruit trees, a few of which can fit on most properties. Standard varieties of plums and peaches are not so space-consuming, and the bush fruits—strawberries, raspberries, and blueberries—require the least space of all.

CROSS-POLLINATION FOR FRUIT FLOWERS—Though decidedly pretty in bloom, apple trees, whether dwarf or standard, that do not bear fruit are a disappointment, once spring is past. When fruit trees flower but do not form fruit, it is usually because their pollen is not self-fruitful and there were no neighboring trees with compatible pollen to fertilize the blossoms.

Peaches and sour cherries are self-fruitful, but sweet cherries (except for a variety called 'Stella') always require a different sweet cherry variety as a pollinator nearby. If you have space for only one apple tree, you can buy a tree that has two or more different apple varieties grafted on it. These trees are often called

5-in-1 or 3-in-1 and supposedly solve the cross-pollination problem for small properties. These trees are available in both standard and dwarf sizes. Nursery catalogues that specialize in fruits
give detailed information on pollination requirements of their
varieties.

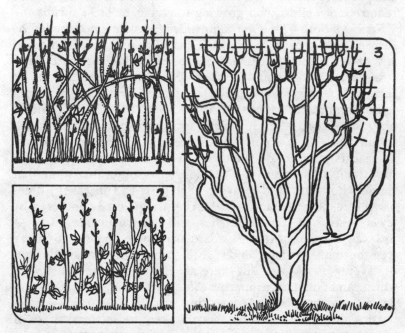

Pruning red raspberries. A tangle of old canes (1) remains after
fruiting ends. Removal of old fruiting canes (2) leaves space for
healthy development of new canes. Blueberry bushes (3) require
very little pruning and not annually, as do raspberries. Older bushes
can be renewed by cutting back branches as shown (in early spring)
and occasionally removing very old stems at the base.

PRUNING AND TRAINING—Raspberries and other bramble fruits
require annual pruning to keep the bushes productive and within
bounds. Blueberries are very low in maintenance needs, but
eventually some renewal pruning will be necessary every few

years to force new growth. Dwarf fruit trees may require supports and some training but far less pruning than standard-size apples, for instance.

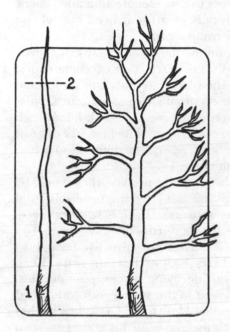

Early training of dwarf fruit trees: graft point (1) should always be above ground. Top (2) of new tree (left) should be cut back to achieve a pyramid shape (right).

▨▨▨▨ A SAMPLER OF FRUITS ▨▨▨▨

DWARF FRUIT TREES—By now you have probably realized that dwarf-size fruit trees are the sensible choice for most home orchards. Their fruit is easier to pick, the trees can be pruned from the ground when it is necessary, and they come into bearing at a much earlier stage than standard trees. Fruits from dwarf trees are the same size as those from large trees.

Dwarf fruit trees owe their dwarfness to the rootstocks on which each variety is grafted. Several different rootstocks are used, and in the case of apples many so-called dwarf trees turn out to be not so dwarf. If you have space for 10- to 15-foot-high trees with an equal spread, these semidwarfs will be satisfactory.

Otherwise, seek apple trees that are truly dwarf. The best dwarfing stock for such trees is known as M-9. Dwarf trees on M-9 stock should remain between 6 and 8 feet tall.

Other types of small fruit trees to consider are spur and genetic dwarfs, varieties that are naturally dwarf and need not rely on dwarfing rootstocks for their compact size.

When planting fruit trees, follow the nursery's instructions.

BLUEBERRIES—The highbush blueberry is an excellent choice for the fruit garden because the plants are easy to care for and each one uses about the same eventual space as an azalea. Blueberries do have special soil requirements, an acid, humus-rich soil that retains moisture but is not soggy. The best way to grow them is as an informal hedge of three or four different varieties, to achieve the best cross-pollination.

Once the berries begin to show their blue color, they should be protected from birds with a plastic net covering (available from garden centers and mail-order sources). If you have extra space, plant a few blueberry bushes for the birds—they will thank you and put on quite a show. (Blueberries are attractive enough to grow as ornamentals.) Blueberry bushes last for years. Keep them mulched year round with decaying leaves, pine needles, compost, or wood chips, and feed in the spring with cottonseed meal or an organic fertilizer called Hollytone. Occasionally, thin out old branches at the base and top vigorous shoots to keep them low enough to reach for harvesting the berries.

RASPBERRIES—One reason for growing raspberries is that the supermarket simply cannot handle the fragile berries. And if you have a surplus, you can freeze them as easily as a commercial processor.

Raspberries do require more care than blueberries and as the plants sucker freely (that is, send up new shoots all around the original plant), they can take over the garden if not checked. Set raspberry plants about 2 to 2½ feet apart as a row or hedge. Don't let suckers grow beyond a width of 2 feet for the row—ruthlessly cut them off with a rotary mower—or your hedgerow will soon become a raspberry patch, ever widening in every direction. Not only will you be unable to reach the inner berries, but the production will be less because the outer plants prevent necessary sunlight from reaching the center. You also will be unable to prune out the old canes.

Pruning is also important: after fruiting in early summer the canes should be cut off at the base. New canes soon appear and carry on the fruiting sequence for next year. If you neglect to cut out these old canes that have fruited, they will die anyway, but if left in place they harbor pests and diseases and can be in the way of the new growth.

STRAWBERRIES—Strawberries are the true dwarfs of the fruit world, as the fruits are produced on low, leafy plants only a foot or so high. Although you can try growing strawberry plants in hanging baskets and old-fashioned strawberry barrels, for a meaningful crop grow them in the earth. A good place is in a patch at one end of the vegetable garden, preferably in soil where tomatoes, eggplants, and peppers have not previously been grown.

A sandy soil high in organic matter (see Compost) is better than a stiff clay. Set out strawberry plants in the spring. There are far more do's and don't's to strawberry growing methods than most fruits, and it is quite possible to get an Excedrin headache while reading some instructions. In a nutshell: the "matted row" system is probably the easiest way for most new gardeners to grow the plants. The plants are set about 18 inches apart in rows 18 to 24 inches wide and 48 inches apart. To plant a strawberry plant, dig a hole large enough to spread out the roots, then cover with soil so the crown or center of the plant is barely above the surface. Press soil firmly around the plant—you can use your feet. Water each plant thoroughly.

When the first flowers appear, pick them off so the plants do not form fruits the first season. Strawberry plants form offshoots, called runners, that form new plants. Runners formed outside of the 18- to 24-inch row should be cut off. Remove any weeds that appear.

The first fall after you plant strawberries and after the first freeze, mulch the plants with straw, hay, or wood shavings, thick enough so you can barely see the plants. In spring, after heavy frosts end, remove the mulch from over the plants and pack it around them to keep the berries clean and suppress weeds. An application of 5-10-5, 5 pounds to 100 square feet, can be applied after fruiting and promptly watered in.

For more detailed information on fruit growing for your region, consult your cooperative extension agent.

G

GARDENS. See Annuals, Biennials, Border, Herbs, Perennials, Roses, and Vegetables.

GENUS. See Nomenclature.

GRASSES. See Lawns.

GREENHOUSES. Greenhouses have been known as glasshouses and solar structures so long that it is difficult to picture the sixteenth- and seventeenth-century forerunners that were built with very small windows and used as holding houses for tropical plants over winter. Once it was discovered that a glass-walled building made an ideal growing environment for many different kinds of plants, the greenhouse, much as we know it today, was born.

Even with the emphasis on solar concepts, the sun becoming the source of as much heat as possible for the greenhouse and adjoining house as well, designs have not changed drastically. Modern greenhouses can be operated more efficiently, with much of the day-to-day operations of watering and opening and closing vents being automatic. The free-standing and lean-to greenhouses are still being offered, with the lean-to, which attaches to a wall of the house, being the better, more economical choice in northern climates. In mild climates, the free-standing is usually preferable because light enters the greenhouse from all sides.

One new word is being used today in connection with greenhouses. It is "sunspace," a fancy word for modern variations of the Victorian conservatory and sunroom of the 1920s. In many cases, it has more to do with life-style than gardening and can encompass a swimming pool or hot tub, elegant wicker furniture and perhaps an orchid plant or two, and tubs of big tropical treelike house plants as background and random accents.

The idea of buying a greenhouse usually evolves as gardening interests and experience progress, but even seasoned gardeners are well advised to do their homework before signing on the dotted line. Can you locate the greenhouse close to your heat source? With a lean-to, you may be able to run a duct from your oil burner to it, but only if your burner has sufficient capacity. Other heating possibilities are propane gas and of course electricity, which can be very expensive. The means of heating your future greenhouse should be thoroughly investigated. What about the size of your greenhouse? A decision here depends on what you can afford and available space, and also how you plan to use the greenhouse. Are you a budding plant collector? Are you interested in propagation? And, of course, you must have the right exposure—no winter shade, but a site with some protection from wind.

Before you decide on a permanent greenhouse, you might try experimenting with cheaper, more temporary enclosures. The cold frame (see Cold Frames) is a good introduction to greenhouse gardening, although you must look into its special environment rather than being part of it.

The plastics revolution has made it possible to build temporary shelters in various shapes—A-frames and Quonset-hut-shapes being two common ones much used in nurseries. These can be fairly permanent, with the plastic sheeting lasting a few years before replacement is necessary. Others can be glorified cold frames, perhaps not large enough to enter but easily moved about according to gardening needs. In cold and not-so-cold climates, these home-made frames or houses give protection to various cold-hardy plants, such as kale, cabbage, lettuce, and pansies. Their usefulness for seed sowing and growing seedlings can really be appreciated as the spring season arrives.

GROUND COVERS. Almost any spreading plant can become a ground cover, but usually the definition refers to very low-growing or ground-hugging plants that can be substituted for grass. Ground-covering plants are sought for shady areas and for banks where it is difficult to establish grass and even dangerous to try to mow it. They are also planted on other sites where the soil is unsuitable for grass, such as very sandy places encountered at the seashore or in desert regions and rock-strewn locations.

Sometimes ground covers are introduced for purely aesthetic reasons, perhaps to contrast with grass (the prime ground-covering plant) or to emphasize or complement other types of plantings.

Certain annuals can make temporary but satisfactory ground covers. Some of the most popular bedding plants, such as sweet-alyssum, wax begonia, impatiens, Madagascar periwinkle or vinca, and petunia give spectacular summer color displays when planted in masses.

However, the majority of good ground covers are perennial and should last indefinitely once established. Many are vines. Some are evergreen, which makes them doubly useful in the North.

Ground covers generally take longer to fill in than grass, so patience is necessary. They will take care of themselves eventually, but for the first year or so, some weeding may be required, and water when rainfall is scarce. Before setting out ground covers (usually in spring or fall, except for certain container-grown plants that can be put in the ground throughout the growing season), prepare the soil by digging with a fork or use a rotary tiller for large areas. If the soil is poor, incorporate about a 3-inch layer of peat moss or compost. (See also Digging, Peat Moss, and Compost.)

▨▨▨▨ SAMPLER OF GROUND COVERS ▨▨▨▨

Ajuga or **Carpet Bugleweed** *(Ajuga reptans)*. Perennial 4- to 8-inch creeper with spikes of pretty blue flowers above foliage rosettes in spring. There are other ajugas, but this one really gallops over humus-rich soil in shade or sun.

Bearberry *(Arctostaphylos uva-ursi)*. Creeping and vinelike, its woody stems clothed in shiny evergreen leaves and red berries in fall. For acid, sandy soil in sun. Slow-growing at first. This is a native, widely distributed over North America.

Creeping Thyme *(Thymus praecox)*. Creeping woody plant to 3 inches that tolerates light traffic. Try it between stepping-stones in sun and in fairly dry soil. Self-sows.

Day-lily *(Hemerocallis fulva* and others). Popular perennial with long ribbons of leaves and summer lilylike flowers. Though tall, up to 3 to 5 feet, day-lilies make effective covering in seminaturalistic areas in shade to sun. The flowers are a plus. Accepts dry to very wet soils.

Dichondra *(Dichondra micrantha)*. Creeping perennial with small evergreen leaves, commonly used on West Coast. Sun or part shade. Must be watered in drought.

English Ivy *(Hedera helix)*. Evergreen vine remains at about 8 inches as ground cover. Humus-rich soil speeds its growth, and it can become rampant where winters are not too severe. Part to full shade.

Epimedium or **Barrenwort** *(Epimedium* species). Clump-forming perennial to 15 inches with semievergreen foliage and airy flowers in spring. Beautiful in woodlands and partly shaded areas. Drought-resistant once established.

Heath *(Erica carnea)*. Low-growing (8 to 12 inches) spreading evergreens with needlelike foliage and spring flowers. Acid, rather sandy soil in light shade to sun. Mix peat moss in planting holes.

Japanese Honeysuckle *(Lonicera japonica)*. Rampant twining vine with partially evergreen foliage and fragrant yellow and white flowers in summer. Blue-black berries in fall are beloved by birds. Now a weed over much of the Northeast, but the fragrance is powerful and the vine is useful in semiwild situations. (See Vines.) Sun or shade, any soil.

Lily-of-the-valley *(Convallaria majalis)*. An old favorite often associated with damp, shady corners, often around the base of shrubs like the lilac. Fragrant white bell-like flowers in spring nestled among lance-shaped dark green leaves 8 inches above creeping roots.

Pachysandra or **Japanese Spurge** *(Pachysandra terminalis)*. Creeping evergreen to 12 inches, very common in the Northeast. It is tolerant of shade and grows well under trees, even those giving as dense shade as a maple.

Periwinkle or **Myrtle** *(Vinca minor)*. Ranks after pachysandra as one of the hardier, most ornamental ground covers for shade. Shiny evergreen leaves on creeping plants with lovely blue or white flowers in early spring. Less formal than pachysandra.

St. Johnswort *(Hypericum calycinum)*. Evergreen to semievergreen shrubs to 1 foot for sun or part shade and rather sandy soil. Yellow flowers in summer.

Stonecrop or **Gold-moss** *(Sedum acre)*. Tiny-leaved succulent perennial that forms dense mats about 3 to 4 inches high. Sunny, dry areas. Yellow flowers in early summer.

Sweet Woodruff or **Asperula** *(Galium odoratum)*. Ferny-leaved spreading clumps to about 8 inches with white flowers in spring. Humus-rich soil in shade to part shade. Leaves and flowers give the flavor to May wine.

H

HEDGES. Shrubs or trees planted close together in straight or curved rows form hedges that can be both practical and decorative. However, before planting any kind of hedge, the small-property owner should consider whether he or she can afford to sacrifice the space that a hedge requires. A fence may be a better solution for gardens with little space.

UsES OF HEDGES—Hedges can define boundaries, screen undesirable views, or at least parts of them, give shelter from wind, provide privacy, and make a background for other plantings. Most low-clipped hedges have no function except to be decorative and may be part of the design in herb, rose, and flower gardens. But most hedges are multifunctional. For instance, one privet hedge on your place might serve as a boundary definer, a screen, and according to recent studies, act as a psychological barrier that deters vandalism and robberies. This same hedge, on its inner-facing side, could also provide a background for a flower border, providing that you leave 3 to 4 feet between hedge and garden to allow space for pruning and to keep the privet's roots from creeping into the garden.

WHAT'S AVAILABLE—Hedges can be of needle-leaved and broad-leaved evergreens and deciduous (leaf-losing in winter) trees and shrubs. In southern and mild-climate regions, the choices among broad-leaved evergreens are wide, but narrow as one moves northward.

Hedges are classified as formal and informal. Formal hedges contain plants that are naturally formal in shape, such as some of the columnar yews and junipers, and other shrubs and trees that are restrained or trained in their habits by shearing and clipping. Informal hedges are only pruned to keep wayward growth in check. They often contain a mixture of different kinds of shrubs. Such hedges can be very attractive in their flowering seasons, examples including azalea, camellia, forsythia, glossy abelia, bush honeysuckle, mountain-laurel, and rhododendron. Unclipped holly and tallhedge or buckthorn hedges can provide a handsome berry display.

Informal hedges generally require far less maintenance, although not all formal hedges need annual pruning or shearing. Both privet and tallhedge can be allowed to grow naturally—if you have the space—and perhaps topped every few years. Boxwood can be sheared or grown in its naturally graceful forms.

Visit local nurseries and consult county extension agents for regional recommendations on hedge materials. Sometimes it pays to buy from a mail-order source that offers quantities of plants in small sizes, which are also easier to plant. Starting with a full-grown hedge can be more expensive than buying a fence.

PLANTING SUGGESTIONS—Hedge plants can be set in single rows, usually satisfactory for today's generally smaller properties. But for country properties and small estates where an impressive, impenetrable hedge is desired, plant double rows, staggering the plants in each row.

Planting distances within the row depend on the type of plant and its size, and may vary from 3 to 4 feet for pines and spruces, 1½ to 2 feet for arborvitae, most yews, and hemlocks, 12 to 15 inches for privet, and 15 to 24 inches for most other material in young sizes. Small plants can often be set out quite quickly in a trench that has been first dug by hand or by a rotary tiller. (See Digging and Planting and Transplanting.)

PRUNING AND SHEARING—The aim is to keep your hedge as dense as possible and to avoid bare areas at the base that can develop when sunlight is excluded. To prevent this condition from happening as the hedge develops, keep the lower growth wider than the top.

Most shearing should be done after the plants have made new growth in the spring. Use hedge shears or an electric hedge trimmer (don't cut the cord!) and remove a portion of the new growth rather than cutting it all off. If you follow this procedure, the hedge should develop a thick, uniform wall. Avoid cutting into old wood on hemlock. However, yews and most junipers often make new growth from old wood. Privet hedges can be cut down to the base, leaving stubs, and started all over again if they have become bare and leggy.

▨▨▨ SAMPLER OF HEDGE PLANTS ▨▨▨

Abelia, Glossy *(Abelia* x *grandiflora)*. Informal hedge to 5 feet. Semievergreen. Small pink flowers all summer. Zone 6.

Arborvitae, American *(Thuja occidentalis)*. Formal evergreen hedge or screen. Needs good, moist soil. Zone 2.

Barberry *(Berberis* species). Many choices for mild and cold climates. Useful barrier because of thorns. Many are evergreen.

Boxwood *(Buxus* species). English box is the glory of southern gardens but venerable specimens exist to Cape Cod, Mass., and Long Island, N.Y. Korean box is more hardy. Zone 6.

Buckthorn or **Tallhedge** *(Rhamnus frangula* 'Columnaris'). Excellent tough, hardy hedge or screen. Part shade. Zone 2.

Cherry-laurel *(Prunus laurocerasus)*. Broad-leaved evergreen for informal hedge. White spring flowers. Part shade. Zone 7.

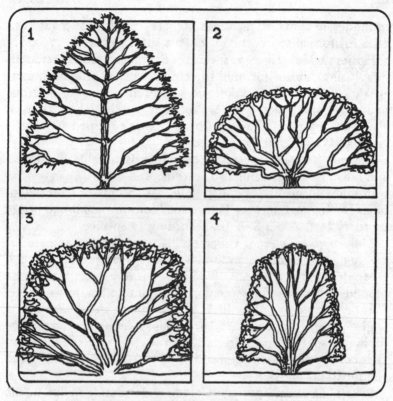

Shapes of hedges: **1** Japanese yew, white pine, and hemlock. **2** Japanese barberry and mugo pine. **3** Japanese yew (spreading forms). **4** Privet (notice that hedge is pruned wider at the base than top).

Forsythia *(Forsythia* species). Large shrub with yellow flowers in spring. Informal hedge for large properties. Zone 5.

Germander *(Teucrium chamaedrys).* Low hedge for herb and flower gardens. Can be clipped. Zone 5.

Hemlock *(Tsuga canadensis).* Outstanding informal to formal evergreen hedge but needs space. Sun to part shade. Zone 3.

Holly *(Ilex* species). Evergreen kinds usual for hedges. For mild to moderate climates. Japanese holly *(I. crenata)* has many varieties for formal to informal use. Part shade. Zone 6.

Honeysuckle *(Lonicera* species). Evergreen and deciduous (leaf-losing) shrubs for mild to cold climates. Tartarian honeysuckle *(L. tatarica)* has pink flowers and red berries for informal hedge in ample space. Zone 5. Box honeysuckle *(L. nitida),* small evergreen leaves and fragrant flowers. Can be clipped. Not hardy north of Washington, D.C. Zone 7.

Juniper *(Juniperus* species). Several kinds suitable for formal and informal hedges and also screens. Red-cedar *(J. virginiana),* with many forms, is very adaptable. Also forms of Chinese juniper *(J. chinensis),* such as 'Pfitzeriana,' for informal broad hedge up to 10 feet. Zones 3 to 10, according to species.

Lilac *(Syringa vulgaris).* Common lilac is often used as an informal hedge along drives and walks on larger properties. Zone 4.

Maple, Hedge *(Acer campestre).* Tree up to 25 feet but can be topped well below for screening or desirable height as hedge. Can be clipped or left natural. Yellow foliage in fall. Zone 5.

Pine, White *(Pinus strobus).* Forms dense, high screening hedge for ample space. Zone 3. In cold, windswept regions of the West, Colorado spruce *(Picea pungens)* is widely used for screening and windbreaks. Zone 3.

Privet *(Ligustrum* species). Common deciduous hedge in the North, and other evergreen species used in mild climates. Usually sheared one or two times a season. Best choice for sturdy, fast-growing wall of greenery.

Rose *(Rosa* species). Rugosa rose *(R. rugosa),* rugged, prickly shrub for sand and seaside (Zone 2). Other shrub roses used as barrier hedges and screens. Lower-growing floribunda roses make attractive flowering hedges. (See Roses.)

Russian-olive *(Elaeagnus* species). Large evergreen or deciduous shrubs with fragrant flowers, silvery leaves, and fall fruits. Most grown as informal hedge or screen. Thorny elaeagnus *(E. pungens)* is often clipped. Zone 7.

Yew *(Taxus* species). Needle-leaved evergreens of various heights respond well to shearing and training. Many spreading and upright forms of both Japanese yew *(T. cuspidata)* and *T.* x *media* (both Zone 5).

(See the Zone Map, page 229.)

HERBS AND HERB GARDENING. Just a few herb plants—lavender and basil are good examples—placed where you brush their leaves as you move about the garden can please the senses with their mingling aromas. Of more practical value are the several herbs you can grow for flavoring foods, either in their fresh state or dried for later use.

The easiest way to get started with herbs is to buy a few seedling plants in spring at a local garden center. But since most herbs are annuals and perennials (a few others are shrubs), they can quite easily be grown from seeds and handled as you would marigolds and zinnias. (See Annuals, Perennials, and Propagation.) You can grow herbs in the vegetable garden, chives and basil along the path, for instance. Or set aside a corner of the vegetable garden for a patch of mixed herbs. Rather than scattering the seeds randomly, at first sow them in rows or blocks, well labeled, so you will know which is which.

Most annual herbs combine well with annual flowers. The purple-leaved basil 'Dark Opal' is ornamental—as well as flavorful—and makes a contrasting background for lower-growing yellow French marigolds. Seeds of the taller dill can be scattered over the soil in the background of an annual garden.

On smaller properties, where space is precious, tuck a few herb plants here and there—wherever there is sun and good drainage. (See the following Sampler of Herbs for the herbs that tolerate some shade.) For those who do most of their gardening on a patio or apartment terrace, the bushy, lower-growing herbs can be grown in pots or planters. You can maintain a nearly complete herb garden in a squat 7- to 8-inch-wide clay pot (herbs seem to look and grow better in clay, but if you do not tend to overwater, a plastic container should be satisfactory). Plants to stuff into the pot could be a plant or two of basil, parsley, chives, summer savory, and dill. Harvesting the tips of plants to keep them bushy and frequent feeding with a liquid fertilizer should keep this little herb garden productive all summer.

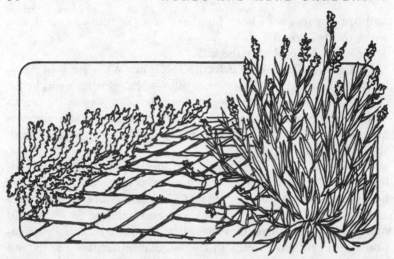

Place a lavender plant (right) along a walk or near the terrace so its distinctive scent can be appreciated. Creeping thyme (left) can withstand some foot traffic, releasing its fresh aroma as it is trod upon.

As you delve into herb lore, you will find that many herbs, once grown for sachets, medical, and other nonculinary purposes, are widely used today simply because of their decorative value. Lavender, rue, lavender-cotton (santolina), germander, clove pinks, and catmint *(Nepeta* x *faassenii)* are some of the major herbs seen in perennial borders. They of course continue to be used in all-herb gardens along with the culinary herbs.

The majority of herbs like all the sun they can get and a well-drained, not overly fertile soil. Rosemary, lavender, and clove pinks often do better in a near neutral soil, one to which ground limestone or wood ashes have been added. (See Soil.)

HARVESTING AND DRYING—Annuals, such as basil, become bushier when the stems are partially cut, as needed. If you harvest the entire plant, that is, cut it off at ground level, that will be the end of the plant—unless of course you are drying it.

Perennial plants like the mints can be drastically cut back and

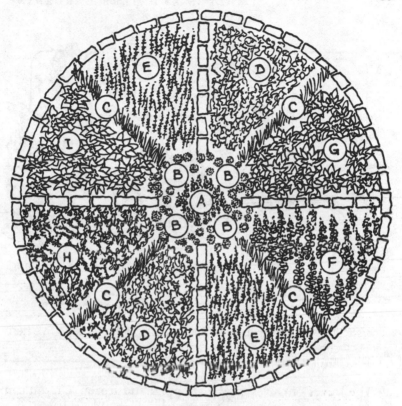

Plan for a herb garden wheel: use bricks on their edges for the
outline of the wheel and major spokes.
KEY: **A** Lavender. **B** Dill. **C** Chives. **D** Thyme. **E** Summer savory. **F**
Sweet marjoram. **G** Green basil. **H** 'Dark Opal' basil (purple-
leaved). **I** Parsley.

will just continue to make new growth. The needlelike leaves of
rosemary can be cut off, or you can remove partial stems to
induce bushiness. When harvesting parsley leaves, you can cut
the entire stem off at ground level. The leaves of chives should be
cut off at ground level. New growth will follow.

The smallest herb garden: a container stuffed with three to five herb plants—chives, basil, rosemary, and parsley.

The leaves of chives can be chopped and frozen. Or you can chop and freeze a mixture of herbs—basil, parsley, chives, tarragon—and thaw later to add to herbed bread, egg dishes, or whatever. Tarragon leaves can be preserved in vinegar (white is preferable). Remove the leaves as you need them and use the flavored vinegar for salads.

The easiest way to dry herbs is to hang the stems, tied in bunches, upside down in a dry, airy room for a few weeks. If you enclose the cut herbs in paper bags (make a few holes in them for ventilation), you won't have to crawl around the floor gathering the leaves that have dropped off as they dry. Of course, you can place newspapers on the floor beneath the hanging herbs.

After the leaves have dried, strip and crumble them and keep them in tight glass jars.

▨▨▨▨ A SAMPLER ▨▨▨▨
OF CULINARY HERBS

Basil *(Ocimum basilicum)*. Annual, about 12 to 18 inches, depending on variety. Bushy, with fresh green, pungently fragrant foliage especially suitable for tomato dishes. 'Dark Opal' has purple leaves; 'Green Bouquet,' very small leaves. Easy to grow from seeds sown indoors or outside after soil warms.

Chervil *(Anthriscus cerefolium)*. Annual or biennial with ferny foliage on 12- to 18-inch plants. Leaves have licorice flavor and go well with fish and egg dishes. Withstands shade and likes humus-rich soil. Sow seeds in early spring or late summer. Self-sows.

Chives *(Allium schoenoprasum)*. Perennial with grassy foliage and attractive purple flowers in early summer. Buy a plant and increase your supply by division (see Propagation) in spring or fall. Or sow seeds in spring. Essential, easy to grow. Garlic chives *(A. tuberosum)*. Leaves taller and wider. Pretty white flowers in midsummer. Also a perennial that self-sows.

Dill *(Anethum graveolens)*. Tall annual to 3 feet with fine-cut foliage as flavorful as the seeds. Scatter the seeds in early spring (no need to wait until soil has warmed) where plants are to remain, as transplanting seems to stunt their growth (for me, anyway). Resow in late summer through fall.

Mint *(Mentha* species). Vigorous spreading perennials that can become pests. Nevertheless, you'll want a patch or two somewhere, especially of peppermint *(M.* x *piperita)*, spearmint *(M. spicata)*, and perhaps some of the others—if you are a mint fan. Mints like moist, rich soil and some shade, yet they grow well enough in almost any situation.

Parsley *(Petroselinum crispum)*. Grown as an annual but technically a biennial, as plants often survive winter to flower, then disappear. Sow seeds in spring after soaking in a glass of water overnight. Or buy seedlings and place in humus-rich soil. Grows in part shade. A good edging plant for annual or vegetable garden, perhaps interplanted with basil and nasturtiums.

Rosemary *(Rosmarinus officinalis)*. Evergreen shrub grown as pot or tub subject indoors in winter in North. Buy plants and overwinter in a cool, sunny window or place small pots under fluorescent lights.

Sage *(Salvia officinalis)*. Perennial, often shrublike, up to 2 to 3 feet or more, with grayish, aromatic leaves and spikes of purple-blue flowers in summer. Buy plants. Cut back woody stems in spring to force new bushy growth.

Summer Savory *(Satureja hortensis)*. Annual to about 18 inches with small flavorful leaves. Pink flowers in summer can be attractive. Sow seeds or buy plants.

Sweet Marjoram *(Origanum majorana)*. Perennial but usually started anew from seeds each spring. Sprawling plant that thrives in hot, dry soil.

Tarragon, French *(Artemisia dracunculus)*. Bushy perennial, not reliably winter-hardy in most northern regions, up to 2 to 3 feet. Buy plants and mulch over winter. (See also Mulches and Mulching.)

Thyme, Common *(Thymus vulgaris)*. Evergreen sprawling or semicreeping shrub to 12 inches with very small, highly flavorful leaves. Other thymes can also be used for flavoring, including the well-known mother-of-thyme *(T. praecox)*, used as a ground cover. Buy seeds or plants. Most plants of all thymes will self-sow.

⬛⬛⬛⬛ SPECIAL PROJECT ⬛⬛⬛⬛
A KITCHEN HERB GARDEN UNDER LIGHTS

What better place for an indoor herb garden than the kitchen? This little garden can be maintained there all year by those who do not have access to the outdoors. Or it can be started in fall for a source of fresh green herbs all winter by those who prefer the fresh product to the dry.

The herbs will do moderately well in a south or southeast window, but I have found the most reliable results are from ever-shining (no cloudy days) fluorescent tubes. (See Indoor Gardening.) A tabletop fixture 24 inches long with two 20-watt tubes (available from mail-order sources or most garden centers) is just the right size to stand at the back of a kitchen table or on a cabinet. (If you do not have space in the kitchen, find another location, but it is convenient—and inspiring to the cook—to have the herbs so handy.

For a beginning, limit your herb selection to those that grow quickly from seed and have wide culinary use. Basil, dill, parsley, sweet marjoram, and summer savory fit this category. In addition to the seed packets, you will need four or five small flats or containers (about 5½ by 7½ inches are the standard seed flats available), a bag of soilless mix such as Redi-Earth or Jiffy Mix or any general purpose potting soil that is sterilized, and a shallow pan or tray that will fit under the light fixture and catch leaking moisture from the seed flats.

Moisten the soilless mix or soil (one way is to pour water—not too much—into their plastic bags and wait a few hours until the medium has become damp but not soggy), then fill the flats to their brim, firming the medium to achieve a level surface. Sow one or two kinds of herbs in each flat, either in rows about half an inch deep or scatter the seeds over the surface. (This is one occasion when thick sowing is allowed, as the purpose of this garden is to harvest young herbs quickly rather than to grow large specimen plants.) Cover the seeds lightly, slip the flats into plastic bags, and wait until the seeds germinate. The parsley may be slow, basil and dill fairly quick, with sweet marjoram and summer savory close behind.

As soon as germination begins, remove the flats from the plastic protection and turn on the fluorescent tubes for 16 hours a day. A timer is convenient for keeping the light consistent. The tubes must be lowered so they are 3 to 4 inches above the seedlings, then raised as they develop.

As the flats dry out, water by placing them in a basin of water for a few minutes or until the surface is damp. There will be some fertilizer in the soilless mix, but when the plants are 3 inches or so high, start feeding them with a dilute fish emulsion or some other liquid fertilizer mixed according to directions.

Begin harvesting as soon as there are enough leaves to add flavor to scrambled eggs, butter, or whatever you wish. I clip off my herbs with scissors and never bother to wash them. If you want larger, chunkier plants, you can always transplant a few seedlings into 3- to 4-inch pots, but you can also thin out some of the crowded seedlings to leave more space for the others to develop. Or just make new sowings as you deplete the supply of seedlings.

Pots of rosemary or bay can be squeezed under the fluorescent tubes to give flavor variety. You can also pick up pots of chives at supermarkets. The more adventurous herb gardeners rely on their established chives clumps from the garden for indoor use in winter. This is a little more complicated and involves the technique of forcing. In the fall, lift a clump of chives, digging deeply to reach the roots. Gently separate the clump into a few sections (not individual plants) in a size that can be stuffed into 3- to 4-inch pots, retaining much of the original soil around the roots. If necessary, add enough soil to fill the top of the pot around the chives, then sink the pots in soil up to their rims. The green tops will die down. Wait until the plants have had a rest and undergone about 6 to 8 weeks of cold temperatures. Dig them up, clean off the soil on the pots, and place them in a sunny window or under the fluorescent lights. Water as necessary. Be patient and the plants will soon break into growth. Harvest the leaves by cutting off with scissors. In the spring, the clumps can be replanted in the garden and soon will be as good as new.

HOUSE PLANTS. See Indoor Gardening.

HUMUS. See Compost and Soil.

I

INDOOR GARDENING. Today there is far more to indoor gardening than growing a few nondescript house plants. Houses are better lighted, windows are larger, and where natural light is inadequate you can use fluorescent lights. Better light conditions have increased the variety of flowering and foliage plants that can be successfully grown indoors and have also made it practical to start seeds indoors for later planting outdoors. (See Propagation.) Indoor gardening makes gardening a yearlong activity in cold climates and gives apartment dwellers the chance to grow plants under fluorescent lights.

THE ENVIRONMENT FOR PLANTS INDOORS

LIGHT REQUIREMENTS—A few house plants can survive in subdued light, a famous case being the well-named cast-iron plant, but the majority need all the light they can receive. Most flowering house plants require 4 or more hours of sun during winter, such as comes from an east, south, or west window. Then when spring arrives, a south or west window may be too bright for flowering plants like the African-violet, which may have to be switched to a north window or moved back so it is shaded by larger plants.

When natural light is deficient, fluorescent lights can be used. However, many foliage plants, including the beautiful variants of the Boston fern, do very well in a north-facing window. One plant, the spathe flower, even will produce its odd ghostly flowers for you.

PLANTS FOR NORTH-FACING WINDOWS AND LOW LIGHT

ASPARAGUS-FERN	NERVE PLANT
BABY'S-TEARS	NORFOLK-ISLAND-PINE
CAST-IRON PLANT	PALMS (most kinds)
CHINESE EVERGREEN	PEPEROMIA
DRACAENA	PHILODENDRON
DUMB CANE	POTHOS
FALSE-ARALIA	PRAYER PLANT
FERNS	SCREW-PINE
FIGS (most kinds)	SNAKE PLANT
GRAPE-IVY	SPATHE FLOWER
KANGAROO VINE	SPIDER PLANT
MONSTERA	STRAWBERRY-GERANIUM
NEPHTHYTIS	WANDERING JEW

FLUORESCENT LIGHTING—You have the choice of seeking special wide-spectrum tubes that have been developed specifically for plants or you can settle for ordinary fluorescent tubes, which give satisfactory results. Bargains in shoplight units, which are 48 inches long, are often available from hardware and department stores, and these make a sensible investment for a beginner in light gardening. They are not very good-looking and must be suspended over a bench or table with chains that can be adjusted to the heights of the plants. If you are growing plants of varying heights and pot sizes, you can stand the lower-growing plants on bricks or inverted pots, as obviously the light level is not going to be suitable for all plants.

Special kinds of fluorescent light units are available from some house plant suppliers and seed companies and locally from garden centers. These are often tabletop units, from 24 to 48 inches long, with the adjustable hood and tubes supported on legs. Then there are fancy systems with tiers of shelves, which have the advantage of being portable, but they are very expensive. You can also find special spotlights and vertical fluorescent lights, one being called a "sun stick."

You may wonder why fluorescent light is preferable to incandescent. Incandescent bulbs give off too much heat for most plants at the distance the plants must be to the light. They are generally more expensive to operate. However, you can take advantage of the evening light of an incandescent lamp on a table by placing a plant or plants about a foot under it. African-violets and most foliage plants will do well under this modest light.

Although fluorescent light is a satisfactory substitute for sunlight, it still is not as powerful, so you must keep fluorescent tubes burning about 15 to 16 hours daily. The best way to handle this is to buy a timer that puts the lights on early in the morning and automatically shuts them off in the evening.

The tops of most plants should be about 4 to 8 inches beneath the tubes, although foliage plants can be as low as 12 inches. As the light is stronger toward the center of fluorescent tubes, you can concentrate your flowering plants there and your foliage plants at the ends. Seedling plants should be placed near the center. The foliage and flower parts of most plants that touch the tubes eventually burn.

You can grow any plant under fluorescent lights. Some that do especially well are African-violets and their many relatives (referred to as gesneriads, after the name of the family, *Gesneriaceae*), miniature roses, miniature geraniums, impatiens, begonias, cacti and succulents, azalea, bulbs, orchids, and annuals such as petunias and sweet-alyssum. Foliage plants always look healthier than when subjected to anemic light conditions and those with variegated foliage become much brighter in their coloring. Large plants in large pots either will not fit under most fluorescent tubes or simply take up too much space. Even healthy, well-grown African-violets with their brittle, spreading leaves become too large, so the enchanting miniature varieties are a better choice.

TEMPERATURES AND ATMOSPHERIC MOISTURE—Bone-dry, hot interiors have always been bad for furniture, people, and plants. Energy's higher costs have forced most of us to lower our thermostats a few degrees, which has been very beneficial to plant growth. Maintaining a daytime temperature of 65 to 70° F, with a 10- to 15° drop at night and a relative humidity of 40 to 50 percent, will please most plants grown indoors. Those plants that prefer cooler temperatures indoors can often be kept in a room with less heat or close to window glass, where temperatures are always colder.

Maintaining humidity in the air can be a problem in some apartments and is always a problem if you heat by wood-burning stoves. Standing pots on pebble-filled metal or plastic trays, with the water level kept beneath the bottoms of the pots, can usually solve the lack of humidity problem with plants growing under lights and in windows and other locations. The trays are almost a necessity anyway to catch the water that flows from pots after watering.

Humidity devices on furnaces increase humidity throughout the house. And house plants grouped together anywhere tend to increase the humidity in their vicinity. Some indoor-outdoor thermometers include a humidity indicator, and, of course, you can buy small indicators that can be placed near all your plant collections.

Spraying with a fine bottle mister (available in garden centers in various sizes) provides temporary air moisture, but use lukewarm water and avoid spraying African-violets in sunshine, as this can cause spotting.

PLANTS THAT THRIVE IN COOL (55–65° F) DAYTIME TEMPERATURES

AUCUBA	GERANIUM
AZALEA	IVY, ENGLISH
BULBS (spring)	KENILWORTH-IVY
CAMELLIA	MARGUERITE or BOSTON DAISY
CAST-IRON PLANT	NORFOLK-ISLAND-PINE
CHRYSANTHEMUM	PITTOSPORUM
CINERARIA	PODOCARPUS
CYCLAMEN	PRIMROSE
CYMBIDIUM	ROSEMARY
FREESIA	STRAWBERRY-GERANIUM
FUCHSIA	SWEET BAY TREE
GARDENIA	VELTHEIMIA

WINDOW GARDENS

A south, east, or west window can become an indoor garden—a place to display house plants from fall to spring. The first thing you may have to do is widen your windowsill (unless you are fortunate enough to have a bay with built-in wide shelves on which to place watertight trays). Do this by adding a board about 10 to 12 inches wide, its length depending on the window width. This board should be screwed to the windowsill and given additional support from two or more wooden legs. Of course you can make the shelf narrower, but then you will have less space for plants. Larger flowering plants can use up a lot of window space.

You will require plastic or metal trays a few inches deep—1½ to about 2½ inches—to hold a layer of pebbles on which the plants will stand above the water level. You can have metal trays

The addition of a board can widen a narrow window sill, giving more space for displaying house plants. The board will require support from legs or brackets.

made to your specifications locally or buy plastic trays at garden centers or from mail-order sources.

ARRANGING THE PLANTS—The fun begins when you plant the garden, that is, add the various potted plants. Select trailing plants like ivy or ferns for the foreground, which will mask the trays and shelf legs. Fill in behind them with begonias, impatiens, African-violets, azaleas, amaryllis, and other flowering plants mixed with foliage plants.

Try to keep flowering plants close to the window so they receive as much light as possible. Accent certain plants and also give them more light by standing them on inverted flower pots. If window temperatures are cool, African-violets, which do better with 70° F daytime temperatures, may stop flowering. Move them to a warmer location for recuperation, preferably under fluorescent tubes. Plants in a window soon grow and lean toward the source of light. Give the pots a partial turn every few days to keep their growth symmetrical. Rearranging the plants fairly often is a good idea.

HANGING PLANTS—Even with a large window, you may soon find that available space for additional plants is lacking. The solution is to take to the air. Suspend plants from a horizontal

Metal or plastic trays filled with gravel and water increase humidity
around the plants and make watering less messy. Stand the pots on
top of the gravel rather than submerged in the water.

pole at the top of the window. You can also use brackets set at the
sides of the windows. Hanging plants contribute an elegant touch
to the window garden and thrive in their well-lighted atmosphere
kept moist from water evaporated by the trays and plants below.

It is not necessary to choose vining plants to hang unless you
wish to, but especially graceful plants with airy foliage should be
considered. Possibilities include ferns with lacy fronds, orchids in
bloom, spider plants, asparagus-ferns, orchid cacti in bloom,
scented geraniums, impatiens, and any plant with long-stemmed
leaves, such as many begonias and the piggyback plant (*Tolmiea*).
Toward spring, as the sun gets stronger, the air space in an east,
west, or south window may become too strong for ferns and some
foliage plants, but during the winter they make a glorious display.

One of the pleasures of window gardening is that the scene
changes as the seasons progress—just as in an outdoor garden.
In time you will work out your own succession of bloom calendar,
but for a start—and as a way of adding to your plant collection—

There is no wasted space when plants are suspended from a sturdy
rod or pole placed at the top of a window.

---

keep in touch with local garden centers and florists. Chrysanthemums are now available nearly year around, but the bargains and
greatest variety are usually found in the fall, then Thanksgiving
and Christmas cacti in November (they are now collectively referred to as holiday cacti), poinsettias and kalanchoe through
Christmas and New Year's, cyclamen in January, azaleas in February, and cinerarias in March. Others include amaryllis and forced
spring bulbs, such as tulips, daffodils, and hyacinths.

In my window garden I rely on a succession of paper-white
narcissus bulbs all winter. I purchase a few dozen of the bulbs in

the fall with my outdoor bulb order and then start about five bulbs at a time into growth in a bowl of pebbles and water every 3 weeks or so.

CARE OF HOUSE PLANTS

WATERING—Potted plants require water when their soil or growing medium becomes dry. Only a few plants—mostly cacti and succulents—can survive long after this. Unfortunately, there is no magic formula to pass on to new gardeners for how to know when to water.

Some gardeners can tell by the "feel" of the soil, that is, by inserting a finger into the pot. Others lift the pot: dry soil will be lighter, especially noticeable with the synthetic mixes that can look dark and wet when they are decidedly dry. A wilted plant can be the sign of a dried-out soil, but it can also be misleading, as saturated soils also cause wilting. (See also Watering.)

The environment indoors does have an effect on how quickly plants dry out. Potted plants dry out much faster in warm rooms with low humidity. Plants under fluorescent lights and in sunny windows also need water more frequently. Generally, small-size pots dry out faster, as do sandy soil and some soilless mixes. Any nonporous container of plastic or glazed pottery dries out less quickly than a clay pot.

While it is important to water plants before drought settles in, overwatering must be avoided, too. Most new gardeners tend to overwater. Do not let pots sit in the water of trays—fill the trays with small pebbles so the pots rest above the water level. Remove excess water from the pots' saucers after an hour or so.

Eventually you will get the hang of watering for your conditions. Rarely do plants require daily watering, but it pays to check, just the same. As growth accelerates in the spring, more frequent watering is usually necessary.

Just remember: avoid "wet feet," the affliction that sets in when pots sit constantly in water.

PRUNING AND PINCHING—Even under the best of growing conditions, many house plants that live on year after year eventually need some pruning or pinching back to induce new vigorous growth and to maintain a bushy, compact appearance. Usually about one third of the old straggly growth can be cut off. In the case of flowering plants, this can be done right after the plant has finished—or is about to finish—its blooming, either in the spring or in the fall. With some plants, such as the vining grape-ivy, philodendron, and wandering Jew, timing is not important and excessive growth can simply be snipped off when it is noticed.

Examples of flowering plants to trim back in spring include the poinsettia, gardenia, Chinese hibiscus, begonias that have been flowering all winter, and azalea. A word of caution regarding the azalea: do not prune drastically into the old wood; restrict pruning to pinching back tips of new growth, especially more vigorous shoots, and cease in early summer when new flower buds begin forming. Flowering-maple *(Abutilon)* blooms in spring and summer, so growth can be reduced about one half in the fall. Continue some pinching during the winter to induce more spring flowers.

Many African-violet fanciers prefer to maintain their plants with a single crown. In very early stages, developing crowns can be removed with tweezers; later on, a small knife may be necessary, although I have seen professional growers pinch out excessive crowns with their fingers without any mayhem to the rest of the so-brittle plant.

FERTILIZING HOUSE PLANTS—Potted plants in active growth, those growing under fluorescent lights or in sunny windows in the spring, benefit from fertilizer applications given in reasonable amounts. There are many kinds of fertilizers (see Fertilizers) that have been packaged for house plants, including fish emulsion types and others that are diluted in water. You can also use plain garden-type fertilizers, such as superphosphate, 5-10-5, and the like.

I have largely solved the fertilizer problem by giving little amounts often—usually as I water the plants. One kind to use in this manner is Schultz Liquid Fertilizer (7 drops in a quart of water), which gives a constant but light supply of nutrients.

Lack of fertilizer is not what usually ails plants indoors. More often, the plant is not receiving enough light, is being roasted to death or the other extreme, frozen, or is being under- or overwatered. Or it may have a pest problem.

PESTS ON INDOOR PLANTS—There is a long list of insects and diseases that can plague house plants—mostly the same ones that exist outdoors—but it is unlikely you will encounter all of them. Eventually you will probably see aphids, mites, and possibly scales and white flies. Diseases are often less of a problem, but mildew sometimes appears as a white-grayish mealylike growth on begonia leaves. If you decide to grow miniature roses under the lights, as you should since they are a delight, you must spray the foliage for black spot disease. Both mildew and black spot can be controlled by Benlate or Karathane and a recent control, Ortho's Funginex.

Aphids, soft, sucking insects of various colors, appear on new growth or on undersides of leaves. Wash them off or use one of the house plant spray cans of malathion or rotenone, formulated to control them.

Mealybugs are white fluffy pests that may infest African-violets, amaryllis, begonia, cacti, coleus, jade plant, ferns, fuchsia, gardenia, piggyback plant, poinsettia, and rubber plants. Spray with pressure can containing rotenone, pyrethrum, or malathion. Swab small infestations with a Q-tip dipped in alcohol. Sooty mold is a sticky black fungus that sometimes grows on residue (called honeydew) from mealybugs and scales. It can be washed off and disappears when its host pests are controlled.

Red spider mites, truly tiny spiders, make grayish webs on leaf undersides of ivy, azalea, cacti, citrus, and certain other plants. Badly infested leaves lose color and soon drop. The correct indoor environment and culture are the best controls: cool rooms with reasonable humidity and the avoidance of overwatering the potting mix. Or wash the leaves and spray with Kelthane according to directions.

Cyclamen mites are so tiny that you need a microscope to see them, but their damage is plain enough: curled, distorted leaf and flower growth. They are most common on cyclamen and African-violets. Badly infested plants might as well be thrown out, but Kelthane, used as a spray or dip, can work. When dipping Afri-

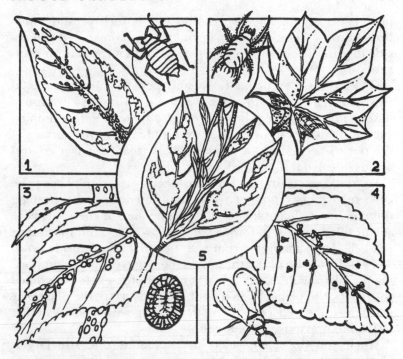

Some common pests of indoor plants: **1** Aphids. **2** Red spider mites.
3 Scales. **4** White flies. **5** Mealybugs (within white waxy covering).

can-violets, use tepid water. There are other mite sprays you may
use—look in your garden centers and read the labels.

Scales of various kinds can be insidious. They are waxy, often
oval or round little humps on stems and leaves and can infest
citrus, orchids, ferns (don't mistake fern spores, which occur in
regular patterns and cannot be flicked off, for scales), bromeliads,
cacti, ivy, palms, figs. The control is malathion, mixed and
sprayed according to instructions on the package. Better control
is finally achieved if severe infestations are first removed with an
old toothbrush dipped in malathion solution. (Do not use malathion on ferns; use a pressure spray containing resmethrin.)

White flies are small flying insects that rise in a cloud when the plant is disturbed. Their special favorite is fuchsia, and sometimes citrus, coleus, gardenia, geranium, and tomato—if you decide to grow a vegetable indoors. Spray with a resmethrin pressure can.

One way to keep plants reasonably pest-free and clean is to swish the plant in a bath of lukewarm water with dissolved soap flakes. Larger plants can be bathed with a sponge. Before dipping smaller plants, wrap newspaper over and around the surface of the pot to keep the soil in place. This treatment can control aphids, mealybugs, and red spider mites.

POTTING AND REPOTTING AND SOIL MIXES—You don't have to be concerned about repotting a plant until you notice roots pushing through the drainage hole in the bottom and/or the roots have solidly filled the pot to form a dense network around the plant's soil ball. To examine the root ball, turn the plant upside down and gently tap the rim of the pot on the edge of a table, supporting the plant with one hand. When the pot is excessively filled with roots, the plant is called pot-bound. Even so, the plant may get along quite well if you follow the feeding-with-every-watering technique previously mentioned.

When you do repot, select a pot that is one size larger. Overpotting a plant, that is, placing it in a much larger-size pot than its previous pot, can slow flowering and cause rotting if the soil is overwatered.

You can buy soil mixes, either synthetic or true soil, in varying proportions of sand, humus ingredients such as peat moss, and soil, usually labeled for general purpose potting or for special plant groups, such as cacti, African-violets, or azaleas. If these soil mixtures are marked sterilized, they are safe to use for seed sowing. (Among house plants to grow from seed are African-violet and relatives, coleus, geraniums, begonias, coffee plant, and impatiens.)

You may prefer to mix your own basic potting soil, and this is very simple to do. Start with 2 parts garden soil and add 1 part sand and peat moss, leaf mold, or compost or a combination of these three humus sources. If you know your soil is excessively sandy, increase the humus content. Mix these ingredients to-

1 To remove a plant from its pot, tap the rim on the edge of a table.
2 If the soil is excessively filled with roots, the plant can be moved
into a larger pot. **3** Soil (indicated by dotted line) has been added to
new pot. Some drainage material or a stone or two can be placed in
the bottom to prevent new soil from slipping through drainage hole
or holes, but must not impede excess water from passing out of pot.
4 Potting an amaryllis bulb: Despite their large size, bulbs prefer a
tight, rather cosy potting relationship. A 6-inch pot is usually about
right. Always allow 2/3 of bulb to protrude above soil.

gether. However, do not use this potting soil for starting seeds, as it is not sterile.

Before potting or repotting, soak clay pots—if new—in water for an hour or so. This is to prevent them from drawing moisture from the soil to the detriment of the plant's roots. The potting procedure itself is considerably simplified from the good old days when layers of broken crocks (pieces of clay pots) and roughage were layered in the bottom of the container, supposedly to aid drainage. All you have to do is place a stone or piece of crock over the drainage hole to confine the soil mix, particularly the often fine synthetic mixtures. Then add enough soil so the crown of the plant will be about 1/2 to 1 inch below the rim of the pot. Before filling with the remaining soil, be sure the plant is centered in the center of the pot. If the plant being repotted is extremely root-bound, loosen or comb out some of the roots. Do not leave any air pockets in the soil around the sides—use a pencil or dowel to ram the soil firmly around the plant. Water the plant. If the soil level falls below the 1/2- to 1-inch level after watering, add more soil.

VACATIONS FOR YOU AND THE PLANTS—Most indoor plants appreciate a summer vacation outdoors. Expose them gradually to the stronger light, and of course do not place foliage plants in sunshine. If you have a partially shaded terrace, use foliage plants as part of the decoration. Plants in clay pots can be sunk in the open ground so they do not dry out so fast. African-violets and other fuzzy-leaved plants and many ferns prefer a more sheltered location, where they will not be exposed to winds and rain.

As for your vacations—if you do not have a plant sitter—most plants in winter will survive quite well if you lower the thermostat and give them a good soaking before you leave. If you expect to be away for more than a week, cover the plants with a thin layer of plastic. For longer vacation periods, individual plants can be slipped into plastic bags. If you close the tops, the plants must be kept from bright sunshine.

INCREASING HOUSE PLANTS—They are propagated in the same ways as outdoor plants—cuttings, division, and seeds. These techniques are described under Propagation.

▨▨▨▨ A SAMPLER OF FAVORITE ▨▨▨▨
INDOOR PLANTS

African-violet *(Saintpaulia* species and many cultivars). Not related to hardy violets *(Viola).* For fluorescent lights or diffused winter sun. Needs warmth and high humidity. Use tepid water; avoid wetting leaves.

Amaryllis *(Hippeastrum* species and hybrids). Sun. These large bulbs should not be overpotted; use a 5- to 6-inch pot; allow 2/3 of bulb to protrude after potting. Keep dry until flower bud shows, then water. After bloom, water as necessary until fall to keep foliage growing, then let bulb rest by withholding water.

Avocado *(Persea americana).* Bright light, partial shade in summer. To start from seed: suspend in water until green shoot and roots appear, then pot.

Azalea *(Rhododendron* hybrids). Bright light, cool location. Needs acid, humus-rich soil. Summer outdoors in part shade.

Baby's-tears *(Soleirolia soleirolii).* Bright or diffused light in winter, part shade in summer. Needs lots of water.

Begonia *(Begonia* spp. and cultivars). Sun (4 or more hours) in winter, diffused sun to partial shade in summer. Flowering begonias, such as wax, need more bright light than foliage types.

Bulbs, Spring. Potted tulips, daffodils, and hyacinths can be forced for indoor bloom. Buy them in bud from florists. Daffodils and hyacinths can be planted outdoors in spring, if foliage is retained. Sun. Cool windows.

Cacti, Desert types. Many kinds, some remaining very small. Ideal for hot, dry rooms with sun or fluorescent tubes. Water sparingly during winter—just often enough to prevent the plant from shriveling. Increase water in spring.

Cacti, Orchid or Jungle types. Best known are Thanksgiving cactus *(Schlumbergera truncata)* and Christmas cactus *(S.* x *buckleyi),* with flattened, crablike jointed stems and colorful orange, red, magenta, or white flowers. Both bloom freely at proper seasons if subjected to short-day treatment (no light after dusk) or cool temperatures in fall. These require more water than desert cacti and more humus in potting mixture.

Cast-iron Plant *(Aspidistra elatior)*. Withstands poor light, but better with bright light to diffused sun in winter. Variegated form is more attractive. Avoid overwatering in winter.

Chrysanthemum *(Chrysanthemum* cultivars). Sun and a cool window. Discard after flowers fade, unless you have a greenhouse.

Coleus *(Coleus blumei)*. Sun or fluorescent lights. Part shade in summer. Pinch off tips to maintain bushiness. Cuttings will root in water.

Cyclamen *(Cyclamen persicum)*. Sun or fluorescent lights and cool temperatures. Moist (not soggy) soil. Difficult.

Dracaena or **Corn Plant** *(Dracaena* species and cultivars). Outstanding foliage plants for bright to diffused winter sun. Gold-dust dracaena *(D. surculosa)*, with handsome white-and-yellow-spotted leaves, is a tough plant tolerant of warm and cool temperature extremes.

Dumb Cane *(Dieffenbachia maculata)*. Bright light, even sun in winter, part shade in summer. Prefers warm, humid location.

Ferns. Many kinds, the Boston and its variants being very popular. Prefer high humidity and cool temperatures but tolerant of varying indoor environments so long as they are watered as necessary. Winter sun, part shade in summer. Repot in humus-rich soil.

Figs *(Ficus* species and cultivars). Many excellent foliage plants here, from large rubber plant *(F. elastica)* to treelike weeping fig *(F. benjamina)*, down to slow-growing mistletoe fig *(F. deltoidea)* and creeping fig *(F. pumila)*. Bright to diffused winter sun. Avoid overwatering, especially in winter.

Gardenia *(Gardenia jasminoides)*. Diffused winter sun, part shade later. Needs high humidity and acid, humus-rich soil.

Geranium *(Pelargonium* species and cultivars). Scented-leaf kinds give indoor fragrance. All geraniums like cool, sunny windows. Grow miniatures under fluorescent lights.

Grape-ivy *(Cissus rhombifolia)*. Sun to diffused sun in winter windows. Kangaroo vine is close relative.

Impatiens *(Impatiens* species and cultivars). Sun or fluorescent lights. Do not overwater. Can be as attractive indoors as out. Easy to propagate by cuttings.

Ivy, English *(Hedera helix).* Sun or bright light in winter. Dislikes hot, dry rooms. Avoid overwatering. Part shade in summer. Stems grow and last well in bottles of water.

Jade Plant *(Crassula* species). Succulent for hot, dry rooms with sun to bright light in winter. Let soil dry out between watering.

Norfolk-Island-pine *(Araucaria heterophylla).* Sun in winter, part shade in summer. Prefers cooler rooms. Eventually becomes large, handsome small tree for tub. Humus-rich soil.

Orchids. A huge, diverse plant group. Many do better in greenhouses than in most homes. However, there are quite a few that can thrive as house plants, including cattleya, cymbidium (choose miniature varieties), laelia, and lady-slipper *(Paphiopedilum).* They need 4 to 5 hours of sun in winter (such as in a window or under fluorescent lights), but partial shade in spring and summer. Many require cool conditions at night (50 to 60° F). Orchids need a quick-draining growing medium, usually composed of bark, sometimes combined with peat moss and other plant fibers. (These mixes are available from orchid specialists and sometimes from garden centers.)

Peperomia *(Peperomia* species and cultivars). Small succulents for bright to diffused sun. Do not overwater. Allow soil to dry out between waterings.

Philodendron *(Philodendron* species and cultivars). Bright light. Avoid overwatering. Several kinds including the overused but tolerant of poor light heart-leaf to Swiss cheese monstera.

Poinsettia *(Euphorbia pulcherrima).* Sun to bright light. Modern hybrids are tough and long-lasting. Avoid overwatering. Let soil dry out between waterings. Its red, pink, or white "flowers" are really bracts around small yellow true flowers.

To rebloom old plants at Christmas, cut back the stems to leave stubs about 6 inches high, which should force new, vigorous growth. Water as necessary. When frost danger has passed and weather is warm, put the pot outdoors in sun (if the pot is clay, you can sink it in soil to its rim, which will prevent its drying out too quickly). Continue to cut back (pinch off) new growth—only a few inches—through early summer, but no later. Of course you can keep pinching back new growth as long as you wish, but this will prevent flowering, which is our aim here. To obtain Christmas flowers, you must give short-day treatment to the poinsettia for about 6 weeks beginning in midfall, when you must bring the plant indoors, as nights become cold. The short-day treatment consists of the plant being given 14 hours of darkness per day by being placed in a dark closet or covered by a cardboard carton beginning in late afternoon. In the morning, the poinsettia must be placed back in a well-lighted situation, preferably where it receives 4 or more hours of sun. A lot of trouble? Well, yes, but perhaps worth it, when the floral bracts finally show color.

Schefflera or **Umbrella Tree** (*Brassaia actinophylla*). Treelike foliage plant for sun to bright light in winter, part shade in summer. Tolerant of warm rooms and low humidity. Avoid overwatering.

Snake Plant (*Sansevieria trifasciata*). Tough foliage plant that tolerates poor light, drafts, hot and dry interiors. Under better conditions may bear small, scented flowers. Avoid overwatering.

Spider Plant (*Chlorophytum comosum*). Graceful, grassy plant for hanging containers in bright windows. Easy and intriguing with its spidery offshoots that can be removed and potted for new plants.

Strawberry-geranium or **Strawberry-begonia** (*Saxifraga stolonifera*). Also known as mother-of-thousands because of its offshoots on thin runners that can be removed and potted. Susceptible to cyclamen mites, which cause distorted growth. Prefers cool day and night temperatures. Avoid overwatering.

▩▩▩▩ SPECIAL PROJECT ▩▩▩▩
ORCHIDS FOR THE WINTER WINDOW GARDEN

Can anyone grow orchids? If the Sunday newspaper features and almost annual articles in various magazines are to be believed, the answer is a definite yes. At the other extreme is the purist who does not believe it possible to grow a decent orchid

DEREK FELL

MARJORIE J. DIETZ

(Above) Gazebos, arbors, and other garden structures function as ornaments as well as shelters from sun and wind. They can bring intimacy and charm to larger gardens, as does this gazebo that is a focal point of two extensive flower borders. (Left) Annuals provide masses of color all summer, as is shown by these yellow zinnias and red salvias.

(Left) Perennial grouping for late summer features a tall clump of yellow goldenrod and chrysanthemums. (Below left) Sweet William, a biennial, is available in white, pink, salmon, and rich red colors and fills the early summer garden with fragrance. (Below right) The flowers of daffodils appear in spring, but the bulbs must be planted in the fall. They are most effective in informal groupings.

(Above) The author's perennial garden in early summer includes the ornamental blue-flowered catnip (Nepeta x faassenii), white astilbe, lupine, and for later bloom, phlox, day-lilies, and globe-thistle. (Right) A plant group of spring flowers in the same garden shows yellow euphorbia or cushion spurge, tulips, and dwarf iris.

(Above) English-style border of sweeping grandeur. White Shasta daisies and blue Siberian iris clumps are used freely to give contrast in color and form. (Left) Day-lilies are the stars of the summer garden, whether used in combination with other perennials or alone in their own border.

under normal house conditions. The truth is somewhere in between these two views. Nevertheless, as most orchids are more
suited to greenhouses because of their high light and high humidity requirements, growing them as house plants *is* a special
project. The new gardener who wants to grow orchids will find
out that they are quite different from other plants and even have
their own vocabulary.

To begin with orchids, start with a plant or two in full bloom
that the salesperson thinks will fit your indoor conditions. De-
mand full instructions on the plant's care. Try to find a beginner's
book on orchids as house plants, although few such books seem
to exist. (One is Rebecca Tyson Northern's *Orchids As House Plants*,
2nd revised edition, Dover Publications, New York.)

My greatest success with orchids as house plants has been with
cymbidiums. These orchids have long, ribbonlike leaves and
spikes of durable, beautiful flowers that look as though they had
been molded from wax. They are often used in corsages. My
seven mature cymbidium plants are grown in 8-inch clay pots
(exceptions are two miniature cymbidiums in 6-inch pots) in an
east-facing over-sized window in winter, along with other house
plants. The main—often spectacular—flower display in this window garden is provided by the cymbidiums. The first flowers
appear in November on a variety named 'Bethlehem' because it
always is in bloom at Christmas, and weeks before and after. As
all my varieties are different and do not bloom at the same time, I
have some cymbidium flowers from November to mid-May.

Cymbidiums do require cool indoor temperatures. My house
in winter averages about 65° F during the day, with a 10- to 15°
drop at night, but the area of the window garden is often colder,
which seems to suit the cymbidiums just fine. During winter,
when maintaining indoor humidity levels is often a problem, I try
to mist the plants several times a day, most often in the morning
when the sun streams in. The pots are watered as often as the
bark-peat moss-perlite growing medium dries out. All the plants
in the window garden sit on top of pebbles in water-filled trays,
which help to keep the humidity close to 50 percent on most days.
(The pots must not sit *in* the water.) Orchid specialists would

probably say that my east window does not provide the maximum amount of light that cymbidiums require, but it is all I can give— the plants are much too large to fit under my fluorescent fixtures —and the plants do bloom and bloom well.

The rest of my cymbidium care is rather casual. As each plant finishes blooming, it is moved to other windows in other rooms wherever there is space. A cymbidium out of bloom is not a thing of beauty, and the large pots with their fountains of lengthy leaves require much space.

In midspring the plants are hustled outdoors, first for a few weeks on a semishaded, protected terrace, then to a more open area where they receive nearly full sun. Apart from watering during droughts and occasional feeding with a liquid fertilizer, the plants are on their own. The plants are kept pot-bound, as this condition seems to encourage more flower spikes, but eventually they need division and repotting, which should be done in spring.

During the fall, the plants get more tender care, such as being moved into sunnier areas, applying a high-phosphorus fertilizer, and watering as the pots dry out. The cool autumn nights and ample sunshine seem to be responsible for generous flower-spike formation, and probably help the later-flowering varieties form spikes after being brought indoors about November 1.

Other kinds of orchids you might want to consider growing among your house plants include the slippers (*Paphiopedilum* species and cultivars), which require far less space than cymbidiums and fit well under fluorescent fixtures along with African-violets, cattleyas, laelias, and oncidiums. But these are only a handful of the many kinds of orchids available—to try as house plants or to grow in a greenhouse.

INSECTS. See Indoor Gardening and Pests and Diseases.

J

JAPANESE GARDENS. See Landscaping.

K

KITCHEN GARDENS. See Herbs and Herb Gardening and Vegetables.

L

LANDSCAPING. Although landscaping as a term today is used to describe the casual planting of several shrubs picked out at random at a garden center or such jobs as garden maintenance and lawn mowing, landscaping has traditionally been concerned with planning and designing properties so they are organized and practical as well as beautiful.

A landscape architect is a professional who has earned a B.S. or master's degree in landscape architecture at an accredited university and who has probably passed special state examinations after spending an internship with a firm of practicing landscape architects. Landscape designers or gardeners may be self-taught or may have taken courses in landscaping as well as horticulture. They can often be competent and helpful. They are frequently associated with nurseries and garden centers, and one way to judge their competence is to ask for a tour of some of the gardens they have designed.

Most small properties today do not require elaborate planning for the use of their space. Even so, some common-sense as well as aesthetic planning is desirable before any planting is done, whether you do the planning or consult a professional.

TRENDS IN LANDSCAPE DESIGN

Low Maintenance—The emphasis in low-maintenance landscaping is on the elimination of fussy formal beds that tend to require constant upkeep. Some people manage to eliminate lawn areas and substitute gravel and other surfacings along with ground cover plantings (see Ground Covers) to create textural and pattern effects that are pleasing to look at but require little care.

Discussing low maintenance and gardening together may seem a contradiction. Yet in truth, a well-laid-out property that eliminates or reduces mowing, trimming, raking, and other chores that relate more to outdoor housekeeping than the practice of gardening can give the interested gardener more time for the pleasures of *real* gardening.

INFLUENCES OF JAPANESE GARDENS—Although low-maintenance landscaping is very much an American phenomenon that has evolved from our frenetic life-styles, much of its essence has been inspired by Japanese or Oriental gardens. Japanese gardens, though man-made, resemble nature's flawless compositions with rocks and stones, water, and plants—all in exquisite harmony. Such gardens may look simple, but they have been carefully planned to the last detail. The American mania for colorful gardens is not usually an aim of Japanese gardeners, who prefer to live with various hues of green.

Although the Japanese gardens on display in public gardens in this country seem formidable and extensive, their elements and artistry can be adapted to modest properties. In fact, most Japanese gardens are found on lots smaller than most of our suburban properties. But before plunging into the creation of a Japanese-type garden, study the many excellent books on its art and philosophy that are available in bookstores and libraries.

NATURAL LANDSCAPING—This is a recent trend, really another aspect of low-maintenance landscaping, but also an outgrowth of the environmental concerns of the 1960s and 1970s. Yet natural landscaping is related to Japanese gardening, too, in its emphasis on imitating nature's best landscaping efforts.

If you are a new property owner and wish to become a disciple of natural landscaping, begin by surveying your lot and planning how to retain and take advantage of its best existing features and plantings (if any). Changes, of course, are permitted and may be necessary, but the idea is to avoid total stripping of the land and then introducing alien plantings that may be a rubber stamp of others in the neighborhood.

PLANNING A LANDSCAPE DESIGN

For a new property that may be nothing but bare ground or for the renovation of an old one, heeding the following points as you survey the site will help before you draw a rough plan or call in an expert:

EXISTING FEATURES AND PLANTINGS—Large trees, shade from them or any source, slopes, rock outcroppings, scenic views, and the like can influence your planning. (See also Rock Gardens, Wild Flowers, Naturalizing, and Shade.)

PROVIDING PRIVACY—Fences or hedges or informal shrub groupings. (See Shrubs and Hedges.)

PARKING AREAS, WALKS—Also steps and possibly retaining walls if property slopes.

OUTDOOR LIVING SPACE—If the builder has not provided one, you will want to consider a terrace or deck for relaxing and entertaining. Is a swimming pool planned? If so, its location should be part of the plan even if its installation is in the future. You may be able to relate the patio area to the pool. (See also Terraces and Outdoor Living Areas.)

SPECIAL GARDEN INTERESTS—A herb garden? A flower garden? Borders of shrubs and flowers, perhaps. And a small vegetable garden if space permits. (See Annuals, Perennials, Roses, and Vegetables.)

LAWN AREAS AND GROUND COVERS—A combination of these may be the solution, especially the latter for shaded areas. (See also Lawns and Ground Covers.)

STORAGE AND SERVICE—The clothesline is now passé (unless energy costs skyrocket again!), but there are garbage and trash cans, woodpiles, and how about a storage shed for garden tools?

SHRUBS TO PLANT NEAR THE HOUSE—These days, generally the fewer the better. (See Shrubs.)

LAWNS. A lawn sets off the house and provides background and foreground for shrubs and flowers. It is pleasant to walk on and restful to contemplate from the patio. Grasses that make a lawn help to keep mud from being tracked indoors and prevent erosion on gently sloping land. If lawn areas are planned carefully, not interrupted by scattered, unrelated plantings and features, mowing can be done quickly and efficiently. When lawns are cut up by flower gardens or abut a wall or other obstacle, the laying of a foot-wide paving, such as cobblestones, flagstones, or even cement, is worth considering. Such mowing strips prevent injury to plants and speed up the job.

KINDS OF GRASSES—Turf experts have divided lawn grasses into two groups: cool-season grasses, Kentucky bluegrass being a good example, for most of the northern regions and warm-season grasses for the South and other mild climates. Kentucky bluegrass, the fescues, and perennial rye grasses and others have many varieties, and new ones are constantly being tested. A current aim in many regions is to find grasses that require less water and fertilizing to maintain the purity of groundwater supplies.

In northern regions most grasses are propagated by seeds, but in mild climates grass is often started from divisions, called plugs and sprigs (see Propagation). Selections of one grass, zoysia, planted in much of the North as well as in warmer climates, are planted from plugs.

The grasses that are best for each region are stocked by garden centers. Unless you wish to become a lawn hobbyist, there is really no reason to know the merits of each variety. However, for those who want this information in detail, cooperative extension experts have it along with specific grass recommendations for each area and purpose. (See Cooperative Extension Agents or Specialists.)

WHEN TO SOW OR PLANT A LAWN—The best time in northern regions is in late summer to early fall, the second best time early spring. Sods of established grasses can be laid for an instant lawn in summer, although late summer and early spring are still more ideal times because of cooler temperatures and usually more rainfall.

Spring is the recommended time for planting zoysia plugs and for such warm-season grasses as St. Augustine, carpet grass, bahia, and Bermuda.

SOIL PREPARATION—It is a waste of time and money to throw grass seed on hard ground that has not been cultivated. You can prepare the soil for small areas or for spot renovation by digging the soil with a fork (see Digging), but for whole new lawns and larger areas, a rotary tiller, which can be rented if you don't own one, is the quick, efficient solution.

For the acid soils east of the Mississippi River, the United States Department of Agriculture recommends applying about 50 pounds of ground limestone to 1,000 square feet, along with 30 to 40 pounds of superphosphate at the same rate. (If you have any questions about the liming requirements of your soil, consult your extension agent for recommendations, which would probably be based on a soil test. See also Soil.) Both the lime and superphosphate can be distributed by a fertilizer spreader. The two ingredients must be spread separately, as superphosphate is likely to be coarse. Till or dig them into the soil.

Then rake over the area to remove stones and any other debris that might impede the germination of grass seeds. If the soil is excessively sandy—and you can afford it—by all means add peat moss or Michigan peat or any other source of humus that is available. Even a layer applied a few inches thick and raked or lightly tilled in the soil with a rotary tiller can be beneficial. At the same time you can add a complete lawn fertilizer, such as 10-6-4 (at a rate of 10 pounds to 1,000 square feet) or 20-10-10 (5 pounds to 1,000 square feet) or any other formula available in your region.

Do not overcultivate the soil! It should not have a dustlike consistency but be crumbly in texture to give the seeds a toehold.

Seeds or plugs are planted next. Seeds can be spread by a spreader more successfully than by hand. If you must sow by hand, divide the seeds in half, sowing one part in one direction, the second at right angles to it. The rate of sowing the seed should be on the package, but usually about 1 to 2 pounds of bluegrass or fescue seeds are recommended for 1,000 square feet.

After sowing seeds or planting the sprigs (sprigs are usually planted 6 to 12 inches apart), whisk the seeds over with a bamboo rake to about a 1/4-inch depth, and then it is time to water. If pools of water begin to form that can wash the seeds about, turn off the water. Water again when the top few inches are dry—don't wait too long. Frequent sprinklings rather than long soakings are better for seeds and newly planted sprigs and plugs. If you have had turf installed, follow the watering instructions given by the contractor.

MOWING AND MAINTENANCE—Don't "scalp" the grass at its first mowing (make the first mowing of new grass when it is about 2 1/2 inches high), or for that matter, at any mowing. The advice from experts is never to remove more than 1/2 inch of growth at a time. This may mean more frequent mowings in spring, especially after fertilizer has been applied. Do not mow the grass when it is wet. A lawn may look better when it is cut short, but in the long run this can be an injurious practice. Close-cut lawns, especially in summer, dry out faster, are more susceptible to diseases, and encourage weed growth.

It is not necessary to "catch" lawn clippings while mowing or to rake them after you are finished. They will quickly decay and in so doing return nutrients to the soil. An exception to this might be in spring, when the grass is very tall, but as recommended above, when mowing has been neglected, it would be better to remove 1/2 inch or so of growth and repeat this every few days until the grass is at its correct height of about 1 1/2 to 2 inches.

Annual fertilizer applications are recommended for established lawns at the beginning of the growing season and possibly again in fall. Use a fertilizer that is formulated for lawns and that is high in nitrogen. The nitrogen should be partially in slow-release form (called ureaform) so it is parceled out over a period of several weeks. Do not apply fertilizers when the grass is wet, to avoid burning the leaves.

Crabgrass is one of the most annoying weeds in lawns. It is an annual, and after the plants die in the fall, they leave a superabundance of seeds behind—just waiting to germinate in midspring. Just before this germination occurs is the time to apply preemergent crabgrass herbicides that prevent germination. (Do not apply a herbicide at the time of sowing grass seeds, as most will also inhibit germination of the grass seeds.) Broad-leaved weeds can be killed with "weed and feed" formulations in spring. Always read the instructions and do not overdose.

In the long run, the best way to control weeds in the lawn is to take reasonably good care of it: water deeply when necessary, avoiding light sprinkles (except for newly sown seeds), and do not cut the grass too short, especially in summer.

LAYERING. See Propagation.

LEAVES. See Mulches and Mulching.

LIGHT, FLUORESCENT OR ARTIFICIAL. See Indoor Gardening.

LIME. See Soil.

M

MANURES. Animal manures are an excellent source of organic matter (see Compost and Soil) and contain varying amounts of nitrogen, phosphorus, and potash as well as trace elements. Horse and cow manures, which are the most bulky and therefore the most valuable for increasing the humus content of soils, are in fair supply beyond most city limits. Riding stables often bag horse manure and sell it on a cash-and-carry basis.

Other manures that may be available locally are poultry, sheep, and goat. They are less valuable as a source of humus but do contain higher ratios of nutrients than horse and cow.

All fresh manures can be toxic to plants when applied around them during the growing season. Fresh cow or horse manures can be spread over vegetable and flower gardens in the fall at the rate of about 15 to 30 bushels per 1,000 square feet. About half that rate of poultry and other more concentrated manures should be applied. Partially decayed manures can be applied in early spring if thoroughly mixed in the soil and should not damage plants. Fresh manures can be layered in the compost pile, where their leaching nutrients help speed decomposition and increase the nutrient content and organic matter of the pile.

Green manure is another term for cover crop—any plant, such as ryegrass or winter rye, alfalfa, or clover, that is sown on farmlands, often in the fall after harvesting of summer crops. Its purpose is to cover the bare soil to prevent erosion from wind and rain and loss of nutrients through leaching and to add to the soil's organic matter after it is plowed under in the spring.

Although the sowing of cover crops is more associated with farming than with small-plot gardening, it is a perfectly viable practice for gardening on any scale. Winter rye seeds can be sown in the fall in the home vegetable garden right after such summer crops as squash, corn, and beans have been harvested. They then are tilled or dug back into the soil in spring to decay before it is time to sow summer vegetables again.

MULCHES AND MULCHING. One of the best ways to reduce maintenance time in the garden is to place layers of leaves and other organic materials around plants. These coverings, called mulches, help prevent weed growth and conserve moisture and, as they decompose, increase the humus content of the soil. Nature herself invented mulches and is still its foremost practitioner—that is, when overneat gardeners do not interfere by removing every leaf and other debris that she deposits around plantings.

Many mulching materials may be available on your own property or nearby, fallen leaves being one of the best. They can be spread in 4- to 6-inch layers among shrubs to form a perpetual mulch, more leaves being added as the layers decay. Rhododendrons, camellias, evergreen and deciduous azaleas, mountain-laurel, blueberries, which are all shallow-rooted plants, especially revel in a constant leaf mulch. However, all shrubs benefit.

Home vegetable plots of any size, where weeds seem to spring up overnight as the weather warms, can be kept nearly weed-free and require less watering during drought when protected by mulches. It is true that some weeds always push through a mulch, but the few that do are more easily plucked from the soil.

Mulching materials for vegetables include pine needles, hay, straw, seaweed, decayed animal manures, tobacco stems, compost, and leaves. Some people use newspapers. At the end of the season, these materials can be tilled or dug into the soil to supply humus as they continue to decay. A synthetic mulch is black plastic, especially recommended for use around such plants as melons and squash, which like a warm soil. Black plastic is available in rolls at garden centers and from mail-order seed houses.

A better-looking mulching material than most of the others is buckwheat hulls, often used around rosebushes. It is fairly long-lasting and can be applied about 1 to 2 inches deep. Bark of various sizes, the smaller being preferable, is also quite long-lasting but is more expensive than the materials you collect yourself. Bark chips are usually applied about 2 inches deep. Not quite as neat as bark and buckwheat hulls but less expensive are wood chips, often available free or at a bargain from tree-pruning companies. They also last a few seasons before decaying. Apply them around blueberry bushes and shrubs about 3 inches deep.

Certain woody mulching materials, such as wood chips and sawdust, the various grades of bark chips, and buckwheat hulls, should not be mixed into the soil until they are partially decayed, as the soil bacteria that feed on these materials deplete available soil nitrogen needed by the plants. This is less of a problem when these woody materials remain as a surface mulch. If you notice any yellowing of foliage or obvious stunting in plant growth, spread a fertilizer high in nitrogen over the area and water it in.

Peat moss is sometimes recommended as a mulch but it is better used in the soil than on top of it. It is a light material that blows away, and it can also form an almost velvety caking that repels water. Eventually peat moss as a mulch builds up and may encourage shallow rooting of plants. Then later, when the peat moss becomes extremely dry, as in a drought, the roots are injured. (See also Peat Moss and Soil.)

WINTER MULCHING—In much of the North, mulches are applied in the fall to protect plants of borderline hardiness, such as pansies, many heaths and heathers, Canterbury bells, sweet William, and strawberries. Flower gardens are sometimes mulched after the soil freezes as a measure to keep the soil frozen so plants are not injured by the alternate freezing and thawing that takes place. Chrysanthemums, which have shallow roots, are often winter killed because of being heaved out of the soil. The mulching materials—leaves, compost, hay—can be applied about 3 inches deep. Applying the mulch after the ground has frozen is also supposed to deter mice. However, if you live in a region where mice and voles are a problem, they may find your winter mulch and the plants it is protecting a cosy home, whether the ground is first frozen or not. Evergreen boughs, if you have access to them, may not appeal to the mice as much as leaves, hay, and straw, and the boughs are much easier to remove in spring than are leaves.

N

NATURALIZING. When a gardener sets out a number of daffodils in an informal pattern in a lawn, meadow, or at the edge of a woodland, he or she is naturalizing them, imitating the way they might be found growing in nature. A plant that is described as being naturalized in a region is a plant that has escaped from cultivation and now grows as though it were wild or native. An example of such a plant is the tawny day-lily (*Hemerocallis fulva*), a native of Asia and Europe that has become naturalized along roadsides throughout the Northeast. For natural gardening, see Organic Gardening, and for natural landscaping, see Landscaping.

NOMENCLATURE—NAMES OF PLANTS. Botanical names often try the patience of new gardeners, who may beg for common, sensible names they can understand and pronounce. While many of the pleasures of gardening can be enjoyed without the intrusion of botanical names, sooner or later their existence must be recognized. And the nomenclature system is not as bad as it may seem.

Many people who shy away from botanical nomenclature are using it when they talk about a rhododendron, a narcissus, or a forsythia. These are all generic names (being used as common names) that are understood all over the world.

But first of all, there is the family. All plants with definitely similar characteristics are classified into families, examples being the daisy or composite family, Compositae, and the heath family, Ericaceae, to which rhododendrons and mountain-laurel belong. Another is the legume or pea family (Leguminosae), a large family that includes peas, beans, sweet peas, and many trees.

After its family affiliation, a plant has two names, the first being its genus (or generic name), and the second, its species (or specific name). Examples are *Rhododendron maximum, Delphinium grandiflorum,* and *Forsythia suspensa.* These names, whether their origin is Latin, Greek, or from some other source, are written in italics and must be Latinized with correct Latin endings that agree in gender.

A plant may also have a variety or many varieties, now correctly called a cultivar or cultivars (derived from the term "cultivated variety"). The offspring of cultivars retain the characteristics of the parent cultivar, whether the reproduction is sexual or asexual. Cultivars are usually set off in single quotes. (See also Propagation.)

The old term "variety" is now reserved for variations of a plant that may occur in the wild and may or may not be stable enough to reproduce its differing characteristics. There does seem to be overlapping between varieties and cultivars and the terms are still used interchangeably, but these are the rules of the International Code of Nomenclature for Cultivated Plants and the International Code of Botanical Nomenclature.

Unlike the rules for botanical names, there are no rules at all for common names. They can differ from region to region and of course country to country. Common names like love-in-a-mist *(Nigella damascena),* Joseph's coat *(Amaranthus tricolor),* and mother-of-thousands *(Saxafraga stolonifera)* can be descriptive and intriguing and are a part of gardening folklore, but for accuracy and worldwide understanding, botanical names are more reliable.

O

ORGANIC GARDENING. Methods of gardening in which plants, especially food crops, are grown without synthetic or inorganic fertilizers, chemical pesticides, and weed killers. Organic gardening is also known as natural gardening.

The serious organic gardener works to maintain a balance of nature in his or her garden, whether it is a farm or suburban lot. The emphasis is on conservation of the soil and its year-to-year improvement by additions of a large amount of organic materials in the form of compost, decayed animal manures, and other natural matter. These are bolstered by ground dolomitic limestone and slow-acting fertilizers, such as bone meal, raw phosphate rock, cottonseed meal, and others.

Organic gardeners are less concerned with harvesting unblemished fruits and vegetables. Rather than resorting to spraying and dusting with chemicals, they try to keep pest damage to a minimum by using biological controls, picking off insects by hand, encouraging birds, and using sprays and dusts derived from plant extracts such as rotenone and pyrethrum and other less deadly sources.

The movement has gained some credibility among former disbelievers because evidence is accumulating that many pesticides have endangered birds and other wildlife and can be a threat to our own health. Also contributing to interest in organic gardening methods have been environmental abuses in general and the knowledge that our natural resources are not infinite. (See also Compost, Manures, and Soil.)

P

PEAT MOSS. Although there are several kinds of peat mined from bogs, peat moss, composed of partially decayed sphagnum moss, is the best. It is fibrous and crumbly in texture, a pleasing earthy brown in color, and very light in weight. It is widely available, making it useful for those who do not have access to other forms of organic materials. It can be obtained in small bags or much larger 4-cubic-foot or 6-cubic-foot bales and, though expensive, is worth every bit of its cost.

Peat moss is sterile and free from weed seeds, but its great value is its tremendous capacity for retaining moisture—as it adds to the humus content of the soil. It contains a negligible amount of nitrogen and is acid in reaction, so is often recommended in the soil mixtures for rhododendrons and azaleas, gardenias, and other plants that prefer an acid soil. However, it can be safely used with all plants and all soils.

There are two ways in which peat moss can be incorporated in the soil: one is in spot plantings, as in the planting holes for trees and shrubs; the second is spreading a layer 2 to 3 inches over the area being prepared for flower and vegetable gardens, lawns, or shrub groupings and borders and then tilling it into the soil with a power tiller or forking by hand. (See Digging.) Peat moss is also an important ingredient for potting mixes and synthetic soils, such as Redi-Earth and Jiffy Mix. (See also Propagation and Soil.)

The material is very light and easier to work with when moist. Keep the bags and bales open so rain water can help to moisten the peat moss. Although it is sometimes recommended for mulching, this is not a good use of peat moss as it tends to cake and repel water. Its best use is as a soil amendment, that is, mixed into the soil to add humus. (See also Mulches and Mulching.)

Michigan peat is another kind of peat, derived from decayed sedges—grasslike plants that grow in bogs. It is very dark in color and fine in texture and is also a source of humus.

PERENNIALS. Along with annuals, biennials, and bulbs, perennials are the plants that make a flower garden. A perennial reappears each spring, its tops having died back in the fall but its roots surviving underground. This is the typical perennial, but there are exceptions, with some plants retaining their evergreen foliage all winter. Examples of these plants include hardy pinks (*Dianthus*) and candytuft (*Iberis sempervirens*).

The appeal of perennials for many is in their permanence, compared with annuals that have to be planted new every year. Yet how perennial are perennials? The truth is that some last for only a year or so, their longevity equal to or not much better than that of annuals and biennials. Fortunately, a goodly number are more lasting, especially when the gardener helps to renew them by dividing their clumps every few years. The peony is the prize example of a long-lived perennial, surviving through generations of gardeners. Some other especially durable perennials are astilbe, butterfly weed, candytuft, day-lily, gasplant, hosta, and monkshood.

In addition to their permanence, perennials offer substance and refinement in their foliage and flower forms and varying heights and growth habits. Taking these traits into account and assembling groups of perennials in a border can be challenging. When the results are successful, a work of art has been created.

PLANNING GARDENS OF PERENNIALS

The traditional use of perennials has been in sweeping, often majestic borders back when properties and labor were in ample supply. Perennials slipped somewhat in popularity, being shunned in favor of the longer-blooming, more carefree annuals that became the darlings of hybridizers. Happily—and quite contrary to the maintenance-free mania of recent years—there is a renaissance in perennials that includes their use in gardens and borders. (See also Border.)

PERENNIALS FOR WHICH SEASON?—Planning today's version of the herbaceous border, perhaps a garden 25 to 35 feet long and 4 to 5 feet wide, does require some preliminary thought, more than running to the local garden center and picking up a few flats of annuals for random planting.

For one thing, perennials cost enough to justify planning. For another, perennials are not everblooming. They can be divided into the seasons in which they bloom: spring, early summer, summer, and fall. So you should decide for which season you are planning, certainly taking into consideration vacation times. Or you may want an all-season perennial garden, a worthy goal if you have the space. Yet no matter which seasons you choose for the main display, there will be times when you must be content with only intermittent patches or accents of color rather than masses, as there will always be perennials whose time to flower has passed or has not arrived. This is why it is important to choose some plants whose foliage and growth habit are of textural interest even when out of flower.

GARDEN LOCATION—The location and surroundings of the garden should also be thought about before any plants are purchased. Today's mostly smaller properties do not permit much flexibility in site or size, but the flower garden should be planned in harmony with the rest of the landscape. (See also Landscaping.)

Choose a sunny site, avoiding tree- or building-shaded areas, as the majority of perennials need as much sun as possible. There are some perennials that grow in partial shade, which can be grouped in sections of a garden that receive some shade during the day.

A hedge, fence, or informal shrub grouping makes a pleasing background for perennial gardens. The size of the garden depends on available space and how enthusiastic you are about perennials. A border of 25 feet or so with a 4- to 5-foot width will allow a balance among tall, medium height, and low perennials, with some overlapping of bloom periods among them to extend the color succession beyond one season. If you wish to start off more cautiously, make a shorter border and, because of less space, choose plants that bloom at the same time.

MAKING A PLAN—It is helpful to make some lists, dividing the perennials into season of bloom. After each plant, jot down its height and flower color. Assembling this information is not difficult with a few nursery catalogues at hand. Catalogues that specialize in perennials give a surprising amount of information, although they are often overly optimistic about the length of bloom periods.

Next is the making of a plan. For borders or gardens 20 feet or under, use a scale of 1/2 inch equalling a foot; for longer borders, use 1/4 inch to a foot. With your list of perennials as reference, start blocking in the positions of various plants, placing the tallest, 3 feet or so, in the rear, those in the 2- to 2½-foot range in the midsection, and the lowest in the front. Of course, if you are planning an island bed, one that can be viewed from all sides, the tallest plants go in the center.

Except for the largest plants, which make strong accents, such as peony, globe-thistle, baby's-breath, and the like, use from three to five plants of the same kind in a group and even more in the front of the garden. In a really long border, you can make the groups even larger and by repeating them at intervals achieve the sweeps and drifts of colors, textures, and forms that are the hallmark of perennial or herbaceous borders. Try to vary the skyline of the border by swinging some low-growing plants toward the center and some of the medium-height plants toward the rear. By doing this, you avoid a rigid stepped-down effect and instead have a graceful, undulating mixture of heights and forms.

The spacing of individual perennials varies according to the ultimate spread of each plant (not usually achieved in the first growing season), but this is influenced by the soil and its fertility and moisture, regional temperatures, and even just the luck of the gardener. (Personally, I like to crowd my plants a bit because I am more interested in overall effect than in displaying each plant. Crowding also leaves less space for weeds.) For your paper planning, assume that smaller plants in the foreground will be set about 8 to 12 inches apart while the larger ones from 14 to 18 inches or more apart.

You may want to consider leaving space in your garden for some strong annuals and bulbs, such as the flowering onion and tulips. This makes the garden a mixed one and helps to maintain a succession of color over longer periods as the flowers from perennials come and go.

PERENNIALS THAT MAKE STRONG ACCENTS

DAY-LILY *(Hemerocallis)*
FALSE-LUPINE *(Thermopsis caroliniana)*
GASPLANT *(Dictamnus albus)*
GLOBE-THISTLE *(Echinops ritro)*

MONKSHOOD *(Aconitum* species)
PEONY *(Paeonia)*
VERONICA *(V. longifolia subsessilis)*
YUCCA *(Y. filamentosa)*

TALLER PERENNIALS FOR BACKGROUND

ASTER, HARDY, tall cultivars *(Aster)*
BOLTONIA *(B. asteroides)*
BUGBANE *(Cimicifuga racemosa)*
DAY-LILY, tall cultivars *(Hemerocallis)*
DELPHINIUM, PACIFIC GIANTS *(Delphinium)*
FALSE-LUPINE *(Thermopsis caroliniana)*
GOAT'S BEARD *(Aruncus dioicus)*
GLOBE-THISTLE *(Echinops ritro)*
GRASSES, ORNAMENTAL, tall kinds
LYTHRUM 'MORDEN'S PINK' *(Lythrum)*

PERENNIALS FOR A SUCCESSION OF BLOOM

	Color	Garden Position
SPRING		
CANDYTUFT *(Iberis sempervirens)*	white	front
LUNGWORT *(Pulmonaria* species)	blue	front
PRIMROSES *(Primula* species)	various	front
DWARF IRIS *(Iris pumila)*	various	front
CUSHION SPURGE *(Euphorbia epithymoides)*	yellow	front to middle
BLUE PHLOX *(Phlox divaricata)*	blue	front
BLEEDING HEART *(Dicentra spectabilis)*	pink	middle
TULIPS *(Tulipa)*	various	middle to rear
EARLY SUMMER		
SIBERIAN IRIS *(Iris sibirica)*	blue, white	middle to rear
BEARDED IRIS *(Iris* x *germanica)*	various	middle to rear
PEONY *(Paeonia)*	various	rear
CATMINT *(Nepeta faassenii)*	lavender	front to middle
ASTILBE *(Astilbe japonica)*	various	front to middle
SHASTA DAISY *(Chrysanthemum* x *superbum)*	white	middle to rear
SUMMER		
THREADLEAF COREOPSIS *(C. verticillata)*	yellow	front to middle
DAY-LILY *(Hemerocallis)*	various	middle to rear
GLOBE-THISTLE *(Echinops ritro)*	blue	rear
PERENNIAL PHLOX *(Phlox)*	various	middle to rear
LAVENDER *(Lavandula angustifolia)*	lavender	front to middle

	Color	Garden Position
FALL		
MONKSHOOD *(Aconitum)*	blue	rear
ASTER, HARDY *(Aster)*	various	front to rear
CHRYSANTHEMUM *(Chrysanthemum)*	various	front to rear

PERENNIALS HERE AND THERE

SMALLER GARDENS—There are other ways to use perennials if you lack the space or inclination for a flower border. There can be miniperennial gardens that fit into your space, such as in sunny corners, or small island beds surrounded by lawn or gravel, or dooryard gardens enclosed by a picket fence. The last can be filled with a mixture of perennials, some annuals, dahlias, and perhaps a rosebush or two. Small groupings of perennials show off very well in the bays formed by informal shrubs. A few perennials can be mixed in with annuals planted around a patio.

Rock garden plants are mostly perennial and can often be used to as good advantage in all-perennial gardens as in rock gardens and walls (see Rock Gardens).

One of the best-known uses of perennials is as a ground cover. Ajuga is a popular ground-covering perennial, but its pert blue flower spikes in spring go well with basket of gold alyssum in the foreground of flower gardens. Ajuga is a vigorous spreader and may invade the lawn from the garden.

PERENNIALS FOR PART SHADE—One of the handsomest perennials that will endure shade is the hosta, with its exotic variegated forms and stunning blue-toned varieties, some with puckered and striated leaves and others with lovely lavender-blue or white flowers. Some thrive in full shade, but most of the many cultivars —and more are being introduced all the time—need light shade with several hours of sun to do justice to their leaf variations.

Use large specimens of hosta as single accents under high-branched trees. Others can be planted in drifts along partially shaded walks or drives, in containers or in the ground near terraces, in sections of a partially shaded flower garden, at the edge of a woodland, or in a shaded wild-flower garden.

Other perennials for part shade are monkshood *(Aconitum* species); columbine *(Aquilegia* species); astilbe; bleeding heart *(Dicentra eximia* and *spectabilis);* epimedium; day-lilies; Jacob's ladder *(Polemonium caeruleum);* lily-of-the-valley *(Convallaria majalis);* blue phlox *(Phlox divaricata);* primroses *(Primula* species), which need sun in spring, some shade in summer; and ferns and many wild flowers native to woodlands. (See also Wild Flowers and Shade.)

PLANTING AND CARE OF PERENNIALS

GETTING STARTED WITH PLANTS—Perennials are usually planted in the spring or fall and are available then from local outlets or mail-order specialists. Mail-order plants are usually shipped as dormant or semidormant plants, while the plants from garden centers are usually potted and may be already in active growth. In fact, perennials in containers, in common with most other nursery stock, are now available throughout the growing season in fairly varied supplies at most garden centers. These plants are convenient for filling in vacancies in the garden scheme and reassure new gardeners who are unsure of planting procedures. It is simple to dig a hole and then plant a container-grown perennial (after removing it from its container, of course).

However, in many parts of the country few if any container-grown plants are available, so mail-order remains an important source. They also often offer a wider selection.

If you wish to save money and are patient, you can plant your garden in stages, buying fewer plants the first few years than your plan on paper calls for. After a few years, these plants can be increased by division. Savings can be substantial, too, when you grow certain perennials from seed, sown about the same time you start annual seeds. (Many cultivars—named varieties—do not breed true from seeds, examples being 'Hyperion' day-lily, 'White Admiral' phlox, and veronica 'Red Fox.') Some perennials to grow from seed include Russell hybrid lupins, painted daisy or pyrethrum, most primroses and columbines, delphinium, basket of gold alyssum, blue flax *(Linum perenne),* and Shasta daisy. It usually takes a year or so before most perennials grown from seed are ready to flower. But the delphinium will flower in six months if the seeds are sown in early spring indoors. (See Propagation.)

PLANTING—After preparing the soil and adding organic materials, such as peat moss, compost, and possibly ground limestone, bone meal, or superphosphate, and a complete fertilizer, such as 5-10-5 (about 4 pounds to 100 square feet), or whatever a soil test has indicated is needed, you should be ready to plant. (See also Soil.)

Keep any bare-root perennials covered until you are ready to plant them. In the planting of a long border, it sometimes helps to roughly mark out the areas to be planted with outlines of limestone, using your plan as a guide.

To plant bare-root plants that are often merely divisions—with little if any top growth showing—dig a hole (with a large trowel or short-handled spade) deep and wide enough to accommodate the spread-out roots, keeping the crown of the plant at soil level. Fill the soil around the plant and firm well. The dormant tuberous roots of peonies often look more dead than alive, with the only signs of life being pinkish "eyes" or buds, usually from three to five. Cover these buds with no more than 2 inches of soil. Always read the planting directions sent along with your plants before setting them out.

Plants in pots and plastic or metal containers are easy to set out. To remove the plant from its container, turn it upside down, supporting the plant with one hand, and tap the edge of the container against something hard, like the rim of a bucket or the side of a wheelbarrow. Then in a prepared hole, set the plant at approximately the same depth as it was in the pot, taking care to keep the crown of the plant at soil level.

Water all plants thoroughly after planting. (See also Planting and Transplanting.)

FLOWER BORDER CARE—The first season after planting, you may wish to mulch perennials, as there will be more space between plants for weeds. A 2-inch or so layer of compost, if you have it, is excellent. Other possibilities are decayed manures, perhaps mixed with decayed leaves, or very decayed wood chips (do not use them here fresh from the chipper).

Remove fading flowers to prevent seed formation and for the sake of neatness. If you remove fading flowers promptly, cutting off the main flower stem above the foliage, you may be rewarded with secondary flower displays.

In the case of day-lilies and iris, flower removal consists of snapping off fading individual flowers daily until all the buds have opened. Then cut back the entire flower stalk.

Some perennials require staking if their heavy flower stems are not to flop over. The tall flower spikes of delphiniums are an example, with each spike usually requiring its own bamboo stake to hold it securely upright. Peony bushes laden with blooms and buds can be held upright by wire ring enclosures available for the purpose in garden centers. These same supports are usually satisfactory for phlox, globe-thistle, and other perennials that may seem top-heavy.

Most perennials are fairly immune to insects and diseases, with a few—the lovely delphinium unfortunately being one—being inevitable targets of pests. (See Pests and Diseases.)

In the fall, growth slows and the tops of most perennials, which have died back, can be cut off at ground level. Do not cut off evergreen foliage, which will be very apparent after a few hard frosts. Some day-lilies retain their foliage all winter, as do candytuft, Christmas- and Lenten-rose (*Helleborus* spp.), many pinks (*Dianthus*), and biennials. After the cleanup is a good time to plant tulips, which can be so dramatic among perennials in the spring. After the ground freezes, a winter mulch can be applied to prevent plants from being uprooted during thaws. (See Mulches and Mulching.)

Established flower gardens will benefit from early spring applications of a complete fertilizer, such as 5-10-5 (3 to 5 pounds per 100 square feet), scattered over the soil. If you make later applications, keep fertilizer from leaves and crowns of plants.

▨▨▨▨ A SAMPLER OF PERENNIALS ▨▨▨▨

Aster or **Michaelmas Daisy** *(Aster)*. Mostly late summer to fall-flowering hybrids in bright color range, including blue-purple.

Sun. For bushy growth and more blooms, pinch off tip growth in late spring and a month later. Divide clumps in spring every few years (see Propagation). New growth favored by rabbits. Protect plants with mounds of chicken wire in spring.

Astilbe *(Astilbe japonica)*. Early summer spikes of fluffy flowers above ferny foliage clumps. Wide color range. Sun or part shade in humus-rich soil. Tolerates damp soil.

Balloonflower *(Platycodon grandiflorus)*. Summer-blooming, star-shaped flowers in blue, pink, or white. Slow to show in spring, so label its site. Once established, resents root disturbance. Sun.

Bellflower *(Campanula)*. Many kinds, of varying heights. One of the best: Carpathian harebell *(C. carpatica)*, with blue or white flowers in summer on 8- to 10-inch plants. Sun.

Catmint *(Nepeta faassenii)*. Small lavender flowers in spikes above blue-gray foliage mounds, 12 inches high. Reblooms if fading flower spikes are cut off. Part shade to sun.

Chrysanthemum *(Chrysanthemum)*. In addition to fall-blooming hybrids, this genus includes white-flowered Shasta daisy of early summer, painted daisy or pyrethrum of late spring, and nonhardy Boston or marguerite daisy. All are showy in the garden, superb as cut flowers. Require frequent division in spring or, for nonhardy Boston daisy, renewal from cuttings wintered over indoors.

Cushion Spurge *(Euphorbia epithymoides)*. Hardy relative of poinsettia with long-lasting yellow bracts in spring on neat foliage mounds. Sun. Very handsome with purple tulips.

Day-lily *(Hemerocallis)*. Lily-shaped flowers in yellow, orange, tawny red, and near purple, often fragrant, carried well above ribbonlike foliage, in late spring to late summer, depending on variety. Part shade or sun. Long-lived. Does not require frequent division. Drought resistant.

False-indigo *(Baptisia australis)*. Deep lilac flowers on tall stems in early summer. Sun or light shade. Care-free, long-lived plants. It and another perennial in the pea family, the yellow-flowered false-lupine *(Thermopsis caroliniana)*, are reliable substitutes for the often short-lived true lupine.

Some reliable perennials for a summer garden: perennial phlox, day-lilies, and globe-thistle are the tallest, from 3 to 4 feet; balloon-flower, about 20 inches; threadleaf coreopsis, 18 inches

Globe-thistle *(Echinops ritro)*. Tall, impressive background plant with blue thistle flowers in summer. Sun or light shade. Drought-resistant. Good companion for day-lilies.

Hosta *(Hosta)*. Outstanding foliage perennial for shade, part shade, and some sun, with white or lilac flower spikes. Needs humus-rich soil. See previous section, Perennials for Shade.

Peony *(Paeonia)*. Many cultivars in pink, red, and white for late spring to early summer. Sun. Deeply prepared soil with plenty of organic matter and superphosphate. Plant in fall. May not require dividing for years.

Phlox, Summer *(Phlox paniculata)*. Fragrant, handsome clumps of flower heads in wide color range in summer. Place in midsection to rear of border in groups of three to five plants of same variety, fewer in smaller gardens. Sun. Humus-rich soil. Divide every 3 to 4 years in early spring or fall. Blue Phlox *(Phlox divaricata)* is spring-blooming. Several plants make lovely foreground grouping with tulips and candytuft. Sun or part shade.

Siberian Iris *(Iris siberica)*. Refined iris flowers above grassy foliage clumps in early summer in plum-red, blues, and white. Sun or light shade. Humus-rich soil.

Threadleaf Coreopsis *(Coreopsis verticillata)*. Golden daisies and finely divided foliage to 24 inches. Daisies appear in profusion from early summer on, making it one of the few perennials that is nearly everblooming. Sun. Remove fading flowers for even later bloom. Divide every few years.

▨▨▨▨ A SPECIAL PROJECT ▨▨▨▨
A PERENNIAL GARDEN FOR FRAGRANCE

Here is a plan for a perennial border whose emphasis is frankly on fragrance. The selection of plants ensures some color from flowers from spring to late summer, and all the plants have foliage that should remain presentable until fall. You may wish to vary the selections. For instance, no annuals have been included, but basil, including the purple-leaved variety, sweet-alyssum, and snapdragons are all fragrant enough in their own way to be considered. The biennial sweet William *(Dianthus barbatus)* really should be included. Once you get the knack of growing biennials from seed, you will never want to be without sweet William's lovely scented flowers in early summer (see Biennials). Three hybrid tea roses, and about six or seven miniature roses for the foreground, have also been included. Since they must be regularly sprayed or dusted to control black spot and other pests (see Roses and Pests and Diseases), you may decide on alternatives. If you do plant roses, be sure to buy those that have decided fragrance.

Along with the roses, three fragrant shrubs have been selected, not only for their sweet-scented flowers in early summer, but also to provide some background and accents for the perennials. The row could be extended for additional background by planting more lilacs or perhaps shrub roses.

The garden is about 2 feet long by 4 feet wide, but can be adapted to any available space. It could be designed to curve around an outdoor sitting area paved with flagstones. (See Terraces and Outdoor Living Areas.) The major perennials used and their season of bloom are:

HYACINTH *(Hyacinthus* cultivars)—early spring
LILY-OF-THE-VALLEY *(Convalleria majalis)*—spring
BEARDED IRIS *(Iris* cultivars)—early summer
PEONY *(Paeonia* cultivars)—late spring–early summer
HYBRID TEA or FLORIBUNDA ROSES—early summer–summer
MINIATURE ROSES—early summer–summer
DAY-LILY *(Hemerocallis)*—early to late summer fragrant hybrids
LILY *(Lilium* cultivars and fragrant species)—summer
LAVENDER *(Lavandula* species)—summer
GRASS PINK *(Dianthus plumarius)*—early summer
CATMINT *(Nepeta* x *faassenii)*—early summer–summer
PHLOX *(Phlox paniculata)*—summer

PESTS AND DISEASES. Is the pest-free garden possible? Yes, but at a cost. Learning to live with some troubles while controlling a few others keeps gardening an enjoyable pursuit rather than a constant battle with blights and bugs.

Certain plants are more susceptible to insects and diseases than others, and unless you are willing to do some spraying on a regular schedule, you may want to avoid them.

Most fruit trees are a prime example of pest-prone plants, but I must add that for years I grew quite good peaches with no spraying at all. And organic gardeners have been growing fruits for a long time without resorting to chemicals. The U.S. Department of Agriculture has published a bulletin (No. 211), *Control of Insects on Deciduous Fruits and Tree Nuts in the Home Orchard Without Insecticides,* containing a section on beneficial insects, lady beetles, praying mantis, and spiders.

If you do decide to grow fruit trees—and the results can be well worth the effort—contact your cooperative extension agent for a

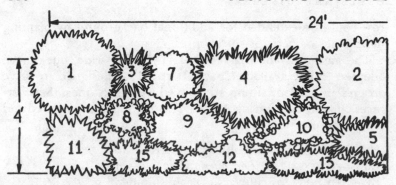

PLAN FOR A FRAGRANT PERENNIAL GARDEN

Fragrance preferences do vary and what may be appealing to some may be cloying to others. Substitutions can be made in the plan or from season to season to suit your own preferences. KEY: **1** Lilac. **2** Mock-orange. **3** Lilies. **4** Day-lilies (early to midsummer varieties).

spray program for your region, as timing is the key to successful controls. (See also Fruits.)

Another plant that invites troubles is the rose, especially hybrid tea and floribunda roses. There are many sprays and dusts formulated for roses, and using one of these faithfully over the growing season will control most pests. (See Roses.) The vegetable garden also has its share of pests, but most people seem able to cope with them. Some vegetable varieties have been bred for disease resistance, the tomato being one prime example.

Any chemical dusts and sprays you purchase should be used with caution. Read all the instructions on the package. Never apply more than the recommended dosage. Generally, it is sensible to wait until the pest appears before springing into action.

The following troubles are by no means the complete picture on insects and diseases, but it would be surprising if you have to contend with more than a few of these.

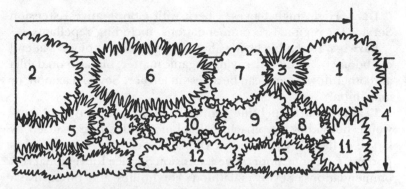

5 Day-lilies (midsummer). 6 Day-lilies (midsummer to late varieties). 7 Peony (choose fragrant varieties). 8 Hybrid tea rose (fragrant variety). 9 Summer phlox. 10 Bearded iris. 11 Hyacinths and lily-of-the-valley. 12 Grass pinks. 13 Miniature roses (fragrant varieties). 14 Nepeta *(N.* x *faassenii).* 15 Lavender.

SAMPLER OF GARDEN PROBLEMS AND PESTS

(For house plant and vegetable pests, see Indoor Gardening and Vegetables.)

Aphids. Soft, sucking insects, often crowded together on buds and new growth. Common on nasturtiums, lupines, roses. Spray or dust with malathion or rotenone.

Beetles. The metallic green and brown Japanese beetles and other kinds chew leaves and flowers. Pick off by hand, dropping beetles into jar of kerosene. Spray or dust with Sevin or diazinon.

Black Spot. Spreading black spots on rose foliage. See Roses.

Caterpillars. Many kinds, including gypsy moth and inch worms. Pick off by hand. Dust or spray with rotenone, malathion, or Sevin.

Crown Rot. Fungus disease causing mushy, rotting crowns of delphinium, columbine, larkspur. No control. Destroy plant. Do not replant infected area with same kind of plants.

Deer. High, high fences. Check with Cooperative Extension Service for regional recommendations, including repellants.

Earwigs. Resemble beetles but have prominent pincers at end of abdomen. Feed on decaying organic matter, but also on dahlia and other flowers and can be a pest in lettuce. Sevin, diazinon, or malathion.

Leafminers. Serpentine tunnels or mines in leaves of boxwood, holly, birch, spinach, columbine, and others, caused by larvae of flies, beetles, moths. Difficult to control. Timing is important. Consult Cooperative Extension Service for regional recommendations. Sevin, malathion. For hollies and birch, use a systemic granule control, such as Di-Syston, sprinkled over the ground in midspring.

Mice. Field mice, pine mice, voles—all can be very destructive in some regions although they do have "off" years. Cats are a help. Some people plant choice bulbs and other plants in hardware-cloth (fine-mesh wire sheeting) baskets. Moles are carnivores.

Mites. Many kinds, red spider and cyclamen being among the more common in gardens. Red spider mites are very tiny, but you can see their webs on undersides of pale, dessicated-looking foliage of hollyhocks, evergreens such as junipers, and many others. Hosing with forceful water spray will wash them off evergreens. Or spray with Kelthane. Cyclamen mites often infest delphinium, monkshood, and other plants, causing distorted growth, especially of flower spikes. Cyclamen mites are invisible to naked eye. Spray with Kelthane fairly regularly through the growing season.

Powdery Mildew. Whitish covering on lilacs, roses, and summer phlox in summer. Unsightly but usually not fatal. Benomyl helps, as do other available fungicides.

Rabbits. Fence in vegetable (and flower) gardens if practical. Damage is worse in spring. Cats help.

Scales. See Indoor Gardening.

Slugs. Shell-less snails that can be ravenous, especially in wet springs. Mulches give them hiding places. Slugs leave slimy trails on the ground that you will spot—even if you don't see the slugs.

Baits are available from garden centers, and sunken saucers of beer are supposed to entice and then drown them.

Thrips. Very small sucking insects that disfigure gladiolus flowers and sometimes others, such as day-lilies. Diazinon.

White Fly. Small white fly that rises in a group when plants are disturbed. See Indoor Gardening.

PLANTING AND TRANSPLANTING. Planting is often the first technique confronted by the new gardener who is frantically trying to fill in a bare property with an assortment of purchased plants. They include seedlings in flats or pots, perennials, shrubs and trees in plastic or metal containers, and perhaps bare-root plants like roses.

The major planting seasons are in spring and fall, but with so many nursery plants being grown in containers, summer and any time that the ground is unfrozen are also possibilities. This is not true for bare-root plants, which are available in spring while still dormant, or in late fall after growth has slowed or ceased.

PLANTING TREES AND SHRUBS—No matter the size or kind of plant, prepare a hole wider and deeper than the present size of the plant requires to allow for future root expansion. In preparing the hole, mix into the soil peat moss, compost, decayed leaves, or other organic material, as once the shrubs or trees are in the ground, there will be no way to add them later. Fertilizer, which will leach through the soil, should be added after the plant is established.

Remove the plants from their containers or plastic wrapping. (Those plants whose roots are wrapped in burlap can be set in their holes with the burlap intact, but before replacing soil, loosen burlap and fold it back. It will eventually rot.) Firm the soil in the bottom of the hole, then measure its depth to be sure it is not too low or too high for the new occupant. The planting depth should approximate the depth of the plant in its container or as it grew at the nursery, and should be deep enough so the top of the root ball is not exposed. Most plants now come with specific planting instructions which should be heeded. Container-grown plants are sometimes pot- or root-bound, that is, the roots are tightly wound around the outside of the soil ball, and before they are planted, require threading or unwinding to encourage them to grow into their new soil situation.

For the planting of bare-root or dormant roses, see Roses.

PLANTING ANNUALS, PERENNIALS, AND VEGETABLES—Seedling plants can be set out quickly, once the soil has been prepared and raked over to make it firm and level. Use a trowel to dig the holes, setting the plants so the first pair of leaves is level with the surface. Both tomato and marigold seedlings can be set deeper, about 2 inches or so above the first pair of leaves, as the stems send out roots that will help anchor the plants in the soil. Water all newly planted seedlings. (See Annuals, Propagation, Soil, and Vegetables.)

Perennial seedlings can be handled as previously described. If mature perennial plants are bare-root, spread out their roots before covering them with soil. Perennials from containers are easily set out in much the same way you would plant a shrub. (See Perennials.)

TRANSPLANTING

TRANSPLANTING—Moving plants from one site to another—is most successful when attempted in spring and fall, while the weather is cool, the soil reasonably moist, and the plants dormant or reasonably so. Deciduous shrubs and trees, those that lose their foliage in the winter, may die when their roots are disrupted by transplanting out of the dormancy period. Needle (coniferous) and broad-leaved evergreens are never totally dormant, but they are also most successfully transplanted in spring and fall.

Never transplant when the soil is very dry. To move a small tree or shrub, first insert a spade to its full depth as you dig a circle around the trunk, approximately under the outer spread of the branches. (With larger shrubs and evergreens, it may be helpful to tie up the branches toward the trunk with soft twine that won't chafe.) In the case of small specimens, it is usually possible to pry up the plant with a spade. Larger plants require more work. It may be necessary to remove soil from the cut circle to form a deep circular trench. This makes it easier to cut under the root ball and insert a piece of burlap, which should prevent the root ball from crumbling and also assist in easing it from its hole. It often takes two people to pry out a large shrub, lift it into a wheelbarrow or garden cart, and then replant it in its new location. The planting process is then the same as planting purchased stock.

TRANSPLANTING PERENNIALS—Some perennials can be successfully transplanted while in active growth, especially if the operation is done quickly. Take as much soil as you can so the roots are not disturbed. Delphinium, phlox, day-lilies, and chrysanthemums do not seem to suffer if carefully lifted and watered well after replanting.

Do not try to dig peonies, oriental poppies, baby's-breath, bleeding heart, or any other perennials with tuberous, brittle roots while in active growth.

ANNUALS AND VEGETABLES—Among annual flowers, California-poppy, larkspur, nasturtium, sweet pea, and annual lupine resent being moved. Do not transplant peas, beans, carrots, beets, radishes, squash, melons, and cucumbers. You can sow squash, melons, and cucumbers in peat pots, then set out plant and pot with no root disturbance.

POOLS. If you yearn for a garden pool and the tranquillity it can bring to a landscape, plastics can provide the means in ways that are less arduous and far quicker than constructing a pool from cement. Not that a well-made and designed garden pool made from concrete (cement, sand, and crushed gravel plus water) can't be an object of beauty, but it is an undertaking that involves a tremendous amount of work and skill. (I have a small, shallow concrete basin at the base of a stone retaining wall and while it serves its purpose of attracting birds and blends into its surroundings, it is a nuisance each spring to have to repair the crack that forms every winter.)

If a mere shimmer of water can satisfy you, perhaps a tiny saucer of a pool in the foreground of a group of shrubs and perennials, in a terrace corner, or in a wild-flower and fern setting, you can get along surprisingly well with a trash can lid, dishpan, or some other vessel that had been designed originally for another purpose. Such a simple little body of water, when its

1 2 3 4 5 6

sides are disguised by surrounding vegetation or a well-placed rock or two, can give the illusion of being more than it is. During the day it will attract birds, chipmunks, and squirrels and during the night probably a possum or raccoon. Adding a layer of pebbles can make this artificial water hole look more natural. A deep container will require more pebbles to bring the water depth to about 2 to 2½ inches, so birds can bathe safely.

PREMOLDED FIBERGLASS POOLS—For a more serious water garden, there are premolded fiberglass pools in several shapes, such as crescent, kidney, round, rectangular, butterfly, and others that should fit quite naturally into a garden plan if care and imagination are used.

Choose the location thoughtfully, keeping in mind that any body of water larger than a few feet will draw attention and be a focal point in the landscape, whether it is formal (that is, rectangular, round, or square) or informal (kidney, lamb chop, or the like). If the pool is to be a true water garden—containing fish and plants, and there isn't much sense in buying a fiberglass pool that won't—the exposure must be sunny for most of the day.

These pools vary in size from 8 feet by 4 feet to 30 inches by 15 inches, with all sizes being from 11 to 15 inches or so deep—deep enough to grow aquatic plants and support fish. Some well-stocked garden centers and nurseries sell fiberglass pools, as do a few specialty mail-order houses. If you have a choice in color, avoid all light blue shades, which look as artificial as the average blue swimming pool, and seek navy blue or black pools, which give the illusion of depth and mystery.

STEPS IN TRANSPLANTING A SMALL TREE OR SHRUB
1 Dotted line shows approximate width of root ball in correct proportion to size of tree. **2** Tying back the branches keeps them out of the way and prevents breakage. **3** Digging the trench to form a root ball. **4** A fairly wide trench around the root ball makes it easier to pry out the tree and to insert burlap. **5** Insert the burlap under the root ball, wrap it around it, and tie or fasten with nails. The reason for using burlap is to keep the root ball intact, but for quick transplanting with a solid root ball, it is usually unnecessary.

Small reflecting pool can be improvised from a dishpan or trash can lid and its humble origin disguised by rocks and plants. It can serve as a birdbath and watering place for other creatures, but will require frequent refilling.

There should be specific instructions accompanying a fiberglass pool for its installation. Dig a hole slightly deeper than the depth of the pool and a few inches wider all around. Remove all stones from the bottom of the excavation and tamp it firmly, making it perfectly level. Add an inch or so of sand. Then lower and position the pool, again checking to be sure all sides of the pool are level with surrounding ground. One way to be certain of this is to fill the pool with about a gallon of water. The other way is to place a board across the pool and place a spirit level on it. If the pool is level, start filling it slowly with water, at the same time replacing soil (free from stones and other abrasive debris) around the sides, being sure it is packed firmly. After about a week of seasoning, the water should be safe for fish and plants.

In the meantime, you can work in the surrounding area of the pool—placing stones and plants in a natural way to hide the fact that this is a fiberglass pool. If the pool is in a formal shape and setting, you can make a raised coping of bricks or paving blocks around the edges.

POOLS FROM PLASTIC SHEETING—Premolded fiberglass pools are expensive but very long-lived. Less expensive and a good introduction to water gardening is the plastic-lined pool, 20-mil polyvinyl chloride (PVC) sheeting being the best. Polyethylene sheeting is not recommended because it lacks the needed stretch and is very short-lived. Although PVC sheeting should last for years, it is not as permanent as an investment in a fiberglass or concrete pool, so if you decide along the way that water gardening is not for you, the sheeting can be ripped out in a thrice.

PVC liners in various sizes can be obtained from the same water garden specialists who handle fiberglass pools, aquatic plants, and fish, or you can usually buy sheeting from local building outlets.

MAKING A PVC-LINED POOL—After outlining the shape of the proposed pool with stakes, a rope, or a hose, obtain its measurements so you can buy the right size PVC. The formula for measuring: the overall length plus twice the maximum depth and the overall width plus twice the maximum depth. A pool 6 feet by 4 feet and 18 inches deep would require a PVC sheet 9 feet by 7 feet.

Excavate the hole, following the outline you have made, making the sides sloping rather than sharply vertical. Remove all stones from the bottom and sides, add a layer of sand on the bottom or use damp newspapers or carpet padding to form a lasting protection for the PVC.

It is most important to be certain that the surrounding edges are level, as you don't want plastic to show after the water is added. Lay the sheeting taut over the hole, taking care not to snag it. There should be at least 6 inches or more overlap all around, which can be kept in place by bricks or smooth stones or other heavy materials that won't snag the sheeting. Then place the hose in the center and start slowly filling the excavation with water. The weight of the water will cause the liner to sag and

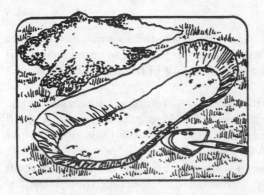

Making a plastic-lined garden pool: after you have dug and leveled the bottom of the pool (top), spread plastic sheeting over the excavation, placing rocks around the edge to hold it firmly as you slowly add water (center). When the pool is filled, use soil and rocks to hide the plastic edges and add suitable plants.

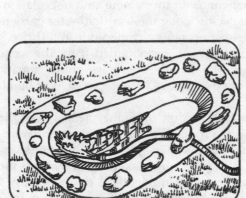

mold to the excavation. You may have to help a bit by smoothing out folds in corners.

After the pool is filled with water, wait about a week, then adjust the edges to hide the plastic overlay by burying it in a shallow trench, covering with soil, and planting shallow-rooted plants on top. Or use flat stones, allowing them to overlap the edges of the pool. A combination of rocks and plants can give a pleasing, natural effect.

If you plan on adding fish, you must include aquatic plants, either floaters or others, including water-lilies in boxes, to provide oxygen for the fish. All of these are available from mail-order sources.

REFLECTING POOLS—Shallow pools can be made of PVC even more easily than deep pools designed for fish and plants. Such pools can reflect the sky and nearby plantings as their appearance changes with the seasons. Such a pool can become even more of a landscape feature when the bottom is covered with small, smooth stones. Look for ideas in the books on Japanese gardening.

If you are determined to work with concrete, a saucer-shaped excavation with very sloping sides can be made into a quite small, presentable pool to entice birds and reflect a plant or two near it. Just be certain it is level!

POTS AND OTHER CONTAINERS. Pots and planters can transform a porch, patio, paved-over city backyard, or apartment terrace into a garden. All kinds of vegetables and fruits, including blueberries and dwarf fruit trees, are being found in containers today, in addition to the plants that have always made good subjects, such as geraniums and many annuals. Container gardening does require more faithful day-to-day attention to water needs than is necessary for most plants growing in the open ground.

KINDS OF CONTAINERS—Clay pots of all sizes are the oldest kind of container and are still preferred by many. Their advantages include their good looks and appropriateness for many settings and plants. Large clay pots always look better on a traditional brick-paved terrace or low brick wall than do most of the concrete and plastic containers. Clay pots are porous and tend to prevent soils from becoming water-logged. This becomes a disadvantage on a sunny, hot deck or terrace or windswept roof, where plants in clay may require daily and often even more frequent watering. Even indoors, house plants in small clay pots can be a nuisance because of their need for frequent watering. Large clay pots can be very heavy, especially if they are filled with soil rather than one of the synthetic mixes, which are considerably lighter in weight.

Bushel baskets make useful containers for most vegetables, as do other utilitarian pots, such as these large fiber pots, left over from purchased nursery stock.

Wooden planters and tubs, of redwood, oak, and other kinds of wood, can be very attractive and have some of the same advantages as clay. Bushel baskets, if lined with plastic, will survive for a few years and are a bargain compared to the cost of more permanent containers. The baskets provide the needed space for larger plants, such as trees and shrubs, and have the right look for little gardens of vegetables and herbs.

Plastic pots and containers are work savers and even the largest can be shifted about without too much strain. Their moisture-retention asset can become a liability outdoors when extensive rainy spells occur. During such wet periods it may even be necessary to turn the pots or containers on their sides to avoid long periods of oversaturated soil or growing mediums.

The African-violet is one of the plants that seems to grow better in plastic than clay pots. The salts that seep from clay pots injure the leaves and stems as they rest on the rims of the pots. Small plastic pots are much better than their clay counterparts for growing flower and vegetable seedlings started indoors. As the seedlings begin to grow faster, filling the soil with their roots, the clay pots dry out faster, which can check the normal rate of growth necessary for their proper development.

GUIDELINES FOR CONTAINER GARDENERS—If you have access to soil and prefer to use it rather than synthetic mixes or other purchased soil mixes, the general-purpose mixture of 2 parts soil, 1 part peat moss, and 1 part sand will be suitable for most plants. If your soil is quite sandy, you can compromise—use half soil and half soilless mix.

The soilless mixes do not contain enough fertilizers to last long (some do not contain any nutrients—read the labels), so a regular feeding schedule must be followed. The frequency of fertilizing depends on the type and strength of the fertilizer used. Follow the suggestions on the package. Using a light dose of a liquid fertilizer every time you water works well for most plants.

Plants growing in a soil mixture will also require extra feedings during the growing season, usually about once a month. (See also Fertilizers and Soil.)

The roots of trees and shrubs grown in containers are more susceptible to winter injury than are plants grown in the ground. Shrubs like privet and lilac can usually tough out winters in their containers, but roses and dwarf fruit trees, for instance, require more coddling, especially where frequent freezing and thawing can be expected. If the plants and their containers can't be moved to a cool but protected shelter, such as a garage, crowd the containers close together and as near as you can get them to the protection of the house or apartment wall. If possible mulch all around them with hay.

Containers not exposed to rain or snow may require watering about once a month. (For suggested plants to grow in containers, see Annuals and Vegetables.)

POTTING. See Indoor Gardening.

PROPAGATION. Most plants can be increased by cuttings, division of old plants, and seeds—with a minimum of anguish. The new gardener, almost before knowing whether his or her thumb is green or black, will have sown some seeds, perhaps for a lawn or for a flower garden. Seed sowing is known as sexual propagation and is nature's major method of increasing plants. Cuttings, division, layering, and other means of increasing plants are known as asexual propagation and are especially important when you want an identical copy of a certain plant whose seeds will not breed true.

SEED SOWING AND SEEDLINGS

STARTING SEEDS INDOORS—Some annuals and vegetables need a longer growing period before they begin to flower or bear fruit, so in the North these are usually started indoors about 5 to 8 weeks before it will be safe to set the plants outdoors, usually after danger of frosts has passed. They can also be sown in a greenhouse and a cold frame. (See Annuals for a list of those annuals best sown early.) Tomatoes, eggplants, and peppers are the vegetables usually sown indoors.

Other annuals and some vegetables do not require as long a growing period and can be just as well sown outdoors after the soil has warmed, but often it is fun to give them a head start indoors.

The seed companies are doing everything possible to make indoor seed sowing easy. For example, there are kits under various names, such as Start and Seed, of all the popular annuals and vegetables, that include a container, seeds, growing medium, and complete instructions to help you succeed.

What these kits can't give you is the proper light. But if you have invested in fluorescent lights for house plants (see Indoor

Gardening) and have space under them for seedlings, you have an important element for successful indoor seed sowing: reliable light for 16 hours a day. You may be able to get along without artificial light if you are fortunate enough to have wide, sunny windows.

You will need clean containers in which to sow the seeds. These can be kitchen and food castoffs (but make drainage holes in their bottoms) or the fiber or plastic flats (about 7½ by 5½ inches and 2¾ inches deep), available from mail-order seed houses or garden centers. Do not attempt to use your own garden soil. It is bound to carry the disease known as damping-off, which destroys seedlings shortly after they have germinated. Instead, buy a sterilized potting or seed soil, or the sterile soilless mixes (see Soil).

Purchased growing mediums are bound to be dry. Moisten according to instructions on the bag or you can pour in tepid water gradually—not too much at a time as you don't want a soggy mass—and wait until the mix is moist. (Or you can fill the containers with the mix and stand them in a basin of tepid water until their surfaces are moist.)

Sow the seeds thinly, either in shallow drills a few inches apart or, if you are sowing one variety per flat, you can broadcast (scatter) the seeds over the surface. Cover the seeds lightly with moist medium. Some seeds should not be covered, including the very fine ones of petunia, impatiens, and others. The seeds of petunia, coleus, impatiens, and lettuce are examples of those that require light to germinate, one of the main reasons for not covering them. Read the instructions on the seed packets for guidance on light requirements. After sowing, mist the surface, then slip the flats or other container in plastic bags or stretch a sheet of clear plastic over the top to retain moisture. This is especially important for the fine seeds that lie on the surface. A temperature of about 70 to 75° F will speed germination of most seeds sown indoors, but do not place the flats on a radiator or any place where they are blasted by hot air.

As soon as seedlings appear, remove the plastic coverings, and place the flats under the fluorescent lights, about 4 inches from the tubes. As the seedlings grow taller, raise the fixture so the

plants are from 4 to 6 inches beneath the tubes. Keep the lights on for 16 hours, beginning early in the morning. Do not leave them on all the time. A timer is the most convenient way to regulate the lights.

Thin the seedlings to about 2 inches apart or transplant each seedling after it has formed two sets of leaves. You have a choice of spacing out the seedlings in the same-size flats or putting them into special compartmentalized plastic ones, which usually have space for six plants. Or you can buy the special peat pots, available in sizes from 2 1/4 to 3 inches, in square or round shapes. Fill whichever container you decide on (2 1/4-inch pots for most annuals, the 3-inch size for tomatoes, peppers, and other vegetables) with fresh sterilized soil or soilless mix. Use a wooden label or a spoon to ease the seedlings from their flats and to make a hole in the new flats or pots that will accommodate the seedlings' roots. Handle the seedlings as little as possible, holding them gingerly by a leaf—not the stem. Water, after gently firming the soil, and replace the flats or pots under the fluorescent tubes or in a sunny window. If you are using the latter, turn the containers every day or so to keep the seedlings growing straight rather than lopsided toward the light.

If any seedlings are "reaching," that is, growing in a spindly, soft way, they probably need more light. Too warm temperatures will also cause unhealthy, weak development. Daytime temperatures of 65 to 70° F with about a 10° drop at night will result in sturdy, chunky growth—if the seedlings are getting ample light as well.

One way to avoid transplanting crowded seedlings, first sown in flats indoors, is to move on to the one-step Jiffy peat pellet method. The Jiffy pellets, along with fluorescent lights and sterile

---

Look around the kitchen for possible containers in which to sow seeds. Paper and Styrofoam cups can be used as pots for tomatoes and other seedlings. Containers left over from frozen pies and dinners, cardboard milk cartons and plastic jugs, muffin tins, and other baking utensils are further possibilities for seed sowing.

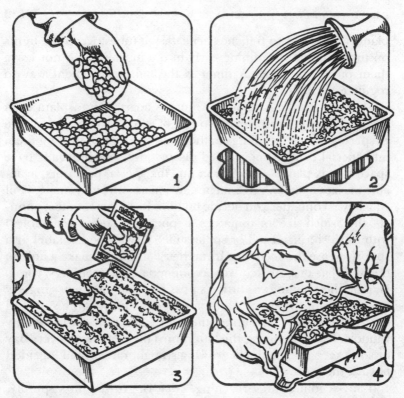

1. A variety of makeshift as well as purchased containers can be used for seed sowing. Some people like to add a layer of pebbles in the bottom of the container, but this practice is not deemed necessary with the synthetic soil mixes. **2.** Moisten the growing medium before sowing seeds by spraying with tepid water as shown, or by standing the container in a basin of water so the water is absorbed through the drainage holes. Another method is to pour water into the plastic bag containing the synthetic mix or potting soil. **3.** Sow the seeds in rows or scatter them over the surface, following the method recommended on the packet. **4.** After covering the seeds (very fine seeds, such as of petunia, need not be covered), slip the container into a plastic bag. No further watering should be needed until the growing medium dries, usually after the seedlings have emerged and the plastic bag is removed.

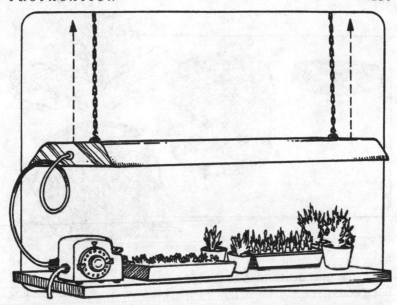

The shoplight fixture containing two fluorescent tubes is reasonable in price and widely available. Once installed, the fixture can be raised or lowered to suit the heights of seedlings and plants. A timer (left) is handy for turning the lights on and off automatically.

soilless mixes that are disease-free, make indoor seed sowing convenient and decidedly worthwhile. When purchased, the pellets are round wafers, but when soaked for a few minutes in a pan of water they at once expand into little peat pots, approximately 2⅛ inches high by 1¾ inches in diameter. They are just the right size for two seeds of tomatoes, peppers, eggplants, marigolds, or whatever you wish. You can also sow a minute pinch of very fine seeds in them. (The reason for sowing more than one seed at once is that one might not germinate—as soon as the two or more seedlings have grown a set or two of leaves, cut off the weaker plant, leaving the strong one to carry on.)

One minor problem with the Jiffy pellet pots is that they are not self-supporting and should be placed in watertight trays, which

Indoor seed sowing is much simplified when Jiffy peat pellets are used. The peat pellet (left), when put in water, expands into a small pot (center), ready for seed placement. The well-developed seedling (right) and its peat pot are then set in a final garden position.

also make watering easier. (Just pour water in the trays and after the pots have absorbed what they need, pour off the excess.) There is some fertilizer in the pellets, enough for a few weeks or so. Thereafter, you can apply a liquid fertilizer, such as Hyponex, Schultz, or fish emulsion (diluted to directions on the container), every time you water. Plants in the peat pellet pots grow very well and should not require any more transplanting until it is safe to set them outdoors.

Indoor-grown seedlings can not be planted outdoors without undergoing the "hardening off" process, which is just what it sounds like. The seedlings must be subjected gradually to the outdoor environment, starting them with a few hours the first days and then lengthening the exposure time. To be on the safe side, I always start with partial sun in an area protected from drying winds. A cold frame can be a help, and since it can be closed at night (see Cold Frames), you can place your seedlings in it earlier. If foliage of the seedlings begins to turn white, the plants have been injured by too much bright light and may or may not recover.

It is safe to plant most annuals in the open ground after about a week of hardening off, as long as frosts have ended. However, some annuals and vegetables can withstand a light frost after their hardening-off adjustment. Such hardy annuals include snapdragons, lettuce, all members of the cabbage family, parsley, onions, leeks, and perennials such as delphiniums. Tender seedlings include tomatoes, eggplants, peppers, petunias, marigolds, zinnias, impatiens, and begonias.

For details on planting annuals and vegetables in the open ground, see Annuals, Planting and Transplanting, and Vegetables.

SOWING SEEDS OUTDOORS—It is possible to sow seeds of many annuals, biennials, some perennials, and the majority of vegetables directly in the soil outdoors.

Some annuals and vegetables can endure frosts and germinate and grow better when the soil and weather are still cold. St. Patrick's Day is the traditional time in much of the North for sowing peas in the vegetable garden. Their close relative, the flowering sweet pea, can be sown a few weeks later. California-poppy, calendula, larkspur, radishes, and lettuce are all very hardy and should be sown a few weeks after peas—just as soon as the soil is reasonably workable and not soggy. The seeds of larkspur, calendula, and California-poppy can be scattered over the soil if it is too wet to lightly cultivate. (See Annuals and Vegetables.)

Most seeds—marigolds, zinnias, beans, and squash—should be sown when the soil has warmed and frosts have ended, about May 15 in much of the country.

If you have the space, it is most convenient to sow flower seeds in a special seedbed, usually a rectangular area, in sun, and convenient to a water source. This is a nursery, a temporary home for seedlings until they are ready to be moved into their permanent locations. The soil should be well drained but contain a goodly amount of peat moss, which will retain moisture and prevent the seeds from drying out before they have germinated and thereafter. The seeds can be sown in furrows at the depths recommended on the packets. Thin sowing means less work later for you, as crowded seedlings must be spaced out to about 2 to 4 inches apart if they are to develop into healthy plants. The seedlings can be moved into their permanent positions in the gardens when they are 3 to 4 inches tall. Don't wait too long, since the seedlings become more susceptible to transplanting shock as they become larger. Replant so the first pair of leaves is at the surface of the soil. Water well after moving.

The procedures are the same for sowing vegetables except that most of the seeds will be sown directly where the plants are to be harvested. You will need a line stretched between two stakes to mark out rows that will run the length or width of the vegetable garden, perhaps 30 or more feet. (Lettuce can be sown in shorter rows and transplanted or harvested from its original rows if the plants are thinned out.)

Stretch out the line and use it to guide your hoe to make a furrow at the depth suggested on the seed packet. Sow the seeds at recommended distances and thin the seedlings later.

DIVISION

DIVIDING PERENNIALS—If you plant perennials, sooner or later you will find yourself dividing a clump of chrysanthemums, or perhaps a Shasta daisy or aster, all three of which require more frequent dividing than day-lilies and many other perennials. Although division is the major means of increasing perennials, especially the named cultivars, which do not breed "true" to their parents from seed, it is also important as a way of maintaining a plant's vigor. Old clumps of many perennials that are not revitalized by division become choked and tend to die out in their centers. A third reason for dividing plants is simply that the plant has become too large for its space and is crowding or being crowded by neighboring plants.

Perennials that bloom in the spring are usually divided in the fall while late summer and fall bloomers are divided in the spring. In practice, though, most perennials can be divided in spring if it is done early. Perennial or summer phlox, for instance, usually needs to be divided every 3 or 4 years to keep the plants vigorous and to avoid woody, nonproductive centers in their clumps. While the textbook recommendation is for fall division, it can be done successfully in early spring when the new growth is only an inch or so high.

To divide a perennial, dig the clump with a spade, going deep enough to catch the entire root ball, and place it on a wheelbarrow or any convenient flat surface. (If you must use the lawn, spread a burlap section or newspapers to protect the grass.) With a spading fork, a knife, or your hands (often all three are involved), split or break up the clump into reasonable sections, discarding all old, woody, decrepit parts and saving the divisions with healthy-looking roots and crowns. Replant the divisions as quickly as possible, following the usual good planting practices (see Planting and Transplanting).

You will find that hard-to-divide perennials (day-lilies, for instance) divide with less mayhem all around if you sink two spading forks into the center of the clump, back to back, then pry them

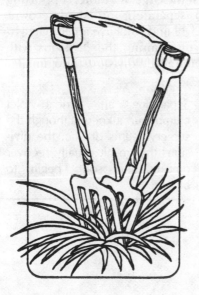

Dividing a day-lily clump by prying apart two forks.

apart, which results in two clumps. (This is an honorable garden practice that never fails—though it must be done on firm ground —and that does not mutilate the roots and crowns.) Repeat the process on each half. The resulting four or so clumps should be about the right size for replanting if you want a decent flower display the next year. Making the divisions too skimpy may mean you must wait a year or more for flowers.

Peonies, which can go for years without requiring division, providing the clumps are flowering well and have no dead centers, should be carefully lifted in the fall, if and when you want to increase the clumps. Examine them, noting the "pink eyes," really buds, and then tease the clump into sections, using a sharp knife and your hands, so each division ends with three to five buds. Replant so the buds are no deeper than about an inch beneath the surface.

DIVISION OF HOUSE PLANTS—Many house plants can be increased or revitalized by division. African-violets often need frequent division to retain their desirable single-crown habit of growth. After removing the plant from its pot (turn the pot upside down and gently tap it against the edge of a table, supporting the plant with your other hand), separate it into single crowns with a knife and your hands. You will find you have an embarrassing number of offspring, even discounting the divisions with broken leaves you can discard. Repot the divisions into smaller

Separating an African-violet clump with a knife: although the surgery seems drastic, the divisions that result usually recover quickly and soon begin to bloom.

pots, about 2½ to 3 inches in diameter, depending on how intact the roots and foliage are. Miniature African-violet divisions can go into even smaller pots.

CUTTINGS AND OTHER MEANS OF PROPAGATION

CUTTINGS—Propagation by cuttings—the old word for a cutting was "slip" and it is still used occasionally—is very important to nurserymen and other horticultural professionals, who increase the majority of trees and shrubs by this method. Yet anyone who has grown African-violets has probably rooted a leaf cutting in water or in a synthetic soil mixture, such as Jiffy Mix. One of the most efficient ways to root an African-violet leaf cutting is to insert the leaf with about 1 to 1½ inches of its stem in a small pot (2¼- to 2½-inch plastic pots) filled with the moist mix, so the leaf is just above the surface. Place it in a plastic bag or propagating box sold at garden centers and by mail-order seed houses. Keep from direct sunlight. Remove the pot from its humid housing when you see a tiny crown of leaves, place the pot under fluorescent lights, and feed with a diluted fertilizer every time you water. Eventually you may have to move the plant to the next-size pot, although many African-violet varieties do very well in small pots as long as they are fertilized regularly.

This African-violet leaf cutting will eventually produce one or more new plants.

Geraniums, coleus, impatiens, and Boston daisies or marguerite daisies are among house plants that can be increased by stem
cuttings. Insert a geranium cutting, about 4 to 5 inches long with
the bottom cut made just below a leaf node, and leave the cutting
exposed to the air for a few hours or long enough so a slight
callus begins to form on the cut end. Then insert the cutting
about 2 inches deep in the moist rooting medium—peat moss
and sand, soilless mix, or peat moss and perlite. Keep from bright
sunshine and do not let the rooting medium remain soggy or the
cutting will rot.

Coleus, impatiens, and other cuttings root quickly in small
plastic flats placed in a propagating box or in a plastic bag. Do not
let the plastic cling to the foliage of the cuttings or they may rot. If
there seems to be too much condensation inside the bag, open
the top for a few hours.

NEW SHRUBS FROM CUTTINGS—A few of the easiest shrubs to
root from cuttings are forsythia, willow, privet, Japanese skimmia, boxwood, winter-creeper, and bush honeysuckles. You may
have noticed that forsythia branches forced for their flowers in
late winter had formed roots by the time you were ready to
discard them. Privet stems up to 10 inches or so can be cut in
spring, inserted in soil, and will be rooted by summer. In fact, this
is a very convenient way to start a new hedge.

Not all shrubs are so casual in their rooting habits, but new
growth of evergreen azaleas, about 4 to 5 inches long, removed
from the parent plant in early summer, roots readily in a flat of
peat moss and sand or inserted in the same mixture in a cold
frame. As with cuttings indoors, constant humidity speeds rooting and prevents the growing medium from drying. Maintain it by
placing a clear plastic tent over a wooden box (form a frame for
the plastic by inserting two wires into the sides of the flats and
then staple the plastic to the sides of the box—the finished effect
looks like a Quonset hut). If the growing medium is well moist-
ened before the plastic is added, no more water should be needed
for weeks. Keep the flat out of direct sun or the cuttings inside
will be cooked. (If you place the cuttings in a cold frame, close the

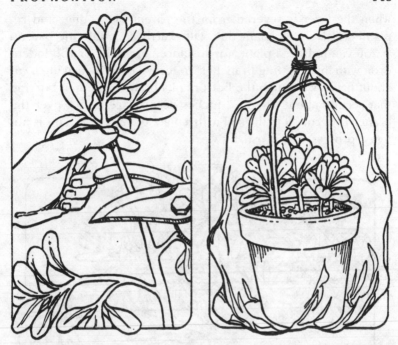

New shrubs from cuttings: cutting material (left) being removed from an evergreen azalea and cuttings (right) placed in a pot to root, which is then enclosed in a plastic bag.

lid.) Overwinter in a protected area, out of direct sun. If the flat is not in a frost-free location, pack leaves and evergreen boughs around it.

The following spring, the rooted cuttings can be planted in a special area in a mixture of peat moss and soil, where they can remain until large enough to transplant.

LAYERING—Some plants propagate themselves by layering, that is, a low branch or stem in constant contact with the soil forms roots. Rhododendrons commonly layer in the lush, decaying leaf mold of their mulch. As with divisions and cuttings, when the layer is severed from the parent plant, dug, and replanted, it is a new plant that will exactly resemble the parent.

You can induce a plant, for instance, an azalea or rhododendron with low-growing branches, to form a layer by making a cut about halfway through the bottom of a branch and then burying that section about 1 1/2 to 2 inches deep. Place a rock over the branch or secure it in the soil with a piece of bent wire. This is not a fast process, but it usually works.

Obtaining a new rhododendron from a layered branch.

INCREASING BULBS—Many bulbs and bulblike plants (see Bulbs) increase themselves by forming small bulbs or offshoots. Tulips are frantic to split into smaller bulbs, while daffodils form offshoots at a slower rate. When daffodils show more leaves than flowers in the spring, it is usually a sign that they can be lifted and their crowded bulbs separated and replanted. Do this as the grasslike foliage is turning brown and water the bulbs well after replanting.

Gladiolus form new corms each year, clearly present on the top of the old corm when it is dug in the fall for storage. The popular amaryllis, grown as a winter-flowering house plant in the North and outdoors all year in the South and other mild climates, forms offshoots, which can be removed from the mother bulb and planted separately.

GRAFTING AND BUDDING—These are important kinds of propagation in the production of fruit trees, both standard and dwarf, hybrid roses, and for certain other plants, such as wisteria. In the case of grafting, a bud or scion (cutting) of the variety you are propagating is inserted or fastened next to a rooted understock's stem in such a way that the cambium layers (the tissue where new wood and bark form) of both are in contact. Grafting is most often used for fruits, while budding is a similar process used for roses. Only related plants can be budded or grafted.

Only the highlights of propagation have been covered here. Readers who wish for more specific information about propagation can find it in *Plant Propagation in Pictures* by Montague Free (revised edition, 1979, Doubleday & Company).

PRUNING. Pruning often seems a mystery to new gardeners and to some more experienced ones, too. Yet with a bit of common sense and advice from experts, such as the county's cooperative extension agents, who can answer questions on how and when to prune specific plants, pruning may not seem so complicated.

First of all, use common sense in knowing what you can do and when you should call in a specialist to do the job. Cutting down large trees or removing large branches are rarely safe projects for the average home owner.

Using common sense can prevent the planting of trees and shrubs in the wrong places where later pruning may be required. One example is the large-leaved rhododendron placed close to the house as part of a foundation planting. While only a few feet high, it may fit its site well enough, but sooner or later it will have reached the window and will continue to shoot up. Then the problem of how and when to prune it arises. With the proper plant in that location, a low-growing shrub or perhaps even better, a ground cover, the concern of reducing the rhododendron's height would be one less mistake to remedy.

Another example: small properties will support few trees, yet many new home owners rush to plant trees without questioning what the ultimate height and spread of the tree will be. (Of course some people deliberately overplant their properties, realizing that later the plants must be thinned out or cut back.)

Actually, many shrubs and trees never require any pruning. Most broad-leaved evergreens, when not used as foundation subjects, like the large-leaved rhododendron just mentioned, or planted too close together, rarely require any pruning back (removal of seed heads after flowers fade is beneficial and is a form of pruning). Dwarf conifers, a few of which are suitable for foundations, make attractive accents elsewhere on the property and do not usually require restrictive pruning. They are a better choice for limited space than their standard-size counterparts. (See also Evergreens.) Pines can be slowed in their growth by cutting the candlelike spring growth at the ends of branches in half, but as the trees continue to grow upward, this becomes almost impossible.

Both hemlocks and yews can be sheared in the spring, often a necessary kind of pruning when they are used as formal hedges. Yews, arborvitae, and junipers have latent buds along their stems, so can undergo drastic cutbacks (best done in spring) when they are outgrowing their space.

Here are a few general guidelines to pruning.

1. When cutting back random shrub branches or removing them to force for cut flowers, try to cut to maintain the looks of the shrub without butchering it. Make the cuts just above a bud, the point at which new growth will come, to avoid leaving a stump.

2. When flowering shrubs, such as lilacs, become overgrown and leggy, spread the removal of old shoots at the base over a few seasons, so the shrub retains some landscape value and produces a few flowers.

3. As for that overgrown rhododendron in the foundation, you can cut it back to the ground in early spring, at which time it is

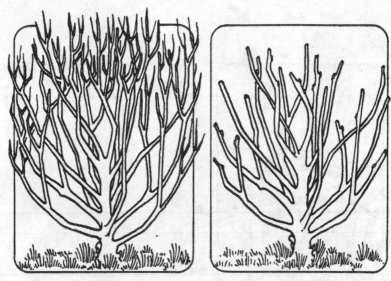

Sometimes an old lilac becomes choked by its own growth (left) and requires rather drastic thinning (right). Not shown are the suckers, random stems that spring up around and beyond the main trunk. These can be cut out or a few can be retained as replacements for older trunks.

most likely to be stimulated to make strong new growth from the stubs, but there will be no flowers for several years. Or you can treat it like the lilac in the illustration, cutting back selected main stems each year rather than doing the job at once. A third option is to cut back the entire plant in spring to the height you want and trust that latent buds will break with new growth. Pruned-back rhododendrons should receive fertilizer in spring, be well mulched (see Mulches and Mulching), and watered during drought. However, the large-leaved rhododendron in the foundation, if all goes well and it continues to grow after being cut back, will soon be once again outgrowing its space.

   4. Mountain-laurel *(Kalmia latifolia)* often becomes leggy and can be handled the same way as rhododendrons. Evergreen aza-

Prune shrubs and roses just above the buds.

leas have latent buds along their stems and usually quickly fill in with new growth after pruning. Azaleas are sometimes sheared right after flowering to keep their shapes chunky and within bounds. Although this sort of training does keep azaleas re-strained and often results in sheets of flower color, the effect can be graceless and artificial. If you want bloom from your azaleas, broad-leaved evergreens, forsythias, and most other spring-blooming shrubs, remember that their flower buds form in early summer, so late summer pruning, not recommended anyway, eliminates that bloom.

5. Fruit trees are pruned while they are dormant. Most dwarf fruits require less pruning than standard-size trees. It is better to err on the side of underpruning rather than overpruning. Follow training directions sent with your trees. Ask your cooperative extension specialists for suggestions and available leaflets. (See also Fruits.)

6. Pruning Trees—Research has shown that some of the accepted practices in pruning trees are out of date. For instance, the "flush" cut, left against the trunk after removal of a large (or small, for that matter) branch, has been amended to preserve the branch bark ridge, or collar, a slight but perceptible bulge just beyond the main trunk. Experts now recommend that the cut be made beyond that point for better healing of the wound. Just a slight bulge is left, which to flush-cut purists may look untidy and like a stump, but it is decidedly better for the health of the tree.

Tree paints and sprays to cover wounds after pruning are no longer recommended, as they do not prevent decay and may impede the healing process.

7. Large shrub roses can be pruned as recommended for other flowering shrubs, that is, as the shrubs mature and show signs of becoming choked, a few canes (stems) can be cut back at the base of the plant in spring or immediately after flowering. Rambler roses, such as the old 'Dorothy Perkins' and 'Paul's Scarlet,' and all others with clusters of small flowers in June, can become a tangle, but will continue blooming for years even under such untidy conditions. Order among rambler roses can be maintained by cutting back the canes that have just bloomed. The new ones that soon shoot up can be partially cut back later in the same growing season if they are outreaching their space.

The faded flowers of large-flowered climbers, those with flowers often as large as those of hybrid teas, should be removed from the lateral stems. Leave three to four buds on these laterals. As the main canes of climbing roses age, they can be cut off at the base, if no vigorous growth appears above them.

For the pruning of hybrid tea and floribunda roses, see Roses.

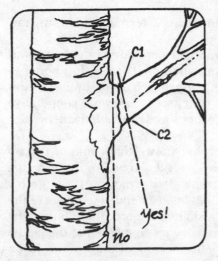

Pruning limbs from trees: do not make the cut flush against the trunk. C1 shows angle at which to start cut, and C2 where to end it.

For pruning and pinching of house plants, see Indoor Gardening.

R

ROCK GARDENS. A rock garden should be an imitation of a natural phenomenon—a series of rocky outcroppings in the foothills of mountains or a higher-up rock-strewn meadow. Usually the most successful rock gardens are inherited from nature, with the role of the gardener being a sort of benign caretaker. He or she can introduce plants and curb and weed out those that become rampant or superfluous, but generally the influence of the gardener is so subtle as to be hardly noticeable. Not that good rock gardens can't be constructed. They can and are made all the time.

MAKING A ROCK GARDEN—If you are fortunate enough to have a rocky slope, a few rock outcroppings, or a hillside and have access to large fissured rocks in your region, a proper rock garden is well within your reach.

Those who do not have any of these fortuitous conditions to start with can build a rock garden on flat land. This may not appeal to rock garden purists, but it is an acceptable way to grow many rock garden plants. Do not make a mound of soil, dot it with round boulders, and then sprinkle a few plants over it!

Instead, think of the flat area more as an alpine meadow. The area can be gently raised by a foot or so of added soil here and there, and the introduced rocks, well sunk to imitate outcroppings, can give the illusion of height. Round stones are hard to use, but unless you live in an area with ample, free-for-the-taking, irregular, weathered rocks, you must make do with what's available regionally. The rounder the rocks, the deeper they must be set.

In some regions, there are nurseries that specialize in rock garden construction. For large rock moving and placement, professional help is necessary. If you want to build your own rock garden on a large scale, study books devoted to the subject and visit public rock gardens. Some of these may be very grand, but they do offer excellent examples of rock gardens along with inspiration and ideas for more modest adaptations. (Good public rock gardens can be seen at the New York Botanical Garden, the Bronx, New York; Cornell University, Ithaca, New York; and Longwood Gardens, Kennett Square, Pennsylvania.)

WALL GARDENS—A retaining wall—a wall constructed to hold back the soil of a steep or even modestly sloping area—offers another possibility for growing rock garden plants. Although a retaining wall should fit into the overall landscape scheme, it is a man-made structure that serves a practical purpose. It is not intended to resemble nature's handiwork, although a wall garden filled with tumbling rock plants can be likened to a sheer, deeply fissured mountain area in which many plants are naturally at home.

The steps in building a retaining wall are similar to those for making a rock garden. The rocks are collected or purchased and should be angular rather than round. A small bulldozer can be hired to loosen the soil and move it as necessary to grade the areas above and below the proposed wall. The larger stones are

kept at the base of the wall, with those in the first row being set
firmly and tilted back slightly toward the slope so water will run
back into the soil. The entire wall should slant back into the
slope. Most of the rocks will be so buried that only one face will
show.

Do not attempt to set plants into the wall as it is being built.
Start planting after the wall is finished and has settled, and you
are sure the soil is well packed behind and between the rocks. You
can then set plants in soil pockets between the rocks and at the
base and top of the wall.

After the plants are well established, you may find that some
plants self-sow, with the happy result that seedlings appear in
small openings you would have found difficult to plant. Behind
these small openings, there is an endless bank of soil for the roots
to penetrate. The tilt of the wall toward the bank helps to catch
rain water, but plants will require watering during droughts and
always after being set out.

PLANTS FOR ROCK GARDENS AND WALLS—Rock garden plants
can be herbaceous perennials, hardy bulbs, shrubs, and dwarf
conifers. Some of the perennials are familiar as foreground
plants for flower borders, but many are rare alpines, tiny gems
from mountainous habitats all over the world. They are sought
out and then coddled by rock garden specialists. (Serious rock
gardeners belong to the American Rock Garden Society, Norfolk
Road, Sandisfield, Massachusetts 01255, membership $15 a
year.)

The following plants are mostly trouble-free perennials, but
many, many more are available from nurseries.

▨▨▨▨ A SAMPLER OF ROCK ▨▨▨▨
GARDEN PLANTS

Basket of Gold or **Alyssum** *(Aurinia saxatilis)*. Clusters of small,
bright yellow flowers in spring and grayish foliage. Sun. Self-sows
if seed heads are not cut off.

Bellflower *(Campanula* species). Blue to white bells, mostly in
late spring to early summer. Sun. Many kinds, some difficult,

DEREK FELL

MARJORIE J. DIETZ

(Above) A sunny stone retaining wall becomes a garden when various creeping plants are encouraged to tumble down its face. (Left) Dealing with shade. Ferns and certain perennials and wild flowers that do not require several hours of sun are the answer. Shown here is the light blue creeping phlox *(P. stolonifera),* a spring bloomer. (Below) Vegetable gardens need as much sun as you can provide. The vegetables here are grown in raised beds, often a solution when soil drainage is poor. Convenience is another of the assets of raised beds, as they make maintenance much easier.

DEREK FELL

(Above left) Brick-walled terrace of good, traditional design. The ground cover of running myrtle or periwinkle is in harmony with the brick pavement and azaleas and rhododendrons along the wall. (Above right) Golden chain or laburnum is a small tree that can be planted close to a building or on a terrace. (Below) Small garden pool made from an oval metal washtub. Blue ajuga, primroses, and hosta are part of the surrounding planting.

(Above left) Container garden by a gate welcomes visitors. (Above right) Bird's-eye view of a pot of culinary herbs for a terrace. The plants, including basil, parsley, and dill, are 10 weeks old. (Below) The small suburban or city lot has space for a wide variety of plant material when it is well planned and organized.

(Above) Plants to grow in a terrarium range from small-leaved foliage kinds to a few that flower, such as the miniature sinningia and certain begonias. (Left) A miniature rose in a cork pot. (Below) One plant of the lady-slipper orchid often produces several waxy-textured, long-lasting blooms. The plant and its pot are the right size to fit under fluorescent lights.

some easy. Start with *C. carpatica*, the Carpathian harebell, and *C. elatines*, and for partial shade, *C. rotundifolia*, bluebells of Scotland.

Candytuft, Perennial *(Iberis sempervirens)*. White flower clusters in spring and handsome evergreen foliage. Sun. One of the best. Easy to propagate from cuttings or allow a few clusters to form seeds and sow in summer as soon as ripe.

Columbine *(Aquilegia* species). Graceful spurred flowers in spring above mounds of attractive foliage. Many available, but start with *A. caerulea*, blue; *A. vulgaris*, blue; *A. flabellata* 'Nana Alba,' white flowers with very gray-tinted foliage. All fairly easy to grow from seeds. Sun to part shade.

Creeping Baby's-breath *(Gypsophila repens)*. Creeper with airy sprays of white to pink flowers in early summer and grayish leaves. Sun. Slightly alkaline soil (mix limestone in soil pocket if your soil is acid).

Moss Pink or **Creeping Pink** *(Phlox subulata)*. Ground hugger with showy flowers in wide color range in spring and tiny evergreen leaves. Sun. Very well-drained soil.

Pinks *(Dianthus* species). Bright flowers in pinks, reds, or white above mounds or cushions of evergreen grassy leaves, often grayish. Sun. Slightly alkaline soil (mix limestone in planting pockets of acid soil). Many kinds. Start with the maiden pink, *D. deltoides*. Most fairly easy from seeds.

Rock Cress *(Arabis albida)*. Sprays of fragrant white flowers in spring, soft gray foliage. Sun. Self-sows.

Sedum or **Stonecrop** *(Sedum* species). Many good sedums. An easy one is *S. acre* with yellow flowers from spring to summer and light green leaves that hug the ground. Sun. Well-drained dry soil.

Snow-in-Summer *(Cerastium tomentosum)*. White flowers in spring above mats of gray foliage. Sun. Self-sows.

Speedwell *(Veronica incana)*. Spikes of blue flowers in early summer above rosettes of gray foliage. Sun.

Yarrow, Woolly *(Achillea tomentosa)*. Bright yellow flowers in clusters above gray foliage mats in early summer. Sun.

ROSES. The rose, of course, is a shrub, but to many, *the* flower is a rose and this has been true for eons. The popularity of the rose endures, and now miniature roses, so suitable for today's smaller gardens, are giving those who never had a chance to grow roses before the pleasure of enjoying these smaller versions indoors as house plants as well as outdoors in special gardens or in containers.

KINDS OF ROSES—The most popular roses remain the hybrid teas, a comparatively recent class as roses go, having come into existence about 80 years ago when crosses were made between the tender true tea roses and the more hardy hybrid perpetuals. Hybrid teas make bushy plants from 2½ to 5 feet tall with large, elegant flowers on long stems. These blooms, often fragrant, are mostly double, although there are some single or semidouble varieties, and are in red, lavender, rose, pink, yellow, orange, white, and blends. Most hybrid teas bloom heavily in early summer, but continue to produce some in summer and often quite heavily in fall.

 SAMPLER OF POPULAR
HYBRID TEA ROSES

(*f* indicates marked fragrance)

BRANDY *f* apricot blend	HELEN TRAUBEL pink blend
CHARLOTTE ARMSTRONG red, pink	PEACE yellow, pink
CHICAGO PEACE pink	THE DOCTOR *f* pink
CHRYSLER IMPERIAL *f* crimson	TIFFANY *f* pink
ECLIPSE yellow	TROPICANA *f* orange

The floribunda class, which originated from crosses between polyantha and hybrid teas, is also quite recent, and its many cultivars are nearly as popular as hybrid teas. Some of the earlier floribundas were very compact, remaining about 3 feet in height, but newer varieties are often vigorous and can reach 5 to 6 feet in mild climates and in the North unless checked by pruning. The flowers are borne in clusters and tend to appear all summer. They provide more massed color effects than hybrid teas, and the bushes are often used as a near-everblooming hedge.

▨▨▨▨ SAMPLER OF POPULAR ▨▨▨▨
FLORIBUNDA ROSES

(*f* indicates marked fragrance)

ANGEL FACE	*f* lavender	FRENSHAM	crimson
BETTY PRIOR	*f* pink	GINGERSNAP	*f* orange blend
EUTIN	red	ICEBERG	*f* white
FASHION	*f* coral pink	IVORY FASHION	*f* white
FRENCH LACE	white	ROSENELFE	pink

Grandiflora roses belong to a new class, still controversial because the flowers often reflect their floribunda parentage. 'Queen Elizabeth' was the first cultivar and is a vigorous rose with pink flowers on nearly thornless stems. The shrubs themselves usually grow over 4 feet.

One of the most famous roses—and still much planted—is 'The Fairy' of the old polyantha class. It is a low, shrubby plant with clusters of pink flowers in early summer and intermittently thereafter. It is resistant to black spot disease.

Tree or standard roses are mostly floribunda or hybrid tea roses grafted onto tall stems of a vigorous shrub rose. In much of the North, they are difficult to get through the winter without special fussy protection.

Rambler and climbing roses have very long canes that must be supported on fences or trellises. Although rambler roses do not seem to be sold any more, they are still very much in existence, rambling over stone walls and low fences in country areas and along the shore in New England and Long Island and no doubt elsewhere.

One of the most popular ramblers was 'Dorothy Perkins,' which can be very pretty with its many clusters of pink flowers in June.

Climbing roses include sports of floribundas and hybrid teas, such as 'Climbing Peace' and 'Climbing Goldilocks,' and another group, large-flowered climbers, such as 'Blaze.'

The miniature rose class is growing in leaps and bounds and it is no wonder. If you have never grown one of these winsome roses in a 4-inch pot, its buds and flowers in perfect proportion to the small leaflets and bush size, and the entire plant an uncanny replica of a full-sized hybrid tea or floribunda, you have an unusual gardening discovery awaiting you.

There is tremendous variety among the miniatures in bud and flower size, shape, and color, as well as in heights that range from 8 inches to nearly 2 feet. The truly miniatures fit well under fluorescent lights. There are also miniature climbers and sprawling varieties that do well in hanging containers, tree roses, and replicas of the old moss roses, whose flower buds have a mossy green or reddish growth of hairs on their sepals.

Another area of special interest for rose zealots, of which understandably there are many, is an overlapping group that includes shrubs and their species and cultivars, and the old roses of history, with such names as White Rose of York and York and Lancaster. Many of the shrub roses grow very large, making them ideal selections for country properties. Many of these roses have delicious and haunting fragrances. Some bloom only once in early summer, others continue intermittently the rest of the growing season.

PLANTING DISTANCES—There are good reasons for generous spacing between rosebushes and other plants. Such spacing provides the necessary air circulation to ward off diseases, gives you access to the plants without being torn by thorns, and prevents the thorns from marring the leaves of neighboring roses and other plants when they are brushed against.

The usual distances between hybrid teas and floribunda roses is 2 to 2½ feet. The often vigorous old roses may need 3 to 3½ feet between plants. Shrub roses, which often grow as tall as a forsythia and have a spreading fountainlike growth, can consume 10 to 12 feet at maturity. Tree roses are usually planted about 5 feet apart. Climbers should be spaced widely if they are grown horizontally on a low fence, but 3 to 4 feet apart is ample when the plants are pruned and trained upward on a trellis. Miniature roses can be set as close as 8 inches for the smallest varieties, with larger ones requiring planting distances between 12 and 15 inches.

ROSE GARDENS—Roses are sun lovers, but a few hours of shade, preferably in the afternoon, can prevent the colors of some roses from fading. Hybrid teas and floribundas prefer an airy location with some protection from the north in the form of evergreens, a hedge, fence, or house. However, keep rose plantings a distance from encroaching roots of hedges and other large shrubs.

Roses, in common with most shrubs, need a well-drained soil, deeply prepared to 18 inches or so. A sandy soil will require generous additions of peat moss, compost, rotted manures, or leaf mold, while clay soils may need the same to lighten them. (See also Compost and Soil.)

Hybrid teas and floribundas give the best effects and are easier to take care of when they are grown in their own special gardens. These can be squares, rectangles, or even ovals, circles, or half moons, carved out of a lawn area. Or they can be planted in a more informal border along the periphery of the property and could combine taller shrub roses and other flowering shrubs as background. Other possibilities are borders around a sunny patio, where hybrid tea and floribunda roses can be enjoyed at near eye level as their perfume wafts through the air.

If you have space for only a few bushes, fit them in where you can, even in the flower garden, if you have enough room so they will not be too crowded there. They can also be grown in containers, although before the ground freezes in winter, the containers should be moved into a cold but protected garage, or the plants should be put in the ground and provided with a mulch.

BUYING ROSES—Patented roses almost always cost more than nonpatented older varieties. Dormant (leafless) roses are available in early spring from mail-order nurseries and most garden centers, and most authorities recommend planting at this time rather than fall. In mild climates, fall is a satisfactory planting time.

Many garden centers now receive dormant roses already potted in fiber containers. All the buyer has to do is dig a hole, make a few slits in the sides of the container to hasten decomposition and supposedly permit the roots to receive more moisture, and bury the plant-plus-pot in the hole so the rim is 2 inches below soil level. With fiber pots that may be slow in decomposing, keep the plant well watered.

Potted roses are generally more expensive than dormant plants from mail-order sources.

PLANTING—When a mail-order shipment of dormant roses arrives in spring, if you plan to plant them the same day, open the box and plunge the bare-root plants into a pail of water for a few hours. If you can't plant them at once, leave the box closed in a cool place.

Whatever you do, don't let the bare-root roses lie around unprotected from wind and sun while you decide where to plant them. If you were smart and planned to be setting out a number of plants, you prepared the soil in the fall or a few days before you expected the rose shipment. You should have dug the soil with a fork or a rototiller, mixing in generous quantities of peat moss, compost, rotted manure, or whatever source of humus you had, as well as superphosphate or bone meal, and perhaps limestone if the soil pH was below 5.5. (See Soil.) After that it is a simple matter to dig individual holes, about 18 inches deep and 12 to 18 inches wide and about 2 to 2½ feet apart.

If you are planting potted roses, follow the instructions on planting depth. If you have bare-root roses, set the bud union (graft), a pronounced swelling or bump on the main stem above the roots (you can't miss it) a few inches above the ground level, so it is exposed to light and air. It sometimes helps to make a cone of soil in the center of the hole, over which the roots can be spread, with the plant being held upright and at the correct depth as the soil is firmed around the roots. Before final firming of the soil, check again to be sure the bud union is above ground. Then water well. It may be necessary to add more soil after the water has settled.

Your plant should have at least three canes: prune back any damaged ones to an outward-facing bud. Then mound about 6 inches of soil or compost over the crown and canes and leave for

When planting a rose, position it so the bud (the bulge in the stem) is above ground and the roots are spread out in the hole.

a few weeks to protect the plant from late frosts and drying winds. Remove as soon as weather warms and green leaf growth shows.

Rosebushes in full growth and flower in containers can be set out throughout the summer, but the longer you wait, the more likely that the roots will be pot-bound, that is, wound around the soil ball in a strangling mass. Too much disturbance, such as trying to unwind the roots, may set the plant back and cause it to wilt and perhaps die.

MULCHING AND SUMMER CARE—All-rose gardens definitely benefit from a mulch, which can prevent wet soil from splashing on lower foliage and spreading diseases like black spot, besides accomplishing all the other known good for plants and gardeners alike. (See Mulches and Mulching.) Since roses are on display, a neat-looking mulch is of some importance.

Most experts frown on fertilizing newly planted rose bushes, except for superphosphate or bone meal, both of which are slow-acting and can be mixed in the planting hole. A light feeding can be given after about 6 weeks. Special rose fertilizers are available in garden centers, some of which even control pests and diseases. Apply according to directions. Keep any fertilizer off the leaves and away from the crown and water it into the soil after applying. Do not apply nitrogenous fertilizers after midsummer in the North.

Established rose plants can be fed in spring as growth starts, again after the early summer bloom period, and finally about 6 weeks later. If using a special rose fertilizer, follow directions on the package. Or if you use 5-10-5, apply about two to three handfuls per plant, observing the cautions just mentioned.

Miniature roses must always be fertilized in proportionately smaller doses.

PEST CONTROL—Probably the most important care you give roses in summer—and actually it starts in spring as the buds begin to swell—is disease control, specifically of mildew and the dreadful black spot (see also Pests and Diseases). The American Rose Society has endorsed Ortho Funginex as the best control for these two diseases. Funginex is a liquid that contains triforine; to apply it you must buy a sprayer. For a start, buy one of the cheaper plastic sprayers you will find in garden centers or from some mail-order catalogues. They work quite well for a time.

Phaltan, Benlate (benomyl), Captan, are among the other chemicals used to control black spot. There are also dusts. Visit your garden center and look over the array of insecticides and fungicides formulated for roses and take your pick.

Many of the shrub roses seem to be resistant to black spot and mildew, as are the following hybrid teas: 'Charlotte Armstrong,' 'Chrysler Imperial,' 'Garden Party,' 'John F. Kennedy,' 'Lowell Thomas,' 'Sutter's Gold,' and 'Tropicana'; also the grandiflora 'Carrousel'; the floribunda 'Sarabande'; the polyantha 'The Fairy'; and the climbers 'Blaze,' 'Cecil Brunner,' and 'Paul's Scarlet.'

For controlling aphids, beetles, mites, and other pests, you have the option of striking when the pest appears, a course often

preferable to those who want to avoid drenching their gardens
with chemicals, or of using one of the systemic granule, dust, or
spray formulations for roses as a preventive measure, applied as
often as recommended on the package, usually weekly. For roses,
I think the latter program is justified, and certainly in the case of
black spot.

WINTER PROTECTION—Unless you live where temperatures regularly drop to −10° F and lower and there is no snow cover,
forget about winter protection for hybrid teas and floribundas,
the various shrub and hardy old roses. (It is assumed that those
who live in northern regions will not be planting tender roses or
those of borderline hardiness.) Many mail-order nurseries offer a
group of roses known as Sub-Zero or Brownell roses that were
developed for the coldest climates, but most are worth growing
in any northern region.

If you are in doubt about protecting your roses, consult the
Cooperative Extension Service for regional recommendations.
When the advice is to mound soil over the crown of each plant,
about 10 inches high, use soil from a different area rather than
scraping it from around the roses.

Tree roses do require protection in most regions north of
Washington, D.C., to save the bud union high on the trunk. One
recommendation is to wrap the top of the plant with burlap or the
like, then enclose the wrapped top and trunk in a trash-can-size
polyethylene bag. The result will resemble the tender fig plants
wrapped like mummies and sometimes spotted in northern areas
in winter.

PRUNING ESTABLISHED ROSES—This is done in the spring while
the plants are still dormant. Use sharp pruning shears, always
making a slanting cut just above an outward-facing bud, which
keeps the center of the plant open. Cut off obviously dead wood
or any that looks diseased. As hybrid teas and floribundas vary in
their vigor and size, you must use your common sense and eventual familiarity with each cultivar in deciding how drastically to
prune back each cane. If you notice strong cane growth from
below the bud union, it is from the understock and should be cut
off.

When cutting rose flowers or fading flowers to prevent seed formation, consider it as part of the pruning process, cutting back to a healthy five-leaflet growth. Removing a lot of healthy foliage with a stem reduces the plant's food source for future blooms and growth.

▨▨▨▨ A SPECIAL PROJECT ▨▨▨▨
GROWING MINIATURE ROSES AS HOUSE PLANTS

This can be a rewarding winter pastime. Although a cool, sunny window is suitable, growing under fluorescent lights (see Indoor Gardening) will provide a reliable light source you can count on every day. For miniature roses, keep the tubes on for 14 to 16 hours a day (never under 12). You can shift the plants out from under the lights to a more attractive and prominent display area as they reach blooming perfection.

A good time to start is in late fall, when you can order miniature roses from mail-order specialists. Try to get dormant (leafless) plants, which can be potted and immediately started into growth under your lights. Follow the instructions sent with the order.

For chunky, floriferous plants, keep them about 3 to 4 inches below the tubes and try not to crowd them unduly. Temperatures around 65° F during the day, with a drop of 5 to 10° at night, have been ideal for my roses, but many growers report that the little plants do well at 70° F. If you pot the roses in a synthetic mix, regular fertilizer applications will be necessary. The light feedings with every watering work well, but any good complete fertilizer used consistently and according to instructions will serve.

Unfortunately, miniature roses are as pestered by black spot and sundry other problems as their larger counterparts, so you will have to spray weekly.

As flowers appear and fade, snip them off to encourage production. In late spring, as house temperatures warm, you can move the plants outdoors, setting them in the open ground. Gradually harden off (see Propagation) the plants to the outdoor

environment for a few days so the stronger light does not burn
the foliage. Keep on spraying!

When fall arrives, you can order new bushes and start the cycle
all over again. Or you can dig the same plants you grew indoors
the previous winter, waiting until their leaves have dropped.
Prune off about a third of their tops and roots and repot—you
may or may not have to move on to larger pots, but only up to
about a 5-inch. (Roses do not like to be overpotted any more than
any house plant.) Then the plants will need a chill period, a rest,
before being brought indoors. Sink the pots in a cold frame or in
a protected area of the garden, covering with evergreen boughs
so the pots do not become frozen in the soil. Leave them there for
about 6 to 7 weeks before bringing inside again to the lights.
After that you may have blooming little beauties in 6 weeks.

Miniature roses are on their own roots, that is, not grafted. You
can easily propagate them by cuttings (unless they are protected
by a patent).

S

SEEDS AND SEED SOWING. See Propagation and Lawns.

SHADE. Some kinds of shade can be welcome. The changing
patterns of light and benign shade on a lawn that are caused by
peripheral trees can be inviting and attractive. Shade from a
grove of trees can result in a low-maintenance, naturalistic landscape in which a variety of plants can be introduced. (See Landscaping, Evergreens, Bulbs, Perennials, and Wild Flowers.)

There are solutions—and plants—for most shady situations.
When planning the landscaping for a new property, note shaded
sections. If there are simply too many trees, remove them before
you do any planting.

A large specimen tree, for instance a maple, oak, or tulip tree,
may be so big that it spreads its shade over a wide area. Its roots
may also be too close to the surface for ground cover plants. If it
is otherwise attractive and perhaps too expensive to remove, a

solution is to make the area into an outdoor living room. Forget about grass and ground covers and instead haul in gravel, wood chips, or flagstones for a surfacing. Some sort of metal edging or railroad or landscape ties (available at garden centers and lumber yards) will be needed to contain the loose materials around the periphery of the tree. Any low branches of the tree can be removed, and if thinning of some upperbranches is possible, there should be enough light to support growth of a few potted or tubbed plants, such as variegated aucuba or gold-dust plant, pittosporum, impatiens, and the tuberous-rooted caladium and elephant's-ear.

A few hours of temporary shade, caused as the sun is blocked by trees, shrubs, or buildings in its movement from east to west, can be endured by most plants. Some shade of this sort, especially if it falls in the afternoon, can prolong the flowering period in hot weather and prevent some delicate colors from fading. However, as tree plantings grow and cast more and more shade each year, vegetable, rose, and flower gardens, as well as many flowering shrubs, suffer and produce fewer flowers. The solution, of course, is to eliminate the source of the shade, and the response to this—the improvement in flower production—can seem almost miraculous after just one growing season. When it is not practical to remove the offending shade sources, the garden must be changed. Sometimes this sort of renovation gives the gardener a second chance to improve the landscape. Flower beds can be replaced by ground covers (see Ground Covers) and the vegetable garden moved to a new site.

PLANTS FOR SHADE—While many plants tolerate shade, some experimenting may be necessary to find the right ones for your particular shade problem.

The majority of annuals and perennials require as much sun as possible, but there are exceptions. Among annuals (and these perform best if they receive a few hours of sun daily) are wax begonia, impatiens, garden balsam, torenia, Madagascar periwinkle or vinca, and coleus (see Annuals). One of the most shade-tolerant perennials is the hosta. For others, see Perennials and Wild Flowers.

Plant grouping for a partially shaded garden: Christmas ferns, primroses, hosta, Jack-in-the-pulpit, and trillium. Hostas bloom in the summer, but together with ferns, provide attractive foliage throughout the growing season. The other plants bloom in the spring.

Although bulbs are not usually considered shade-tolerant, it is comforting to know that daffodils and most other spring-flowering bulbs do well under deciduous (leaf-losing) trees because they bloom and generally are able to ripen their foliage before the trees are fully leafed out in late spring and grown too dense to admit sufficient light.

Among tender bulblike plants for partly shaded terraces are achimenes, caladiums, and tuberous begonias.

Among shade-tolerant shrubs are all the broad-leaved evergreens, but even the cream of these flowering shrubs, such as camellias and rhododendrons, perform best in some sunshine. For other shade-tolerant shrubs, see Shrubs.

SHRUBS. Shrubs are invaluable. In their favor are such attributes as permanence, easy care, beauty from flowers and berries and foliage, and varying growth habits. There is such diversity that there are shrubs for every imaginable landscaping need.

They can form the framework of a property and the backdrop for flower gardens.

Shrubs are evergreen or deciduous (leaf-losing in the fall in northern regions). Where the climate permits, the most pleasing landscapes result when a mixture of both kinds is planted. Mild climates offer the ideal growing conditions for many evergreen shrubs, while the most northernly must rely on deciduous shrubs and some of the needle or coniferous kinds. (See Evergreens.)

USES FOR SHRUBS—The most practical uses for shrubs are as hedges or barriers along property boundaries or walks or drives, and as screens. (See Hedges.)

Large shrubs can be used as substitutes for trees on smaller properties where a tree may soon outgrow its space. Of course shrubs, too, may outgrow their planting situations, but they are easier to restrain by pruning or to cut down than a tree.

Shrubs are the main plantings close to the house that are known as foundation plantings. This is one situation where often too many shrubs and those of the wrong size are placed. All too soon windows are covered and the house looks uncomfortable and even dwarfed in its base of overgrown shrubbery.

The most satisfactory foundation planting today is a spare one, with the tallest shrubs placed as accents at the main entrance and perhaps at the corners of the house. In between them, fill in with ground-covering plants (see Ground Covers). For some kinds of architecture, even these plantings may be excessive, and few houses require much more. It is best to avoid many of the shrubs —even in small sizes, as they are bound to grow—that are too often recommended for this purpose, including such broad-leaved evergreens as rhododendrons and evergreen azaleas, andromeda or pieris, and leucothoe. Also to be avoided are such coniferous evergreens as hemlock, spruce, tall-growing junipers and chamaecyparis or false-cypress, and others. They may invite the unwary while they are baby evergreens, but quickly they become too large. Developers are often prone to filling in around their new homes with young plants of coniferous evergreens.

Often suitable near the house are forms of yew, boxwood,

Japanese hollies, and some of the barberries, all of which respond well to pruning.

Low-growing and creeping shrubs, such as stephanandra, can be used to cover slopes too steep for mowing grass. In partially shaded areas, shrubs can be combined with ground-covering plants to form varying patterns and textures that are much more ornamental than a struggling grass cover.

CHOOSING AND BUYING SHRUBS—If you are planting a new property, the choices of shrubs should be coordinated with your landscape plan (see Landscaping). Consult mail-order catalogues, books on shrubs, and try to visit public gardens in all seasons to observe their special shrub collections. Your neighbors' gardens can give you ideas on what to do with shrubs—and what not to do.

Do not be afraid to experiment with shrubs that may not be available locally, as long as they are possible candidates for your region. Most nursery catalogues now give reliable information on the hardiness of their offerings (see Zones, Climate). Sometimes it can be challenging to plant shrubs of borderline hardiness in your climate—you may be surprised how well they do in protected sections (called microclimates) of your garden.

If you have space for only a few shrubs, try to choose those whose beauty is more than skin deep—that offer other assets in addition to flowers, such as berries, outstanding foliage, either evergreen or that may color in the fall, or an especially attractive form of growth. An example of an out-of-the-ordinary shrub is the winter honeysuckle (*Lonicera fragrantissima*), a rather large shrub (perhaps too large for small properties, although pruning can restrain it) with very fragrant white flowers in early spring that are followed by red berries in early summer. The berries do not last too long, since they are favored by birds, but for bird watchers this is an asset. On the other hand, Japanese skimmia, a fairly compact broad-leaved evergreen, has red berries that last and last because birds turn to them as a last resort. (The female skimmia bears the berries, but the small flowers of the male plant are very fragrant.)

Another outstanding shrub is redvein enkianthus. It bears drooping bell-shaped flowers in spring, has brilliant orange-red leaf colors in fall, and then a rather symmetrical, layered branch arrangement for winter. However, the one-season beauty of the forsythia and the fragrant lilac is undeniably appealing, and when space permits, they deserve a place on your property too.

The best planting time is in spring and fall, but container-grown shrubs, as well as those that are balled and burlapped (called B and B stock), can be planted throughout the growing season. (See Planting and Transplanting.)

The following lists of shrubs for various purposes give an idea of how versatile they are. The list of shrubs for a succession of color shows how long the flowering season can be if a few shrubs from each season are planted.

▨▨▨▨ A SHRUB SAMPLER ▨▨▨▨
SHRUBS FOR A SUCCESSION OF BLOOM

EARLY SPRING

ABELIA-LEAF, KOREAN *(Abeliophyllum distichum)*, white

ANDROMEDA, JAPANESE *(Pieris japonica)*, drooping white panicles

AUCUBA *(A. japonica)*, fragrant white clusters

CAMELLIA *(Camellia japonica)*, white, pink, rose, red

CORNELIAN-CHERRY *(Cornus mas)*, small yellow

DAPHNE, FEBRUARY *(Daphne mezereum)*, fragrant purple or white

FORSYTHIA *(Forsythia* species and cultivars), yellow

HARDY-ORANGE *(Poncirus trifoliata)*, fragrant white

HEATH *(Erica carnea* and cultivars) white, rose

HONEYSUCKLE, WINTER *(Lonicera fragrantissima)*, fragrant white

QUINCE, FLOWERING *(Chaenomeles speciosa)*, white, pink, red

RHODODENDRON *(Rhododendron* species and cultivars), various

SKIMMIA *(Skimmia japonica)*, fragrant white clusters

SPICEBUSH *(Lindera benzoin)*, small yellow

SPIRAEA, GARLAND *(Spiraea* x *arguta)*, small white clusters

SWEET-OLIVE *(Osmanthus fragrans)*, fragrant white

WINTER-HAZEL *(Corylopsis* species), drooping yellow clusters

WITCH-HAZEL *(Hamamelis* species and cultivars), yellow, orange

MID- TO LATE SPRING

AZALEA *(Rhododendron* species and cultivars), various
BARBERRY *(Berberis* species and cultivars), yellow
BEAUTY-BUSH *(Kolkwitzia amabilis),* pink
BROOM *(Cytisus* species and cultivars), yellow, red, white
CALIFORNIA-LILAC *(Ceanothus* species and cultivars), blue, white
COTONEASTER *(Cotoneaster* species and cultivars), pink, red
CRAB APPLE, SARGENT'S *(Malus sargentii),* white
DEUTZIA, SLENDER *(Deutzia gracilis),* white
ENKIANTHUS, REDVEIN *(Enkianthus campanulatus),* yellow and red
FOTHERGILLA, DWARF *(Fothergilla gardenii),* fragrant white
GARLAND-FLOWER *(Daphne cneorum),* fragrant pink clusters
HONEYSUCKLE, BUSH *(Lonicera* species and cultivars), yellow, red
KERRIA *(Kerria japonica),* yellow, orange
LEUCOTHOE, DROOPING *(Leucothoe fontanesiana),* fragrant white
LILAC *(Syringa* species and cultivars), white, rose, purple
PEARL-BUSH *(Exochorda* x *macrantha),* white
PEONY, TREE *(Paeonia* species and cultivars), white, yellow, red, purple
RHODODENDRON *(Rhododendron* species and cultivars), various
ROSE *(Rosa* species and cultivars), various
SHADBLOW *(Amelanchier* species and cultivars), white, pink
SPIRAEA, BRIDALWREATH *(Spiraea prunifolia),* white
SWEET-SHRUB *(Calycanthus floridus),* fragrant maroon
VIBURNUM *(Viburnum* species and cultivars) fragrant white, pink
WEIGELA *(Weigela florida* and cultivars), pink, red, white

SUMMER

ABELIA, GLOSSY *(Abelia* x *grandiflora),* pink
BUTTERFLY BUSH *(Buddleia davidii* and cultivars), white, purple
CHASTE-TREE *(Vitex agnus-castus),* lavender
FUCHSIA *(Fuchsia* species and cultivars), white, pink, purple
HYPERICUM *(Hypericum* species and cultivars), yellow
HEATH *(Erica* species and cultivars), pink, rose, white
HEATHER *(Calluna vulgaris* and cultivars), white, pink, rose
HYDRANGEA *(Hydrangea* species and cultivars), white, blue, pink

POTENTILLA *(Potentilla fruticosa)*, white, yellow, red, rose
ROSE *(Rosa* hybrids), various
ROSE OF SHARON *(Hibiscus syriacus)*, white, pink, red, lilac
SPIRAEA, JAPANESE *(Spiraea japonica)*, pink to rose
SUMMERSWEET *(Clethra alnifolia)*, fragrant white spires

SHRUBS WITH SHOWY BERRIES OR FRUITS

(b indicates bird favorites)

BARBERRY *(Berberis* species and cultivars), red and black   *b*
BAYBERRY *(Myrica pensylvanica)*, gray   *b*
COTONEASTER *(Cotoneaster* species and cultivars), red   *b*
CRAB APPLE, SARGENT'S *(Malus sargentii)*, dark red   *b*
DOGWOOD, SHRUB *(Cornus* species and cultivars), white, blue,
    black, red   *b*
EUONYMUS *(Euonymus* species and cultivars), various   *b*
FIRETHORN *(Pyracantha* species and cultivars), orange, red   *b*
HOLLY *(Ilex* species and cultivars), red, black, red   *b*
HONEYSUCKLE, BUSH *(Lonicera* species and cultivars), black   *b*
JUNIPER *(Juniperus* species and cultivars), blue   *b*
ROSE, RUGOSA *(Rosa rugosa)*, white, pink, rose, red
RUSSIAN-OLIVE *(Elaeagnus angustifolius)*, silvery   *b*
SEA-BUCKTHORN *(Hippophae rhamnoides)*, red
SKIMMIA *(Skimmia japonica)*, red
VIBURNUM *(Viburnum* species and cultivars), red, yellow,
    black   *b*
YEW *(Taxus* species and cultivars), red   *b*

SHRUBS WITH COLORED FOLIAGE IN FALL

AZALEA, ROYAL *(Rhododendron schlippenbachii)*
BARBERRY, JAPANESE *(Berberis japonica)*
BLUEBERRY *(Vaccinium corymbosum)*
CHOKEBERRY, RED *(Aronia arbutifolia)*
FOTHERGILLA *(Fothergilla* species)
ENKIANTHUS, REDVEIN *(Enkianthus campanulatus)*
ROSE, RUGOSA *(Rosa rugosa)*
SHADBLOW *(Amelanchier* species)

SPICEBUSH *(Lindera benzoin)*
SPIRAEA, BRIDALWREATH *(Spiraea prunifolia)*
VIBURNUM *(Viburnum* species)
WITCH-HAZEL *(Hamamelis* species and cultivars)

LOW-GROWING SHRUBS TO COVER SLOPES

COTONEASTER *(Cotoneaster* species and cultivars)
DOGWOOD, RED OSIER *(Cornus sericea* and cultivars)
HEATH *(Erica* species and cultivars)
HEATHER *(Calluna vulgaris* and cultivars)
MAHONIA, CREEPING *(Mahonia repens)*
PINE, MUGO *(Pinus mugo* variety *mugo)*
ROSE, MEMORIAL *(Rosa wichuraiana)*
STEPHANANDRA, CUTLEAF *(Stephanandra incisa* 'Crispa')
WINTER CREEPER *(Euonymus fortunei* and cultivars)

TREELIKE SHRUBS

ASIATIC SWEETLEAF *(Symplocos paniculata)*
CHASTE-TREE *(Vitex* species)
CORNELIAN-CHERRY *(Cornus mas)*
ENKIANTHUS, REDVEIN *(Enkianthus campanulatus)*
HOLLY, JAPANESE *(Ilex crenata)*
HYDRANGEA, HILLS OF SNOW *(Hydrangea arborescens*
  'Grandiflora')
LILAC *(Syringa* species and cultivars)
PHOTINIA, CHINESE *(Photinia serrulata)*
PRIVET *(Ligustrum* species)
ROSE OF SHARON *(Hibiscus syriacus)*
RUSSIAN-OLIVE *(Elaeagnus angustifolius)*
SHADBLOW *(Amelanchier* species)
SMOKE-BUSH *(Cotinus coggygria)*
SNOWBELL, JAPANESE *(Styrax japonica)*
SPICEBUSH *(Lindera benzoin)*
VIBURNUM *(Viburnum* species and cultivars)
WITCH-HAZEL *(Hamamelis* species and cultivars)
YEW *(Taxus* species and cultivars)

SHRUBS FOR PARTIAL SHADE

(e indicates evergreen foliage)

ABELIA, GLOSSY *(Abelia* x *grandiflora)*   semi-*e*
ANDROMEDA *(Pieris* species and cultivars)   *e*
AUCUBA, JAPANESE *(Aucuba japonica* and cultivars)   *e*
AZALEA *(Rhododendron* species and cultivars)   some *e*
BOXWOOD *(Buxus* species and cultivars)   *e*
BARBERRY *(Berberis* species and cultivars)   some *e*
BLUEBERRY *(Vaccinium* species and cultivars)   some *e*
CAMELLIA *(Camellia* species and cultivars)   *e*
EUONYMUS *(Euonymus* species and cultivars)   some *e*
GRAPE-HOLLY, OREGON *(Mahonia* species)   *e*
HOLLY *(Ilex* species and cultivars)   some *e*
HYDRANGEA, OAK-LEAF *(Hydrangea quercifolia)*
JETBEAD *(Rhodotypus tetrapetala)*
LEUCOTHOE *(Leucothoe fontanesiana)*   *e*
MOUNTAIN-LAUREL *(Kalmia latifolia)*   *e*
PITTOSPORUM, JAPANESE *(Pittosporum tobira)*   *e*
PRIVET *(Ligustrum* species and cultivars)   some *e*
RHODODENDRON *(Rhododendron* species and cultivars)   *e*
SHADBLOW *(Amelanchier* species)
SKIMMIA *(Skimmia japonica)*   *e*
SPICEBUSH *(Lindera benzoin)*
SUMMERSWEET *(Clethra alnifolia)*
SWEET BAY or LAUREL *(Laurus nobilis)*   *e*
VIBURNUM *(Viburnum* species and cultivars)   some *e*
WITCH-HAZEL *(Hamamelis* species and cultivars)
YEW *(Taxus* species and cultivars)   *e*

SOIL. Most of us do not have any choice when it comes to garden soil. The soil is inherited with the purchase of the property, and more often than not, it is of average to good quality, and with some amendments, is suited to most gardening requirements.

Of course there are poor soils. Sometimes rather than being regional, they can be local and due to the carelessness of the builder, who spread the excavated subsoil from the house's foundation on top of the existing topsoil, leaving a hard surface. Incorporating quantities of organic materials is one solution for such a situation. In another situation, the new house may have been built on a sand dune. Rather than hauling in truckloads of topsoil, the sensible solution is to encourage native plants that will grow in sand and grow more exotic materials in planters and other containers. The town house with the barren backyard—not even a weed in sight—may also find a pot garden is the answer. But that solution is only workable if the backyard receives good light and at least a few hours of sun daily. (See Shade and Pots and Other Containers.)

COPING WITH SOIL—The new gardener can make a judgment of sorts about his or her soil by looking at the plants already growing on it. Even vigorous weeds can be an indication that the soil has potential for more desirable plantings. You can also get information and help in solving soil problems from the specialists at the county Cooperative Extension Service.

Soil is composed of different sizes of particles of clay, silt, and sand. The ideal soil, usually referred to as loam, is a mixture of 7 to 27 percent clay, 28 to 50 percent silt, and less than 52 percent sand. Quite satisfactory garden soils are made of different ratios of all these materials, such as a sandy loam. Extreme amounts of clay can result in a soil that often acts like cement, while an excessively sandy one means a constant struggle to maintain sufficient moisture and nutrients for plant growth. Short of replacing either of these soils with hauled-in topsoil, an expensive earth-moving operation beyond most of us, the solution is to amend the existing soil. The materials and methods to use are about the same for both soil extremes.

Heavy clay soil can be opened by tilling in coarse sand, the particles being from 1/16 to 1/18 of an inch in size, and applied in a layer of at least 3 inches. Avoid fine sand, which when mixed with clay, will result in even more of a cementlike consistency when the soil dries. Along with the sand, quantities of organic matter should be added.

Sandy soil can also be much improved by the addition of large amounts of organic materials, peat moss being especially suitable and always available from garden centers and nurseries. (See Peat Moss.)

ORGANIC MATTER—Organic matter, materials from decaying plants and animals, can solve almost any soil problem. In addition to binding sandy soil and opening up clayey soil, in its ultimate form of decay, as humus, it releases nutrients, which are absorbed by plant roots, and feeds bacteria so they can free other nutrients locked up in the soil. As organic matter decays, it also releases some nitrogen.

Sources of organic matter, in addition to peat moss, include fallen leaves, animal manures, straw, hay, sawdust, seaweeds, most refuse from the kitchen, weeds (preferably without their seeds), and other locally available materials. All of these materials are among the ingredients of the compost pile. When nearly decomposed, the compost can be mixed into vegetable and flower garden soil, into planting holes for trees and shrubs, and used as mulch. (See Compost.)

FERTILIZERS—Applying organic materials to the soil should not be an off-again-on-again operation, as each year new supplies must be added to replace depleted amounts used by plant growth. Important though the presence of organic materials is to the soil, most garden soils need fertilizers to supply nitrogen, phosphorus, and potash to supplement the amounts of these essential elements already present in the soil.

People in the organic gardening movement rely solely on fertilizers from organic sources—animal manures, seaweeds, fish meal, cottonseed meal, and dried blood. Other gardeners use complete fertilizers from synthetic sources, such as the granular 5-10-5 and superphosphate. Most organic fertilizers have the advantage of decaying slowly, thus releasing their nutrients over long periods (and incidentally adding humus to the soil), while inorganic or synthetic fertilizers are more balanced and usually quicker to become available to the needs of the plants. (See Fertilizers, Manures, and Organic Gardening.)

As with organic materials, fertilizers become depleted, so additional applications must be made. How often this is done depends on several considerations, such as the kind of soil, kinds of plants grown, and how they are grown. Obviously, plants grown in pots and other containers need more frequent fertilizer applications than most plants in the open ground.

A sandy soil, because of its porous structure, is unable to retain nutrients, which leach out, especially where rainfall is frequent and as a result of regular waterings applied by the gardener. (See Watering.)

Nitrogen is usually depleted first in soils, as it is the most important element in plant growth. Phosphorus, usually applied as superphosphate, is also important, but it becomes available to plants more slowly. The ideal time to incorporate superphosphate in the soil is during soil preparation—digging by hand or using a rotary tiller. (See Digging.) This way the phosphorus is in the soil where the roots can reach it rather than just sitting on the surface.

LIME AND SOIL TESTS—The most exact way to find out what fertilizers your soil requires and in what amounts is to have a soil test made. Tests are made by private laboratories or by the county's extension specialists, who will send you instructions on how to collect the soil samples. Complete soil tests are complicated to make and interpret, but anyone can do a test to find out the acidity or alkalinity levels of his or her soil. These simple kits are available at garden centers or from mail-order sources. Their results can tell you whether to add lime to your soil if it is too acid for the plants you are growing.

Lime, available in various forms of calcium carbonate, is a soil amendment that, like humus, performs several functions. It can decrease acidity, thereby making nutrients available to plants, improve the physical texture of clay soils, and, depending on its source, supply in addition to calcium, magnesium, phosphorus, and potash to the soil.

It is possible to determine how acid a soil is by noting the kind of plants that naturally grow in it. For instance, wild blueberries and huckleberries, mountain-laurel, azaleas, and many familiar wild flowers, such as trailing-arbutus, grow in quite acid soils. However, the most accurate way to determine the acidity of soil is by a test. The results of the test are interpreted by the pH scale, which runs from 1 to 14, the neutral point between acidity and alkalinity being 7. All soils that test below 7 are acid, with the lowest numbers indicating the highest degree of acidity. Numbers above 7 indicate an alkaline soil, with the highest readings being for the most alkaline soils. The majority of plants do well in slightly acid to slightly alkaline soils and many will even tolerate more acid soils.

However, if your soil tests at 4.5, very acid, and you wish to grow vegetables and flowers, you will want to add lime, which may be 50 to 60 pounds of ground limestone per 1,000 square feet, to reach a pH reading of about 6.5.

Ground limestone, in the form of dolomitic limestone, is the usual source of lime recommended. It is reasonable in price, breaks down slowly, and also supplies magnesium and calcium to the soil. The best time to apply it is in the fall.

Other sources of lime and calcium are wood ashes, by-products of wood-burning stoves and fireplaces, ground oyster shells, and bone meal. Wood ashes also contain potash, and bone meal and oyster shells contain phosphorus. Bone meal also contains a small amount of nitrogen.

Wood ashes must be kept dry in storage before being used in the garden. They can be applied at the rate of 2 to 9 pounds per 100 square feet. They are fast-acting, both as a soil amendment to raise the acidity level and as a source of potash. Wood ashes can definitely injure plants if applied in excessive amounts. The best time to apply them is in the spring.

A soil that is too alkaline can be made more acid by the addition of sulfur or ammonium sulfate, plus large amounts of peat moss and other materials. These materials, though, will not permanently alter the alkalinity level. Only a soil test can indicate how much sulfur must be added to lower the pH. For instance, if the soil tests reveal a pH of 8.0, add 4 pounds of sulfur or 8 pounds of ammonium sulfate to 100 square feet.

SOILLESS OR SYNTHETIC MIXES—Once upon a time the growing of seeds indoors for both professional and amateur alike was a tricky procedure. A soil-borne disease, known as damping-off, could attack and destroy the seedlings soon after germination, wiping out entire batches of young plants. Prevention of this disease involved the nuisance of sterilizing the soil, a messy, smelly operation for the kitchen, that was not always foolproof.

To the rescue came the Cornell Mix and other university formulas, now referred to as soilless mixes. They are sterile and virtually disease-free, and contain vermiculite, peat moss, or sand, and usually some traces of fertilizers. They are widely available in garden centers and other outlets in various-size bags, under such trade names as Jiffy Mix, Redi-Earth, and Pro-Mix.

In addition to being used for seed starting and cuttings, synthetic mixes are helpful to container gardening because of their light weight and water retention. They can also be mixed with garden soil for various potting needs, usually about half and half. Do not mix soil with soilless mixes for starting seeds, or it is back to the drawing board, as damping-off disease is almost bound to occur.

MIXING YOUR OWN—You can mix your own synthetic soil. There are several recipes. Here is one that makes a peck of mix:

> 4 quarts vermiculite
> 4 quarts peat moss
> 1 teaspoon superphosphate
> 1 tablespoon ground dolomitic limestone
> 4 tablespoons 5-10-5 or similar complete fertilizer.

Sprinkle with water to keep down the dust, which you should not breathe, and mix thoroughly. Store indoors and keep dry until use.

(See also Indoor Gardening.)

SPECIES. See Nomenclature—Names of Plants.

STAKING. The majority of plants remain upright without special supports or stakes. In fact, the most attractive garden borders are those in which stakes are not an intrusion and flower stems have the freedom to sway gently in summer breezes. However, a few perennials must be staked. One is the 'Pacific' hybrid delphinium, from whose leafy clumps several tall flower spikes can rise. One stake cannot do the job—you must use a stake for each flower stem. Insert the stakes around the outside (not through the center) of the clump, then fasten the stems in two or more places to the stakes. (For other perennials that may require staking, see Flower Border Care in Perennials section.)

The trend is to breed lower rather than taller annuals—which helps these plants remain true to their carefree reputation. The slender, green-dyed bamboo stakes, sold in bundles in garden centers, are inconspicuous and useful for temporary supports for snapdragons, the tall 'Sensation'-type cosmos, and any other annuals that seem too floppy for their garden situations. Or, you can improvise twiggy supports from shrub and hedge trimmings. Not only are such supports free, but they require no string or special fastening with Twist-em (green plastic-covered wire for tying plants to their supports, available in garden centers or from mail-order sources).

In the vegetable garden, space is saved if certain crops, namely peas and tomatoes, are held upright by supports. Peas will cling to a length of chicken-wire fencing stretched taut between a double row of peas. The tall-growing (indeterminate) tomato varieties can be supported by a single stout stake, but the wire cages you can make from wide-mesh wire fencing or cages you can buy in garden centers (see under Tomatoes in Vegetables section) are easier to use.

T

TERRACES AND OUTDOOR LIVING AREAS. These have become essential components of the home landscape. (The words terrace and patio are used interchangeably today, although technically the Spanish-derived "patio" is a courtyard surrounded by walls.) A terrace, in addition to being a slightly raised or level adjunct to the house, can also be a terrace or balcony off an apartment house, or a rooftop garden adjacent to a penthouse. Another version of the terrace is the wooden deck, first designed to surround a house at the beach or one in the hills or mountains. Now wooden decks and paved terraces are often combined, the result being elaborate multilevel structures of varying shapes, patterns, and textures. Some of these complex designs are space-filling projections to a swimming pool and do not have much to do with gardening unless the owners are avid container gardeners, which they sometimes are.

Ideally, any outdoor living space, whether adjacent to the house or situated around a swimming pool, or in a rustic retreat in a wooded area, should be considered in the early stages of planning and then marked on your plan. (See Landscaping.) For one thing, you will want to provide for some degree of privacy, either in plants or in structures, such as panels or fences. The sooner shrubs are set out, the sooner they reach screening proportions. Privacy screening is important near outdoor living areas (unless you are fortunate enough to be on several acres), but it should not shut off attractive views or focal points in your own garden. They may not look very inviting in their early stages, but should improve as the garden seasons. Even if screening is not required, some shade may be desirable, especially in the afternoon, so you may want to move in a small tree.

Not all terrace and patio areas are do-it-yourself projects. Rather than ending with an amateurish effort, it is better to consult a qualified designer whose work you have seen and admired. If you are a handy person with cement, lumber, or whatever materials are contemplated, all you may need is a plan that fits your house, surroundings, and needs. If you are neither a designer nor handy, by all means let someone else do the work.

Do-It-Yourself Designs—Simple outdoor living areas can certainly become legitimate projects for new house owners, especially when the terrain is level. Rectangles, L-shapes, and squares have been traditional shapes for terraces, but today any shape or combination of shapes is acceptable, as long as its proportions are right and fit into the adjacent area and overall landscape scheme. Experiment with terrace shapes on paper first.

Several kinds of paving are available. One is grass, suitable in a sunny area, where traffic is fairly light and every night is not a party occasion. The grass's durability will be helped if you lay large flagstones. However, any stone or cement squares you choose will have to be flush with the lawn so you can mow.

Flagstones alone are very durable and distinctive enough to set the area apart from the surrounding landscape. The larger the flagstones, the more firm and comfortable the paving. Various grades of gravel is another widely used surface, which must be contained by some sort of edging, prominent enough so people don't trip over it. Gravel is not really very comfortable to stand around on, although it is a good material for moving traffic, as on paths and drives. For a more stable footing in terraces, gravel can be combined with large flagstone rounds or rectangles, or sections of precast concrete, all usually available from local building-supply outlets and some garden centers. Any random paving materials combined with gravel should be set slightly higher than the gravel so the gravel is kept off the smooth stones. The combination can be slippery.

A traditional surfacing is brick, which, when properly laid and used in curved as well as geometric shapes, can be very elegant. Don't embark on a brick-laying venture without consulting a book on garden construction first.

You will find people in lumber yards and building-supply outlets most helpful. If you are building decks and other structural elements, enquire about pressurized wood. It is usually of pine, weathers to a pleasant color or can be stained, and is highly resistant to decay.

GARDEN OPPORTUNITIES FROM AND ABOUT THE TERRACE—Although gardeners want to relax as much as anyone, outdoor living areas are often related to their gardening interests rather than being mere architectural space-filling extensions of the house. Any terrace or patio should be as attractive to look out on as it is relaxing to sit upon. This is essential in the North, where the looking-out-the-window time is of much longer duration than the few months of outdoor living.

One of the ways to make the terrace inviting to contemplate from within is to add a tree, such as a dogwood, whose layered branch habit stands out as an etching in the winter landscape. The same tree can provide some summer shade, flowers in spring, and beautiful red foliage and berries in the fall. The berries are impressive but short-lived, as birds are attracted to them. Other small trees to consider might be a vase-shaped flowering crab apple or one of the larger viburnums. English and American hollies, where hardy, or coniferous trees (see Evergreens), which can be strung with lights over the holidays, are other possibilities.

More yearlong interest for the terrace can be planned, much as you would plan for a succession of color in a flower garden. Narrow beds around the terrace, the space under the dogwood, or areas left without paving can be filled with spring-flowering bulbs, snowdrops appearing first, with the progression of flower color continuing through spring to summer, when annuals are added. The patio is also the place for pots and other containers. If you lay fairly wide flagstones as a paving, you can plant thyme,

Plants can be enjoyed at close hand on a patio in pots and various containers. Plants can also grow in the patio when a few bricks or a flagstone are omitted in the paving pattern. Creeping thyme can be established in the spaces between flagstones and other random pavings.

chamomile, sweet-alyssum, and perhaps some of the small pinks (*Dianthus*) between the stones. However, to save these plants from an often precarious existence, you must use large enough paving materials so people stand on them rather than on the plants.

TERRARIUMS AND BOTTLE GARDENS. A different, almost magical world seems to exist in the inner gardens of terrariums and bottles. Although house plants are the major but not sole inhabitants of these gardens under glass, the techniques of planting and the aftercare differ from the culture of most indoor plants. Not that there are any special difficulties, except perhaps for teasing plants into a narrow-necked bottle, which has much in common with getting the ship into its bottle. Actually, terrariums are the epitome of low maintenance, for once established they require no regular watering, as condensation supplies their moisture.

CONTAINERS TO USE—Fish bowls and aquariums have always been the standard containers for terrariums, but added to them are brandy snifters, mason, apothecary, and candy jars, and other sorts of fancy glass and plastic bubbles, cubes, and other shapes especially manufactured for the purpose.

Bottle gardens, of course, are made in bottles, with wine jugs (gallon and half-gallon sizes) and smaller wine bottles being readily available and a bargain. Laboratory bottles and any others you can find are also desirable. Avoid colored glass, as it shuts out some of the needed light. Bottles can be hung in bright but not sunny windows.

PLANT SELECTIONS—You may have some of the plants suitable for terrariums or bottles in your house plant collection. If they seem to be too large for the container you have chosen, plant cuttings from them (see Propagation), which will soon root in the humid atmosphere of their glass enclosure. Other plants are usually available in small pots in special displays for the purpose in garden centers, or can be ordered from house plant specialists.

Made to order for terrariums are the miniature African-violets and some of their relatives, including the miniature gloxinia or sinningia. They, along with a few choice and dainty begonias, can

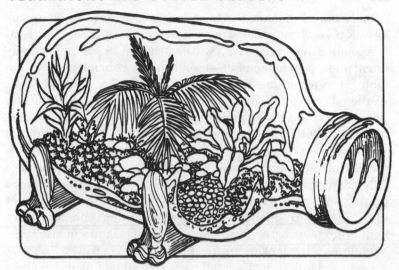

A horizontal bottle garden permits more space for a creative landscape.

---

be the stars of the display, supplying the flower color lacking in most other terrarium plants.

▨▨▨▨ A SAMPLER FOR TERRARIUMS ▨▨▨▨

AFRICAN-VIOLET, Miniature (Saintpaulia cultivars)

ARTILLERY PLANT (Pilea microphylla)

BABY'S-TEARS (Soleirolia soleirolii)

BEGONIA 'BUTTERCUP,' 'CHINA DOLL,' etc.

EARTH STARS (Cryptanthus species)

FERNS, small, various kinds

FIG, CREEPING (Ficus pumila)

IVY, ENGLISH (Hedera helix), small-leaved

KENILWORTH-IVY (Cymbalaria muralis)

MINT, CORSICAN (Mentha requienii)

NERVE PLANT (Fittonia argyroneura)

PILEA (Pilea depressa)

SELAGINELLA (Selaginella species)

SINNINGIA, MINIATURE (Sinningia species)

SPHAGNUM MOSS and other mosses

SWEET FLAG, JAPANESE (Acorus gramineus)

PLANTING A TERRARIUM—One of the smaller rectangular aquariums is a good container size to start with, as it is easy to plant.

Assemble the plants, which will probably be in pots, and experiment with an arrangement—either in the container or on the table. Most terrariums are viewed from the front and both ends, so the tallest plants can be positioned toward the center at the rear—just as you might arrange a shrub or flower grouping outdoors. You don't want too crowded an effect in the beginning, as the plants soon begin to grow very well in their special environment. (I always use too many plants and a jungle soon results.)

In addition to the plants, you will need a package of sterilized potting soil, some crushed charcoal, and living or dried sheet moss, all of which should be available at a garden center or from a mail-order house specializing in house plants. You will also need a few interesting-looking rocks, if you plan on making a "scene," a spoon and fork and/or a small narrow trowel for planting, and a bulb-type water sprayer or plastic spray bottle.

If you have dried sheet moss, soak it for a half hour or so before using. Then press out excess water. Use sections of the moss as a lining—green side against the glass—for the area of the terrarium to be filled with soil. The soil depth can vary from an inch or two to 3 to 4 inches for really large tanks. Don't add too much soil, only enough to adequately support and fit your plants. Some people wet the soil *before* adding it to the terrarium, which may be a good idea, because there is less risk of overwatering later.

Before adding the soil, mix a scant handful of the charcoal with it. You are now ready to proceed with planting. Knock the plants from their pots by turning them upside down, supporting the plant with one hand as you tap the rim of the pot against the edge of the table. It may be necessary to carefully reduce the size of the root ball of some plants.

Start planting from the rear, using your tools or hands to dig the holes and fill in with soil around the plants. Use the lower and creeping plants toward the front. When the front is finished, position a rock or two or whatever other nonplant elements you fancy. Place really large rocks before you plant. Use a mister to help settle the soil around the roots. This is the trickiest part of terrarium-making. You need enough moisture to wet the soil, but no standing water is allowed. If you are in doubt, proceed cautiously with water applications, waiting to see if more is needed. This is why wetting the soil before you start is perhaps the better way. Planting is also easier.

Setting up a terrarium: before planting, experiment with an arrangement, placing the taller plants in the rear and lower-growing ones toward the front.

Finally, wipe the inside walls of the terrarium and mist off any soil that may be clinging to the plants. Then place a sheet of glass or lucite or stretch clear plastic wrap over the top. The terrarium must be in good bright light, but not sunshine, which can cook the plants.

BOTTLE GARDENS—A bottle garden differs from a terrarium

only in the planting and design. Taller plants can usually be used, as long as they fit through the narrow opening. Brittle-leaved plants or plants with leaves and stems that can't be folded upward without breaking or bruising must be avoided.

You will need special tools for planting bottles. Wire the handles of the spoon and fork to dowels, first being sure they will pass through the neck of the bottle. An empty spool, inserted at the end of a dowel, is useful for firming the soil about the plants, provided it fits through the opening. For very narrow-necked bottles, use sections of wire, slightly hooked or bent at the ends, and pointed and flat-end dowels, the first for digging, the second for soil firming.

Cut the sheet moss into small pieces, then form in rolls with green side out so you don't soil the insides and neck of the bottle. Use a dowel to unfold the rolled moss and press it into overlapping sections across the bottom and around the sides as high as the soil will reach.

The amount of soil-charcoal to be added depends on the height of the bottle: for a 5-inch bottle, about 1½ inches; for a 24-inch-high bottle, about 6 inches. You can also make a bottle garden in a bottle in its horizontal position, but as with the ship in a bottle, some sort of cradle or stand must be provided.

Pour the soil into the bottle through a long funnel—a cylinder left over from a paper towel roll, or make your own from rolled cardboard or newspaper stapled together. Measure to be sure these funnels fit through the bottle entrance. After planting and watering, cork the bottle and let nature take its course.

Robert Baur, in his book *Gardens in Glass Containers*, warns that patience is essential in putting together a garden and bottle. If you are in a frazzled state of mind, postpone the project. That is good advice.

FOLLOW-UP POINTERS—If plants show signs of rotting or if the inner walls of terrariums or bottle gardens are covered with sheets of water rather than scattered beads, remove the top or cork to help evaporate moisture. Sometimes this remedy is too late and you must start over, this time being sure the soil is moist but not soggy.

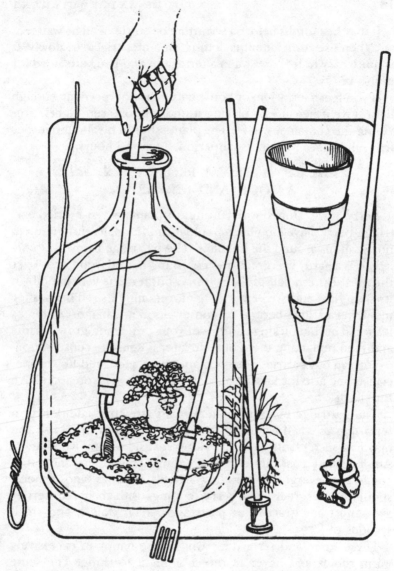

Home-made implements to use in planting a bottle garden.

It may be months before a terrarium or bottle need be watered, and then use scant amounts, letting the water trickle in slowly. It is quite easy to feel the soil in a terrarium and gauge its need for moisture.

If you feel a terrarium or bottle garden is not receiving enough light, give it new life by placing it under fluorescent lights, providing the container will fit. The plants should be about 6 inches from the tubes for the usual period, 14 to 16 hours.

▨▨▨▨ A SPECIAL PROJECT ▨▨▨▨
A WOODLAND TERRARIUM

Berry bowls, stuffed with cuttings or plants of red-berried partridge-berry, have long been popular, traditionally turning up in florist shops around the holidays. The partridge-berry (*Mitchella repens*) is a hardy evergreen creeper found in acid woodlands over the northeastern half of the country, but it exists very happily in its cosy glass-enclosed environment, retaining its red berries for months. Partridge-berry is on conservation lists in most states, as it should be, but picking cuttings of your own home-grown plants and then replanting them outside later is sensible conservation.

You can buy partridge-berry plants from a few wild-flower specialists and also the kits for making a berry bowl if you don't have the plants.

The partridge-berry plant makes an attractive addition to a terrarium of small wildings. If you have country property, you may find such plants close by, along roadsides or in woodlands. Among plant possibilities are seedlings of junipers and other coniferous evergreens, trailing-arbutus, mosses and lichens, spotted wintergreen, bearberry (cuttings with their red berries are almost as attractive as partridge-berry), violets, and small sections of ferns.

These woodland terrariums will not be happy in excessively warm rooms and never in direct sunlight for long. The same cautions on water apply—just don't overdo it and the little woodland in miniature should remain in good condition for months.

TOOLS AND EQUIPMENT. Some gardeners collect tools

and garden gadgets as lovingly as others collect plants. Then there are those who struggle along with a short-handled spade when a long-handled one with a round point to its blade would be far less stressful for most digging activity. (See Digging.) Yet it is surprising how few tools actually are needed.

The essential tools for a small vegetable or flower garden are a steel rake, a fork or spade to loosen or turn over the soil, a hoe, a trowel, a watering can or some lengths of hose, a line between two stakes to mark out rows, and perhaps a wheelbarrow or garden cart. If you have a lawn and an outdoor terrace, you will need a bamboo or light aluminum lawn rake for quick cleanup jobs.

You will, of course, need a mowing machine. For small lawn areas, consider a lightweight, hand-pushed reel mower, which makes a pleasant whirring sound. For large lawn areas, the gas-powered rotary mower is noisy and often difficult to keep sharp, but it is quick and efficient. Also necessary for larger lawns are spreaders for fertilizers and grass seed. There are two types, the broadcast or Cyclone type and the drop type. The latter gives you a better idea of where your fertilizer is going than the Cyclone type, but both kinds have their supporters.

If you are dealing with acreage instead of small space, you will require some heavy equipment. Perhaps the mower will become the riding kind, with attachments such as hauling carts and lawn sweepers. Most of these start at about $1,000 and go up. A rotary tiller, and there are many models in various price ranges, is a lifesaver for preparing new gardens for vegetables, shrubs, and flowers and for cultivating the soil whenever it is necessary. The mechanized leaf blowers are a help for those who want an especially neat garden area that may be surrounded by large shade trees, whose annual leaf fall can be smothering. Leaf blowers can be too efficient and will also blow away leaf mold and mulch, which is desirable all year around shrubs such as the broad-leaved evergreen group.

An electric hedge trimmer speeds the job considerably, but if your hedge is not extensive and you are mainly trimming soft

The essential tools for a vegetable or flower garden.

growth, you can get along very well with the lighter-in-weight cordless hedge trimmer and hand-powered shears.

As your garden interests expand, you will require hand pruners for rosebushes and other shrubs, and possibly lopers, which are long-handled pruners, for thicker, hard-to-reach canes of roses, raspberries, and other shrubs.

Once tools and larger equipment start accumulating, the problem of storage arises. A few tools can usually be hung in the garage or, less conveniently, stored in a cellar or back entry. Often a tool house, a version of the old-fashioned potting shed, is a solution. Unfortunately, many of the prefab metal storage sheds available from local outlets or mail order, while efficient, are just plain ugly. Sometimes they can be repainted to mimic wood and be screened by shrubbery. Wooden tool sheds, usually also pre-fabricated, are also available, and some are fairly innocuous in appearance. If you are handy you can construct your own.

While few gardeners take the time, it does pay to take care of your tools and equipment, beyond giving them shelter when not in use. Hand tools can be cleaned in the fall and coated with rust-inhibiting oil. Do not expect hand pruners to cut through stems large enough for a pruning saw or heavy-duty lopers.

TRANSPLANTING. See Planting and Transplanting.

TREES. Trees have much in common with shrubs. Both are woody plants, making them the permanent elements in a landscape. The separation between trees and shrubs is not always clear-cut, but generally trees are single-trunked (there are many exceptions, though) and larger than shrubs. There are evergreen trees, both coniferous and broad-leaved, with the majority of the latter being found in mild climates, and deciduous or leaf-losing trees.

ESTABLISHED TREES—Starting out with a treed property can be an asset. Established trees imbue the land with a sense of time-lessness. They are a link with the past yet give us something to look forward to as they change their appearance with the seasons. Their presence can help in planning garden details, and the number and kind can shape the overall landscape scheme. (See Landscaping.)

You may have to remove some trees to open areas to light and direct sunshine, but before making hasty decisions about re-moval, evaluate each tree. Many well-treed properties may re-quire only minimal landscaping if you decide on a naturalistic approach. After you do some thinning and removal of lower branches (see Pruning), you have the basic components of a low-maintenance garden, with the trees forming a canopy for wild flowers and other naturalized plant groupings. (See Shade and Wild Flowers.)

PLACES FOR TREES—The raw, treeless property also offers op-portunities. Here is a chance to start fresh, choosing from an array of trees of varying shapes, sizes, and textures. For a large property in the country, one to several shade trees—plantings for the future—may be desired, while the average suburban property may have space for one or perhaps several of the smaller flowering trees. There are favored trees for every region, some native and others introduced. Where space permits, a mingling of both groups can supply diversity and yearlong interest.

It is obviously important to plant a tree in the right place the first time. Although even large trees can be transplanted fairly easily today with special tree-lifting equipment, you don't want to be calling in one of these mechanical monsters every few years as you rue the day you sited a tree too close to the house. Ideally, future tree plantings should be marked on your original landscape plan rather than dotted here and there on the spur of the moment.

An exception to random planting might be the making of a grove of trees for quick shade and a future woodland. Young trees can be planted randomly about 8 feet apart. They will intermingle in their growth, but you can trim off lower limbs and even thin out a tree or two later. A mixture of trees can be used or all one kind, including coniferous kinds. (See Evergreens.)

Trees, along with larger shrubs, are the framework of a property and should be planted to the sides (not closer to the house than 8 to 9 feet) and not plunked down in the center of the front yard. Trees can be placed where they help screen undesirable views or create privacy. At the same time, their mostly vertical growth relieves the monotony of much lower plant groups and varies the skyline of the property. An occasional small but spreading tree can make long, narrow properties appear wider.

One of the most logical places for planting a small tree is on or just off a terrace or patio. Such a tree can be attractive to the viewer indoors at all seasons, yet serve the function of providing some morning or afternoon shade without eventually blocking sun, which must reach other plantings beyond this outdoor living area. Those with city roof and backyard gardens, can plant small trees in large tubs, which often last well for several years. (See also Terraces.)

CHOOSING AND BUYING TREES—Check over lists of recommended trees (call the Cooperative Extension Service for regional suggestions) and consider those that promise more than one season of interest. No flowering tree has a very long flowering period, but many have fruits that develop slowly and may eventually provide food for birds. Others may give a colorful foliage display before the leaves drop in fall. In cold climates, there is the silhouette of the tree in winter and, possibly, attractive bark textures. In mild climates, there are many beautiful flowering trees that remain evergreen.

The 'Bradford' flowering pear is being widely planted as a street tree, but it is compact enough in habit for most home grounds. Its fine display of white flowers in spring is followed by tiny pears that attract birds during the winter. More familiar are three flowering dogwoods, each of which is uniquely suitable for specimen use, that is, either alone or as an accent among shrubbery, or, on the larger property, at the edge of a woodland. The well-known flowering dogwood (*Cornus florida*), native over much of the eastern half of the country, the somewhat similar Pacific dogwood (*C. nuttallii*), and the Japanese dogwood (*C. kousa*) all have outstanding spring flowers, red fall fruits, spectacular fall foliage colors, and interesting patterns of branch growth.

Of course, where space is ample, establishing a small arboretum can be an engrossing project. Here trees and shrubs can be collected for particular qualities even if they do not rate among the wonders of the four seasons.

Trees, being woody plants, are sold in spring and fall when they are dormant. The roots of young plants are often in a bareroot condition; larger trees may be balled and burlapped or in containers. For planting techniques, see Planting and Transplanting.

▩▩▩▩ SAMPLER OF SMALL TREES ▩▩▩▩

Birch, Cutleaf Weeping or **European** (*Betula pendula*). White bark. Slender silhouette with drooping branches. 35 to 50 feet.

Cherry, Autumn Flowering (*Prunus subhirtella* 'Autumnalis'). Spring and fall show of white flowers on graceful, rounded tree to 20 feet.

Cherry, Kwanzan *(Prunus serrulata* 'Kwanzan'). Large double-pink flowers in spring. 20 to 25 feet.

Crab Apple, Flowering *(Malus* species and cultivars). A truly remarkable group of small trees. Very hardy, with beautiful spring flowers and ornamental fall fruits. 15 to 25 feet. Most are quite pest-resistant and vary in form from vase to spreading habits. Some have tinted foliage.

Dogwood, Flowering *(Cornus florida).* Many cultivars now of this white-flowering favorite, including double-flowered, pink to near red, and variegated leaf. 25 feet.

Golden-rain Tree *(Koelreuteria paniculata).* Rather wide-spreading shade tree with panicles of yellow flowers in midsummer. 30 feet.

Hawthorn, English *(Crataegus laevigata).* Neat, compact. 'Paul's Scarlet' has deep red double flowers; 'Plena,' double white. Red fruits in fall. 18 to 25 feet.

Magnolia *(Magnolia* species and cultivars). Famous flowering trees for the South and North, some of which are evergreen. Star magnolia *(M. stellata),* fragrant, early white flowers, often nipped by frosts, 15 to 20 feet; 'Merrill,' hybrid, similar white flowers, 25 feet; saucer magnolia *(M.* x *soulangiana),* spreading form and large pink flowers, 25 feet.

Maple *(Acer* species and cultivars). Magnificent shade trees for ample space. For less roomy properties: Fullmoon Maple *(A. japonicum).* Slow-growing, to 25 feet, with excellent fall foliage color. Japanese Maple *(A. palmatum).* Many cultivars, becoming living works of art when well grown. Partial shade, humus-rich, moisture-retaining soil. 8 to 10 feet. Amur Maple *(A. ginnala).* Tough, fairly fast-growing and very hardy. Often multistemmed, spreading, and 15 to 20 feet tall. Good fall leaf colors. Tolerant of dry soil.

Pear, Bradford *(Pyrus calleryana* 'Bradford'). See Choosing and Buying Trees. Not drought-resistant so add plenty of peat moss to planting hole.

Plum, Newport Cherry *(Prunus cerasifera* 'Newport'). Neat little tree, fairly fast-growing, to 15 to 20 feet. White flowers before red-purple leaves unfold. Very hardy.

Sourwood *(Oxydendrum arboreum)*. Slow-growing native. Often called lily-of-the-valley tree after its white drooping flowers in summer. 15 to 20 feet. Brilliant fall foliage. Humus-rich soil; water in drought.

Styrax, Japanese *(Styrax japonica)*. Small, rounded tree with drooping white bells in early summer. Ideal terrace selection. Needs humus-rich soil.

Viburnum, Siebold *(Viburnum sieboldii)*. Single or multitrunked large shrub or small tree, slowly reaching 10 to 20 feet. White flowers in spring, then slow-ripening fruits, first pink to red, finally blue-black. Very hardy. Not drought-resistant.

TUBERS. See Bulbs.

V

VEGETABLES. Vegetable gardening can be so simple and so quick with results. Sowing a row of bush beans can be child's play compared to some long-term gardening projects. (Vegetable gardening is one way to introduce children to the gardening world, either at home or through programs at some public gardens.) You can grow vegetables on an acre, as many people do, or almost on a postage stamp with minimal equipment and expense. (See Tools and Equipment.)

A FEW REQUIREMENTS—Choose a sunny location, although vegetables tolerate a few hours of shade, especially lettuce in summer. Deep, rich soil is the ideal, but fortunately, when improved by the addition of organic matter and fertilizers, most average soil will serve if the drainage is good. (Celery is about the only vegetable that will grow in constantly wet soil.) If you have doubts about your soil, have it tested. (See Soil.)

GARDEN SIZE AND SHAPE—Once you have selected the location for a garden, decide on its size and shape. Rectangles and squares are the usual shapes, but a triangle, perhaps to fit a sunny corner, or even a circle or an oval are acceptable. A convenient size for a family of two or three would be a plot about 25 feet by 25 feet or

30 feet by 20 feet or thereabouts. Even the postage-stamp size, say about 6 feet by 3 to 4 feet, allows space for three or four tomato plants, two or three summer squash plants, a patch of bush beans, and a row of salad plants. A garden of this size is easily reached from all sides.

FOOD FOR THOUGHT—Most vegetables are annuals, their seeds being sown in the open ground in spring. However, vegetables have different lengths of growing time before their harvesting can begin. Some mature very quickly after their seeds have been sown, while others require a longer growing period. Tomatoes, eggplants, and peppers are examples of the latter, so in northern regions their seeds are given an early start indoors, usually about 5 to 8 weeks before the last frosts end and it is safe to set them outside. (See Propagation.) Those who prefer not to bother with seed sowing indoors have the convenience of buying at garden centers plants that have been grown by bedding-plant specialists.

Some examples of quick-maturing vegetables are most kinds of lettuce, radishes, curly cress, roquette or rocket salad, and turnips.

Vegetables also differ in their resistance to cold, just as do annual flowering plants. Peas, including the edible-podded varieties, are very hardy. Their seeds must be sown outdoors early so the plants reach maturity before hot weather settles in. After their pods have been harvested, the vines are finished and can be placed on the compost pile. The space taken by the peas can be filled with bush or pole beans, summer squash, or a heat-resistant lettuce like 'Salad Bowl.'

Other hardy vegetables are radishes, lettuce, cabbage, broccoli, onions, and spinach. Their seeds can be sown about the same time as peas or soon after, and hardened-off transplants (see Propagation) of lettuce, cabbage, broccoli, and onions can be set out a good month before the frost-free date of the region. (Spinach seedlings should not be transplanted.) Husky young lettuce seedlings will survive temperatures as low as 28° F.

The very hardiness of these vegetables makes them poor candidates for the summer garden in much of the North, although there are heat-resistant lettuce varieties. You can give these cold-tolerant vegetables a second chance by sowing their seeds in summer so they can be harvested in the colder weather of fall, and in mild climates, all winter. Kale is another cold-tolerant vegetable, whose seeds are always sown in mid- to late summer. It is so hardy that the plants survive northern winters, either under the snow or a light protective mulch of straw or leaves.

VEGETABLE SEEDLINGS NOT USUALLY TRANSPLANTED

(t: can be transplanted if seeds are sown in peat pots)

BEANS	PARSNIPS
BEETS	PEAS
CORN	PUMPKIN *t*
CUCUMBER *t*	RADISHES
MELONS *t*	RUTABAGA and TURNIPS
MUSTARD	SPINACH
OKRA	SQUASH *t*

VEGETABLE SEEDS TO SOW OUTDOORS IN EARLY SPRING

CRESS, GARDEN and UPLAND	PEAS (very early)
LETTUCE	RADISHES
ONIONS (also sets and plants)	ROQUETTE (Rocket Salad)
PARSLEY	SPINACH

VEGETABLE PLANTS TO BUY AT GARDEN CENTERS IN SPRING

BROCCOLI	LETTUCE
CABBAGE	PEPPER
EGGPLANT	TOMATO

VEGETABLE SEEDS TO SOW OUTDOORS AFTER WEATHER WARMS

BEANS	CORN
BEETS	CUCUMBER
CARROTS	LETTUCE

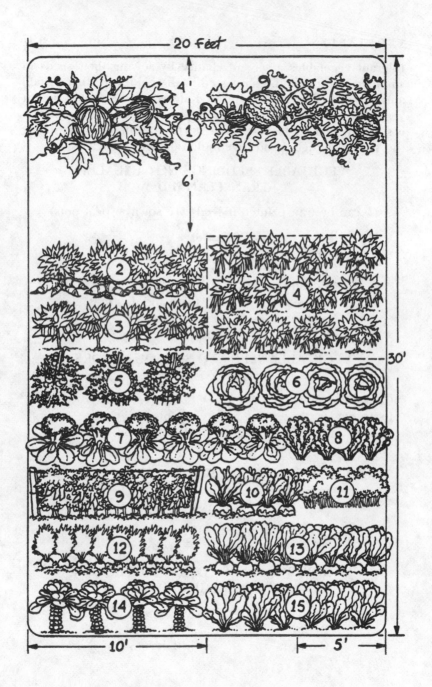

MELON (Cantaloupe)	SQUASH
OKRA	SWISS CHARD
PUMPKIN	WATERMELON

VEGETABLE SEEDS TO SOW IN SUMMER FOR FALL HARVESTS

BROCCOLI	LETTUCE
CABBAGE	KALE
CAULIFLOWER	ROQUETTE
CHINESE CABBAGE	TURNIP

PLANNING AND PLANTING—With seed catalogues close at hand (most of them arrive in January and February), make a list of the vegetables you *do* like and can grow. Then draw a rough plan, based on the size and shape of your garden-to-be, and start filling in your selections. The better seed catalogues will be most helpful, usually picturing the vegetable so you can get an impression of its habit, supplying the number of days from sowing or transplanting to harvest, suggested planting distances, and general how-to-grow tips. Some of this information is on seed packets, too.

PLAN FOR A NUTRITIOUS GARDEN

This garden, adapted from a plan by Gardens for All, a nonprofit association that promotes gardening, contains vegetables of proven nutritional content. Although lettuce is comparatively low in food value, it makes salads of more nutritious vegetables more inviting. KEY: 1 Melons or winter squash. 2 Potatoes or tomatoes and peppers. 3 Peppers (preceded by spinach). 4 Bean area (10 feet by 6 feet): 'Jumbo' snap beans or black-eye peas; lima, pinto, or white beans. 5 Tomatoes. 6 Cabbages (cut first heads carefully and smaller heads will form inside the outer leaves). 7 Broccoli. 8 Kale (preceded by lettuce and/or spinach). 9 Peas. (Follow with more broccoli or heat-resistant lettuce, such as 'Ruby' or 'Salad Bowl.') 10 Turnips. 11 Mustard. 12 Carrots. 13 Beets. 14 Brussels sprouts or cauliflower (preceded by spinach and other greens). 15 Swiss chard (preceded by lettuce).

Tomatoes, especially when staked or grown in wire-mesh cages, pole beans, and corn are tall growers, so try to place them to the north so they do not shade lower plantings.

A little cheating on suggested planting distances is allowed but there must be space for you to reach the plants, usually about a foot between rows. Where space is limited, try planting and sowing in blocks or very wide rows rather than single or close-together double rows. Peas, beans, spinach, lettuce, radishes, beets, carrots, and onions are among the vegetables that are suited to this type of planting. The blocks can be 2 feet or more in width, and while the plants will be close together, there will be fewer if any weeds and mulching will be unnecessary. It always pays to sow short rows of lettuce—as often as every 10 days during spring—to keep a gradual supply over a longer period rather than having the plants all mature at the same time.

If you elect to grow perennial vegetables, asparagus and rhubarb, place them at one end of the garden so their presence in springs to come does not interfere with annual soil tilling. Two or three clumps of rhubarb are sufficient usually—most people tend to overplant it, thus wasting valuable space.

Garden books and articles often emphasize "succession of crops," that is, the planting of another vegetable in the place of one that is finished, so no garden space is wasted. This is not always practical in very small plots, and the practice itself assumes that you have devoted much space to such early-maturing vegetables as peas and spinach. However, if you have skipped these very early crops, there will be a chance to practice succession by filling space first occupied by bush beans or summer squash with kale or broccoli for late fall harvesting.

Another must for old vegetable-garden hands is "crop rotation," again, a good practice and one that makes sense for larger gardens. The idea here is that the same vegetable or its relatives must not be replanted in the same space year after year, thus thwarting diseases and certain other soil pests that hold over. Examples of related vegetables would be broccoli, Brussels sprouts, cabbage, and kale. Another related group would be tomatoes, eggplants, and peppers. Rotating crops is not so easy in a small garden, but even a partial rotation is better than none.

If the vegetable garden is a new one in soil that has not been cultivated before, it will save time and also be beneficial if preparation can be done in the fall. Fallen leaves and grass or whatever other growth was in the area can be tilled or dug under and should be decayed by spring. Fresh manures can be safely applied at that time, also. Ground limestone can be applied if a soil test indicates its need. Of course the same procedure can be followed in spring, but the manures should be partially decayed. (See Digging, Manures, Peat Moss, and Soil.) If your soil is excessively clayey, you should not work it extensively too early in the spring while it is still wet. This can damage its texture, so wait until it is crumbly.

Spring is the time to apply 5-10-5 or a similar fertilizer at the rate of about 3 to 4 pounds per 100 square feet. Fork or till it in, then rake over the area where you plan to sow your first seeds to firm and level the soil.

If you are sowing in a single row, use a line stretched between two stakes to mark it so you can make a furrow or shallow trench. Its depth depends on the size of the seeds and is given on the seed packet. (See Propagation.)

If you were Jack, beanstalks would immediately spring up, but the wait for emergence of seedlings will not be too long. Warm-weather vegetables usually appear quickly, but peas and other cool-soil vegetables are slower.

As spring progresses, you will be doing more seed sowing and also setting out transplants—seedlings of tomatoes, peppers, and eggplants that you have grown yourself indoors or purchased from bedding plant specialists. See Propagation and Planting and Transplanting.

WATERING AND MULCHING—The earliest-sown seeds often grow well enough without the need of the hose or watering can, as the temperatures are still cool and the soil moist from late winter rains. Later, though, as it warms, and depending, too, on the type of soil you have, sown seeds may need a good sprinkling when the rains fail. Transplants must always be well watered after planting.

Applying a mulch about 4 inches deep will help conserve soil moisture and also reduce the weed population that is beginning to burgeon, if you have not been vigilant and lightly stirred the soil with a hoe from time to time. Even with a mulch, you may have to hand-pull weeds close to the vegetables, as hoeing can injure their roots.

HARVESTING TIPS—To maintain production, harvest mature vegetables regularly. Cucumbers and squash simply stop bearing if fruits are not picked and allowed to reach immense proportions with ripe seeds. Pick squash at about 6 inches in length and cucumbers well before the fruits become bloated and yellowish. (Cucumbers differ in size according to variety.) When harvesting spinach, pull the entire plant. Loosehead lettuce varieties, such as 'Salad Bowl,' 'Ruby,' and 'Green Ice,' can be harvested over a long period by picking leaves rather than the whole plant. The Boston or Butterhead types form heads, and the entire plant should be harvested.

Bean pods develop very fast in warm weather, so picking should be done every few days. Freeze the surplus. The bush bean called 'Jumbo' is one snap bean that retains its flavor and quality even when the rather flat pods are 8 inches long.

VEGETABLES IN CONTAINERS—Many vegetables do surprisingly well in pots, planters, bushel baskets, and even in plastic trash bags. The key to success is never letting the soil become bone dry and maintaining a regular fertilizer schedule. While you can grow some of the small-fruited tomatoes ('Toy Boy,' 'Tiny Tim,' and 'Florida Basket') in 6- to 8-inch pots, they do dry out fast once fruiting starts. Other tomato varieties bred for container growing, such as 'Patio' and 'Patio Prize,' need larger containers that will hold 2 to 5 gallons of soil or synthetic mix, or a combination of the two. A pepper or eggplant will do quite well in a gallon pail (a plastic or metal pail that has developed a few leaks is fine for this purpose—the leaks provide some drainage yet the soil will not dry out as fast as in a clay pot).

If you are gardening on a city balcony or terrace, you can grow pole beans in a bushel basket or the like if you provide strings that the plants can twine around to reach a railing or other support.

You can also sow seeds of some of the small carrot varieties in a window box or planter. (See also Pots and Other Containers.)

COPING WITH PESTS—The worst pests may be four-footed—deer, rabbits, woodchucks, raccoons, or playful dogs. A fence is the best solution. Deer, of course, can soar over most fences and raccoons can climb them, while young rabbits can squeeze through openings in wide-mesh wire fencing. Many garden centers now carry wire-mesh fencing with a smaller mesh section at the base to discourage the bunnies. If you are plagued with any of these creatures, consult your county's cooperative extension people. The land-grant universities of each state usually offer special publications on coping with animals. For instance, *Control of Wildlife Damage in Houses and Gardens* is available from Cornell University for $2.50. (Cornell Information Bulletin No. 176, Distribution Center, 7 Research Park, Cornell University, Ithaca, N.Y. 14850.)

If you do fence in your vegetable garden, use the fence as a support for cucumber vines. You will save space by sending the vines upward, and the fruits will be straight and unmuddied. (You could also start with peas as an early crop and follow with cucumbers.)

While spraying is always more efficient in attacking most insect problems in the vegetable garden, it is much more convenient to have a good duster (available in garden centers) handy. It can be whisked out in a second and put to immediate use (but not while bees are present). There are many all-purpose dusts formulated for the most common pests, although you may have to invest in more than one kind. (I keep two dusters, one filled with rotenone and the other a combination dust, and manage fairly well.)

You can buy canister dusters already filled with various chemical dusts, but they do not work very well (for me, anyway) and are expensive compared to a separate duster that will last for years and bulk supplies of dusts.

In addition to wiping out occasional infestations of aphids, a duster will help control the following common vegetable pests.

Green-colored cabbage worms, the larva of small yellow moths that flitter throughout the summer garden, usually in pairs. The worms are partial to all members of the cabbage family. Controls are spraying with Thuricide or Biotrol, biological controls, or dusting with rotenone, rotenone-pyrethrum, or Sevin as soon as you see the tiny worms. Cease spraying or dusting 3 days before harvest.

Flea beetles make small holes in foliage of newly set tomatoes, eggplant seedlings, and new foliage of bean plants. Dust with rotenone or malathion.

Cutworms, fat, dark worms often found in a half-moon position near plants, are the culprits when you find young plants chopped off at ground level or just beneath it. They live in the soil and eat at night, doing most of their dining in the spring. Paper collars or open-ended tin cans are sometimes sunk around newly set transplants. Or dust the soil around the plants with diazinon or methoxychlor.

The squash vine borer tunnels into stems of squash and sometimes melons and cucumbers. It is difficult to control, but often the vines prevail, continuing to produce fruits. Sevin, methoxychlor, or malathion are recommended controls, applied as a dust when the leaves form and thereafter three times at 10-day intervals. In much of the North, a second sowing of summer squash can be made in early July, which will take over as the borer-weakened plants give up.

Slugs are worst in spring and fall and can be very destructive among succulent lettuce plants. Baits are available, and there is also the beer-in-a-sunken-bowl solution. (See Pests and Diseases.)

▨▨▨▨ A SAMPLER ▨▨▨▨
OF WORTHWHILE VEGETABLES

Asparagus. A perennial, but once established, production continues every spring for years. Roots are planted in spring.

Beans, Snap. High quality, nutritious, and bountiful harvests in 40 to 55 days from seed sowing. There are bush and pole varieties. Pole beans are space savers. Tie three or four stout stakes about 6 feet tall together at the top to form a tepee. Vines will twine around and up them. Plant both kinds of beans about 2 inches apart. Try not to handle plants when they are wet.

Broccoli. Buy transplants in spring, or sow seeds in late spring to early summer outdoors for fall and early winter harvest. Plant about 18 inches apart. Pick off by hand or dust worms lurking in leaves.

Cabbage. See Broccoli.

Carrots. Seeds germinate slowly. Mix radish seeds with them to mark rows. Sow seeds a few weeks before last average frost date. For best flavor and texture, pull when small.

Cucumbers. Choose bush types like 'Spacemaster' for limited space, or grow vining varieties against a trellis or fence, as previously suggested. Always plant disease-resistant varieties.

Eggplant. 'Dusty' or 'Ichiban' produce small fruits but many more per plant. Needs lots of sun and warmth. Buy transplants or sow seeds indoors about 6 to 8 weeks before last frost.

Lettuce. You can grow lettuce carelessly, sowing the seeds with only a slight covering because their germination needs light, thinning the plants as necessary to prevent crowding, and harvesting as they mature. Or you can give them more loving care and be repaid with fabulous results. Sow seeds, then transplant seedlings into humus-rich soil, watering copiously as necessary.

Peas. For the early-bird gardener. For a taste treat, grow the edible-podded, bushy 'Sugar Ann' or 'Sugar Bon' snap peas.

Peppers. Buy transplants or sow seeds indoors as with eggplant. You can also grow peppers in an 8-inch or larger pot.

Radishes. Fast-growing root vegetable for cool weather. Sow seeds in early spring and again about 10 days later. To deter maggots in roots, dust seed area with diazinon at sowing time.

Spinach. Sow seeds early in humus-rich soil. Use raw in salads if you lack space for a generous sowing.

Summer Squash. Several kinds here, including zucchini, yellow crookneck types, patty pan, and vegetable spaghetti (a viner that needs lots of space). Prolific and delicious. (Winter squash need more garden space and a longer growing season, but if you have the room, they are most rewarding in flavor and nutrition.)

Tomato. Buy transplants or grow from seed sown indoors about 5 to 6 weeks before last frost date. (See Propagation.) Incorporate liberal amounts of organic matter (compost, rotted manure, etc.) and a scant handful of 5-10-5 fertilizer into planting hole, mixing all ingredients together with a fork. If you are using a special tomato or vegetable fertilizer, follow directions on its package. Otherwise, do not feed plants again until fruits begin to form. To save space, enclose largest-growing varieties (called indeterminate) in wire cages or towers available at garden centers or through mail-order sources. The cages will have to be supported by one or two stakes to keep them from tipping over as the fruits develop.

Do not set tomatoes (or peppers and eggplants) in the ground until it has warmed, although you can plant a few weeks earlier under protection of little "hothouses"—waxed paper Hotkaps (available in garden centers), or plastic gallon-size cider or milk jugs, with their bottoms cut off. These little hothouses will keep the plants cosy even during frost nights, and the plants grow fast. Make a hole in the top of the Hotkap for ventilation as the weather warms. Don't close the tops of the plastic bottles—the small opening is needed for ventilation even during cool weather. Remove both kinds of protection as soon as frost danger ends and weather warms.

Mulch tomato plants, but not before the soil warms, as applying the mulch too early will keep the soil cool. Use grass clippings, half-rotted compost, pine needles, leaves, or black plastic. The mulch conserves moisture needed by the robust plants, and may deter blossom-end rot, a physiological condition manifested by black spots at the blossom end of fruits. It is believed to be caused by uneven soil moisture.

When tomato leaves are overly large and the plants slow to blossom, the problem may be an overdose of nitrogenous fertilizer. (See earlier fertilizer recommendations.)

It is no longer considered necessary to prune tomato plants; doing so may increase chances of sunscald on the fruits.

There are many tomato types and varieties available, enough to dizzy the new and not-so-new gardeners alike. When selecting

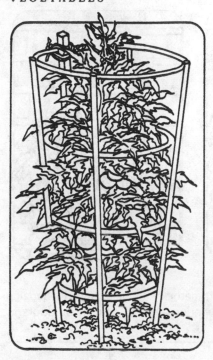

Support tomato plants with towers, available from garden centers, or improvise wide-mesh wire cages you can make from sturdy turkey fencing.

varieties, watch for those that are disease-resistant, indicated by the letters VFN (meaning resistant to verticillium and fusarium wilt diseases and root knot nematodes). Some varieties are resistant to all of these conditions. The well-known 'Floramerica' tomato is resistant to fifteen diseases. Also pay attention to maturity times of tomato fruits, usually given after the name of the variety, and referring to the number of days fruits ripen *after* the plants are set in the open ground. You can extend the tomato season at both ends by growing early, midseason, and late-bearing varieties. Even if you plan to buy transplants, being familiar with the characteristics of varieties can help in making your selections. When growing your own plants, be sparing with the seeds. The seed packets can be kept in a dry location for another year.

Several kinds of small-fruited tomatoes can be grown in hanging containers indoors in a sunny window and, of course, outdoors as well.

⬚⬚⬚⬚ SPECIAL PROJECT ⬚⬚⬚⬚
WINTER SALADS TO GROW INDOORS

Growing some of your salad ingredients indoors during the winter is not going to reduce the grocery bill appreciably, but it will intrigue your friends and give you satisfaction.

Rocket salad or roquette (also called arugula) is not always available during the winter months—at least not in my region—so growing your own leaves from seeds in a sunny window or under fluorescent tubes is definitely worthwhile.

Fresh watercress *is* often available in the supermarket, but it is most convenient to have your own supply for a last-minute garnish or for a teatime watercress sandwich. Another cress, the small-leaved curled cress, is also an easy-to-grow ingredient for salads or sandwiches.

Seeds of watercress are listed in seed catalogues, but a quicker method is to buy a bunch of watercress in the market in fall. Place several stems in a watertight container—I use a 5-inch ceramic basket and then hang it in a west-facing window, although any well-lighted exposure or fluorescent lights should be satisfactory.

Before adding the watercress cuttings and water, place a handful or so of unmilled sphagnum moss with some sand and peat moss in the container. Then fit a section of crumpled chicken wire across the top as a support for the watercress as it grows. It will take a few weeks for the cuttings to form roots, then attractive new vinelike growth begins, which is why I like to hang the container. All you have to do is maintain the water level and harvest the shoots as you need them. Add a liquid fertilizer, such as a fish emulsion, Schultz, or whatever you have, every time you replenish the water or as you think of it, and the growth will prosper.

The seeds of roquette can be sown in handy seed flats or a clay or plastic pot about 4 to 5 inches wide in diameter, or whatever container you have (a depth of 3 to 4 inches is adequate). Use a sterilized potting soil or synthetic mix (see Soil) and scatter the seeds over the surface rather than planting in rows. Cover lightly with the growing medium and keep moist. The seeds should germinate in 5 to 6 days, and soon you can harvest individual leaves or the whole plant. Roquette has a flavor distinctive from other mustards and is usually mixed with lettuce. You will want to make several sowings over the winter.

Curled cress is handled the same way as roquette, but it is even faster-growing. Harvest when the leaves are only a few inches high and make several sowings. Both roquette and curled cress need a cool, sunny window or a place under fluorescent lights.

You might want to experiment with some of the small-statured tomato varieties ('Toy Boy,' 'Tiny Tim') during the winter. They will need warmth and as much sun as possible, or grow them under fluorescent lights for a more reliable source of winter light. Even these small tomatoes need about a 6-inch pot, so you will need a hanging fluorescent shoplight that can be raised as the plants grow in height. Sow the seeds in late summer, fall, or early winter in sterilized potting soil or synthetic soilless mix. (See

Propagation.) Once the plants begin to flower, shake the pots frequently to stir the pollen so fruits will form. And keep a spray for white fly control handy. These little white flies are bound to appear. When fruits form, feed the plants with a liquid fertilizer diluted according to instructions.

VINES. Vines like the large-leaved Dutchman's-pipe once formed curtains of foliage for the verandas that surrounded most houses. The grand porch is no more, but the terrace or patio that has replaced it offers places for vines. The wisteria and less rampant clematis are possible choices for the pergola structures over some outdoor living areas.

DOWN-TO-EARTH USES FOR VINES—In some situations, vines are simply the only plants that will do the job. They can mask unattractive masses of masonry, including the cement block, so useful for building quick, inexpensive retaining walls. Evergreen vines are effective in all seasons, but any clinging vine can be selected. Some pruning back of overreaching stems may be required, but even this may be unnecessary if the walls are terracing rough areas unsuitable for more refined plantings.

The utilitarian chain link fence, a strong structure that makes no claim to beauty whatsoever, cries for camouflage. To fill this need you have several choices, two being Hall's honeysuckle and the silver lace vine. Both are fast-growing twiners that can clothe the fence with foliage (semievergreen in the case of Hall's honeysuckle) and flowers. Some clipping back will be required to keep the honeysuckle fairly compact, if a neat appearance is the aim. The silver lace vine will transform the prosaic fence into a billowing green and white beauty when in bloom. Virgin's bower *(Clematis paniculata* or *C. virginiana)* is faster-growing than most kinds of clematis and might also be considered.

Not all fences are as pedestrian as the chain link, but the stockade fence and certain other wooden fences can be made less austere with a vine covering. Self-supporting vines, such as evergreen English ivy or winter-creeper, can be planted at intervals and controlled so they do not cover every inch of the fence. The vines of Boston-ivy and Virginia-creeper will make a fine network rather than a dense covering.

Attractive wooden fences and stone and brick walls often need just a tracery of vine growth. The small-leaved Boston-ivy known as 'Lowii' can give this effect, although the vine is eventually vigorous and wide-spreading. Also suitable would be large-flowered clematis vines, which would need a trellis or wire supports to which they can cling.

VINES AND THE HOUSE—Vines are still used to dress up old buildings and old fences and walls, but the enthusiasm for planting vines against brick and stone buildings may be on the wane. It has recently been found that the holdfast rootlets that make some vines self-supporting eventually cause deterioration of the cement and perhaps of the bricks, too. The age of the building and the many years that the walls have been vine-clothed must be weighed rather than deciding arbitrarily not to plant vines in new situations. And who can envision academia without ivy-covered walls?

Twining vines should be kept off houses, too. Wisteria, for instance, can force its way under shingles and gutters. If you decide to plant a wisteria over an open structure near a terrace, chop back unmercifully wayward shoots that head for the house and roof. Nor should clinging vines be planted against wooden house walls, as their holdfast rootlets can eventually cause rotting. And, of course, the vines will interfere with painting.

If you want to enjoy the patterns of vinelike growth against house walls, consider training a shrub in espalier fashion, but set forward so air circulation and narrow access (for painting) are maintained. Some espaliers need a trellis for support, but most plants can stand alone. Good subjects for training are yews, pyracantha or firethorn, forsythia, junipers, and viburnums.

Most clematis vines can be grown near the house without fear of the vines becoming a nuisance. Since clematis cling by tendrils, a post wrapped in chicken wire or an open wire or wood trellis for support is needed. If you have climbing roses (not true vines, but merely shrubs with long canes that must be fastened to their support or allowed to ramble over walls, fences, or rough ground), consider growing a large-flowered clematis on the same trellis or fence.

ANNUAL VINES—If you are unsure of what vine to plant, experiment with some of the annual vines for a season. One of the faster-growing is the scarlet runner bean, easily grown from seeds sown in spring after the soil warms. If your growing season is a long one, you may harvest and eat the green pods that follow the cheerful red flowers. The morning glory and its close relative moonflower have always been popular vines for sunny locations. These three vines are twiners and can be supported by open trellises or slender poles. They do not transplant well unless the seeds have been sown in peat pots.

PLANTING VINES—Vines are really shrubs with climbing habits, so planting them is the same as shrubs. Most are shipped in spring and fall when dormant (see Shrubs and Planting and Transplanting), but a few kinds are available in containers for later planting. Clematis are often sold in full flower at garden centers. Follow the planting instructions that should accompany the vines and shift them from pot to ground with as little root disturbance as possible.

▨▨▨▨ A SAMPLER OF VINES ▨▨▨▨

Boston-ivy *(Parthenocissus tricuspidata)*. Fast-growing, robust vine. Clings by means of discs at ends of tendrils. Commonly used on stone buildings. Glossy foliage turns red in fall, blue-black berries that follow are ornamental.

Clematis. *(Clematis* species). Beautiful flowering vines to grow against a trellis to which they cling with tendril-like leaf stalks. For sun or part shade and a deeply prepared soil improved with organic matter. Mulch the root area. The small-flowered virgin's bower *(C. paniculata)* is less fussy and soon engulfs a stone wall, fence, or pergola. Large-flowered hybrids are more refined. Most clematis do not require much pruning. Some bloom on current or new growth, others on previous year's wood.

Honeysuckle *(Lonicera* species and cultivars). Twining vines; some, like Hall's honeysuckle, is so rampant it can become a pest. It can be useful in the country and at the seashore on any rough ground that needs a covering. More refined kinds include *L.*

henryi and *L. heckrottii.* 'Dropmore Scarlet' is very hardy and bears red flowers in summer. Honeysuckles will grow in sun or shade and most have deliciously fragrant flowers.

Hydrangea, Climbing *(Hydrangea anomala petiolaris).* High climbing vine that clings to supports by rootlets along the stems and can safely be allowed to clamber up trees. Handsome large white flower clusters in early summer. Vines are slow at first.

Ivy, English *(Hedera helix).* Evergreen climber as useful above ground as it is as ground cover. When climbing, it clings by rootlets along stems. Best in shade, especially in the North, where the leaves need protection from winter sun. It will climb onto trees and is not harmful, but too many ivy-clothed trunks can be gloomy.

Silver Lace Vine *(Polygonum aubertii).* Fast-growing twining vine with pretty filmy sprays of white flowers in late summer. For sun and grows well in sandy soil.

Sweet Pea, Perennial *(Lathyrus latifolius).* Nonwoody perennial vine with tendrils whose tops die back in winter. White to rose-colored flowers are pretty but lack the fragrance of the annual sweet pea. Rather untidy but useful in informal sunny situations as ground or fence cover. It will naturalize on sand dunes and banks and stabilize the soil.

Trumpet-creeper *(Campsis* species). Clings by rootlets along stems and can be showy with its red-orange flowers in summer along a sturdy fence. Prune back lateral growth to two or three buds in the fall or plants become so heavy they fall down.

Virginia-creeper *(Parthenocissus quinquefolia).* Native woodland vine that clings with tendrils. Brilliant red foliage in fall. Very hardy. Often found with poison-ivy, which has three leaflets, while Virginia-creeper has five.

Winter-creeper *(Euonymous fortunei* and cultivars). Evergreen vines or creepers that cling to supports with rootlets. Shade or part sun. Quite hardy.

Wisteria *(Wisteria* species and cultivars). This beautiful flower-ing vine is a strong-growing twiner. Can strangle a tree. Wisterias need strong support, a pergola or open-top shelter over a sunny terrace, so the beauty and fragrance of the flowers can be appreciated from below. Vines can also be trained along board and split rail fences but need annual pruning—the shortening of new growth in summer. Buy wisteria plants that are grafted or grown from cuttings of known flowering plants. Mix a handful or so of superphosphate in the planting hole and water well and thereafter as necessary until new growth shows.

W

WATERING. It sometimes seems that providing water for house plants, thirsty container-growing plants on a roof top or sunny terrace, vegetable and flower gardens, and newly transplanted shrubs is more time-consuming than any other gardening activity. (For more specific details on watering, see Annuals, Evergreens, Indoor Gardening, Perennials, Planting and Transplanting, Shrubs, Trees, and Vegetables.) One reason for emphasizing the importance of organic matter in the soil (see Compost and Soil) is that it does increase its moisture-holding capacity, which in turn can take some pressure off the gardener. Mulching, also emphasized, will slow water loss from the soil. It also suppresses weed growth, which competes for a share of moisture.

Yet when rainfall fails, the gardener has no alternative but to turn on the hose. It has been estimated that lawns and gardens need about 1 inch of water a week. But since a heavy clay soil is very moisture-retentive and a predominantly sandy one dries out quickly, a suggested rule is to keep the soil moist—not soggy—to the depth of the plants' roots. Making a judgment as to how moist or dry your soil is may not be as easy as it sounds, but with experience, forking into the soil to a depth of 6 to 8 inches or so and examining and feeling the soil should reveal whether it is bone dry or reasonably moist.

One myth about watering the garden seems to have been put to rest: it does no harm to water in the middle of the day in the hot sun, a time once thought to "burn" or injure the plants. However, watering in the hottest, brightest time of the day can increase evaporation, so morning or later in the afternoon may be preferable in that respect.

The reason that plants can be killed or "burned" after overdoses of fertilizers, or even correct amounts that have been improperly applied (e.g., in direct contact with the foliage or stems), is that concentrated fertilizer salts withdraw moisture from the plant tissues. Fertilizer should be thoroughly watered into the soil and washed off the plants immediately after applications.

A thorough watering puts the fertilizer into a dilute, soluble form that plant roots can safely absorb. Insufficient watering or fertilizer overdosing will result in a highly concentrated fertilizer solution near the soil surface, causing damage to roots and stems. This damage shows as leaf burn, yellowing, wilting, and sometimes the death of the plant.

OVERWATERING—There is no point in turning on the sprinkler and letting it run indefinitely. This can be wasteful in the case of sandy soils, which can only hold a limited amount of moisture, even with the addition of organic matter. In the case of heavy clay soils, overwatering fills the air spaces between the soil particles and deprives plant roots of oxygen. This prevents roots from absorbing water and nutrients, which is why potted plants sometimes wilt when their soil is too wet.

WEEDS AND WEED CONTROL. Weeds, part of the dark side of gardening, are bound to appear. A weed, after all, is simply a plant out of place. There is a thin line separating weeds from ornamental plants, and what a fastidious gardener or anxious farmer may disdain can be desirable to a naturalist or creative flower arranger.

Some common weeds are edible, two examples being the low-growing, fleshy purslane and lamb's-quarters. A few flowering plants, considered weeds when they invade a hay field, a suburban lawn, or a golf course, are being elevated to a special place in the sun as elements in the seed mixtures sold for low-maintenance wild-flower lawns or meadows. (See Wild Flowers.)

Many gardeners can live with a few weeds, but this is less tolerable when they get out of control, as in a vegetable or flower

garden, where they compete with the cultivated plants for water and nutrients and spoil the garden's appearance.

FRIEND OR FOE?—Weed seeds begin sprouting in the spring as the weather warms and at the same time that most vegetable and flower seeds are sown. How can the new gardener distinguish friend from foe? One way is to sow the seeds carefully in a row, rather than scattering them over a wider area, and to label each variety. Study the "seed" or first leaves as they appear so you can recognize them in the future when you may want to broadcast the seeds rather than starting them in a row. (See the endpapers.)

Some perennials in a flower garden may look weedlike as they make their new spring growth, but this growth is nearly always in decided clumps. Again, labels are a help, put in place in fall or whenever the plants are set out. Admittedly, it is difficult to keep them in place, especially when a mulch of leaves must be raked out of the garden in spring.

If weed seeds are cultivated out of existence as they appear in the flower garden, half your battle may be won. For as the perennials develop, they tend to shade the ground and crowd out weeds. There is usually more space for weed growth in the vegetable garden, but again, early cultivation with a hoe, then a mulch about 4 to 6 inches thick, set after most seeds have been sown and transplants are in place, should keep the garden reasonably weed-free.

CHEMICAL WEED KILLERS—Many new gardeners wonder why they cannot solve the weed nuisance once and for all by using a chemical weed killer (herbicide) the way farmers and nurserymen do. The reason is that farmers and other professional growers usually specialize in one kind of plant in a large area, while home gardeners grow a varying mixture of unrelated plants, often cheek by jowl. Under such conditions, a selective chemical con-

---

WEEDS
1 Annual bluegrass. 2 Crab Grass. 3 Broad-leaved plantain. 4 Purslane. 5 Ground-ivy. 6 Common chickweed. 7 Spotted spurge. 8 Dandelion. 9 Quack grass. 10 Heal-all.

trol for certain weeds may also injure tomatoes or flowering plants, wiping them out as efficiently as though the chemical had been intended for them in the first place. The chances are too risky to take.

Where weed killers make some sense for home gardeners is on lawns. Crab grass, an annual nuisance, can be virtually eliminated by preemergent chemicals that prevent the seeds from sprouting. Another weed killer, 2,4-D, can be applied to lawns to kill broad-leaved weeds. (See Lawns.)

Nonselective weed killers can be used on driveways and walks *if* there is no likelihood of the chemical running into lawns and areas of cultivated plants.

WOODY WEEDS—Owners of country and seashore properties are often plagued by poison-ivy, Japanese honeysuckle run amok, catbrier, wild grape vines, and Japanese-bamboo or knotweed (not a true bamboo at all, which shows how unreliable common names can be—it is *Polygonum cuspidatum*). These are all perennial, mostly woody plants, the first four bearing fruits attractive to birds, which help disperse the plants all over the place. The chemical glyphosate has proved to be very successful in wiping out these pests. It is available under the trade name Round-Up, for treating extensive patches of these weeds, and as Kleen-Up in a handy premixed spray bottle for spot applications. Follow the instructions carefully. Be patient. Glyphosate is a nonselective herbicide that will kill any plant reached by its spray. It is not a harmless detergent!

Some grubbing-out of wide-ranging roots of woody weeds may be necessary. Remember that every part of the poison-ivy plant (roots, stems, leaves, berries) can cause the itching skin rash at any time of the year.

WILD FLOWERS. Wild flowers can be found in all sorts of expected and unexpected places—along major highways and less-traveled country roads, in woods, next to streams and on bog hummocks, in meadows and overgrown hedgerows, on mountainsides and sand dunes—and more and more in backyard gardens. Although the dictionary defines wild flowers as plants not in cultivation, it is not a contradiction to talk about gardens of

Virginia-creeper (right), a native woody vine often confused with poison-ivy (left), has five leaflets.

---

wild flowers. For as more and more wild plants face extinction as their environments are destroyed, introducing them into the home landscape is one step toward their preservation. This does not mean that every wilding can adjust to a suburban plot. Yet with the diversity of gardens throughout the country in every climatic region, there should be space for an impressive number of wild plants.

KINDS OF WILD FLOWERS—A few native plants have an extensive range and can be found from one coast to another. For instance, the evergreen creeper known as bearberry *(Arctostaphylos uva-ursi)* is native to sandy and rocky land in the Northeast up to Labrador and Alaska, down to Indiana and Illinois, and in the West to New Mexico and California. Others may be confined to one region, such as the beautiful Oconee bells or shortia of the Blue Ridge Mountains.

Wild flowers also include woody plants—native trees and shrubs.

Not all plants found in a wild state are necessarily native to the region or to the country. They may be escapees from cultivation that are indigenous to another country. An example is the lovely weed Queen Anne's lace, which is native to Europe and Asia, but has certainly made itself at home here. Another alien is the tawny day-lily from Europe, but which long ago escaped from gardens. (See Naturalizing.)

Other wild flowers native to one part of our country have become accepted garden flowers in another region, and are often listed in seed catalogues along with the usual cultivated plants. The California-poppy *(Eschscholtzia californica)* is such a plant, being native to sandy soil regions of California, especially along the coast. Hybridizers have added rose, pink, and white flowers to the standard yellow of the wild plant. Just about every plant in its original form was wild somewhere.

GETTING STARTED WITH WILD FLOWERS—Look around and see how wild flowers can fit into your existing or being-planned landscape scheme. Are you striving for a naturalistic, low-maintenance garden for your property? (See Landscaping.) If so, wild flowers are obvious choices, as the majority, once established, require little care. If you have areas with varying amounts of shade, you may have an almost made-to-order habitat for many wild flowers and ferns. Many other wild flowers are found in sunny meadows. If you have areas of full sun, even a small field where you would prefer a flowering carpet in summer instead of a lawn that must be pampered, there are various kinds of wild-flower mixtures now available.

There may even be wild flowers on your property now. On new properties, it is helpful to survey the area in the spring and again a few times in summer, with a field guide featuring wild plants of the region handy, and perhaps an informed neighbor.

Many well-intentioned conservationists and new gardeners become hysterical at the notion of removing any wilding from its habitat. Wholesale plundering of any area not in danger of being developed is wrong, but careful collecting of a few plants for a wild flower garden is harmless and can aid in the preservation of the plants. At the risk of arousing the ire of some readers, here are a few guidelines to follow when collecting plants from the wild for your property:

Explain your mission to the owners of private land and receive their permission before you dig.

Study field guides or books on wild flowers that give the native habitat of the plants to be sure you can reasonably match it on your place. Of course if the wild flowers are growing near you and the environment—exposure and soil—is similar to your own, there should be no problem of the plant's adjustment to a new situation.

Dig at the right time of the year—spring or fall—and preferably after a substantial rain. Some wild flowers are very difficult to transplant because of extensive root systems or tap roots. An example is the bearberry, mentioned earlier, a woody vinelike creeper whose plants are almost impossible to dig successfully. But stem cuttings will root in a peat moss–sand mixture in a flat that is enclosed with plastic. The cuttings can be planted in the open ground in spring or potted for later transplanting. (See Propagation.) Other kinds of plants are best collected in "sods." That is, with a sharp spade, dig a square block around the plant or plants and then replant the entire sod without removing its original soil.

Always water newly moved plants well.

The next way to start a wild-flower garden is to buy plants or seeds, and there are specialists to supply both. A few nurseries still make no effort to propagate wild plants and instead collect rapaciously. Fortunately, the more reliable nurseries now propagate wild flowers as they do perennials.

Spring is the usual time to order and plant, with fall also being satisfactory, except perhaps in the coldest regions. Seeds of most kinds can be sown in spring or fall according to directions on the packets. Fall-sown seeds germinate in spring.

EASY WILD FLOWER GARDEN FOR SPRING—The most simple wild-flower garden can be planted under a small tree, such as a dogwood, fruit tree, or a shrub planting, or wherever there is light to part shade. Such a modest garden is a good introduction to wild flowers and would require little care.

The limited size of the garden makes it possible to practice an artful arrangement of plants, similar to one that might be encountered in a woods. Suitable plants are the Christmas fern (*Polystichum acrostichoides*), Virginia bluebells (*Mertensia virginica*), wild columbine *(Aquilegia canadensis)*, Solomon's-seal *(Polygonatum* species), and perhaps wild lily-of-the-valley *(Maianthemum canadense)*, a low-spreading plant for the foreground and to fill in around other plants at its own pace. These are perennial wild flowers, which should prosper in average soil into which peat moss and/or compost or leaf mold have been mixed.

WOODLAND GARDENING—A giant step beyond the previous wild-flower garden that offers more scope is the making of a woodland garden. This, of course, depends on your inheriting a wooded property, but with many country properties such a likelihood is possible. It can take up half of the land or much of the front yard or be a grove of a few trees, but whatever its size and kind of trees, it offers a challenge and opportunity.

As a beginning, make the suggested survey, noting any wild-flower colonies and desirable shrubs. Then identify the trees. If the shade seems too dense, remove a few trees or prune off lower branches and thin out some of the higher ones. Watch out for poison-ivy, a rampant vine and ground cover in woods and open areas. If you have any doubt of its identification, check with a neighbor or a county cooperative extension specialist. (See Weeds and Weed Control.)

Next, mark out meandering paths. If the area is modest, curving the path or paths can make it seem more mysterious and extensive. Take advantage of any large rocks or hilly terrain as you lay out paths and plan future plantings. Wild plants tend to form colonies, so plan on introducing new plants in groups of three to five, or more if space permits. Use ferns, both in groups and as single accents, just the way they are often observed along a natural woods trail.

A woodland garden can be restricted to the native plants of the region or to suitable natives from more distant parts of the country. Certain cultivated plants that will thrive in partial shade and that fit aesthetically into woodsy surroundings can be included. Personally, I would not add impatiens to a woodland garden, but several perennials, such as hosta (but not too many variegated-leaved varieties), bergenia, primroses, Christmas-rose, epimedium, and perhaps day-lilies, do not look out of place. Among shrubs, there are always many natives to consider, such as shadblow, summersweet or clethra, and deciduous (leaf-losing) azaleas. Alien shrubs that belong include rhododendron hybrids and evergreen azaleas, witch-hazel, and others.

One of the pluses of woodland gardening is that extensive working of the soil is usually impractical and undesirable. Some muscle may be required to grub out roots of weedy interlopers, such as grapevines, poison-ivy (with care, though, and when possible, use a weed killer for this one). Generally, though, soil areas can be prepared piecemeal, as needed for each new planting, by forking through the soil and adding peat moss, leaf mold, or compost, if the soil is essentially sandy and lacks humus. (See Compost and Soil.) Many woodland plants grow in acid to slightly acid soils. If the woods contain oak, sassafras trees, or wild blueberry or huckleberry shrubs, the soil is acid.

Maintenance in a woodland garden is minimal. You don't have to rake leaves in the fall or spend hours weeding. The leaves can remain where they fall, as in a natural woods, to form a mulch. Watering during drought is necessary, but with partial shade conditions and a constant mulch, the soil should become dry at a slower pace than in more sunny, crowded gardens.

⊠⊠⊠⊠ A SAMPLER OF ⊠⊠⊠⊠
SPRING-BLOOMING WILD FLOWERS FOR PART SHADE

BLOODROOT *(Sanguinaria canadensis)*, white, very early

COLUMBINE *(Aquilegia canadensis, A. caerulea)*, red and yellow, blue

FALSE SOLOMON'S-SEAL *(Smilacina racemosa)*, white plumes, then berries

FERN, CHRISTMAS *(Polystichum acrostichoides)*, evergreen, tough

FERN, ROYAL *(Osmunda regalis)*, airy, elegant, moist soil

FOAMFLOWER *(Tiarella cordifolia)*, white, humus-rich soil

GALAX *(Galax urceolata)*, white wands above glossy evergreen leaves

GERANIUM, WILD *(Geranium maculatum)*, magenta-pink

GINGER, WILD *(Asarum canadense)*, hidden brown flowers, early

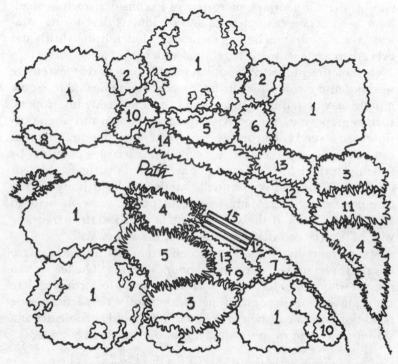

A WALK ON THE WILD SIDE

A walk on the wild side—a curving path among existing trees or large shrubs (or plant them for this purpose)—divides a wild-flower garden of ferns and other plants tolerant of part shade. KEY: **1** Large or small trees or large shrubs. **2** Shrubs, such as clethra, or evergreens, such as rhododendrons or mountain-laurel. **3** Day-lilies. **4** Christmas ferns. **5** Naturalized daffodils. **6** Solomon's-seal. **7** Trilliums or partridge-berry. **8** False Solomon's-seal. **9** Royal fern. **10** Epimedium. **11** Jack-in-the-pulpit. **12** Wild lily-of-the-valley. **13** Hosta. **14** May-apple. **15** Rustic bench, fallen log, large rock or rock grouping, or shallow watering place for birds and wildlife.

IRIS, CRESTED *(Iris cristata)*, blue, white, low
JACK-IN-THE-PULPIT *(Arisaema triphyllum)*, brown and green,
    then red berries
MAY-APPLE *(Podophyllum peltatum)*, fragrant white flower, large
    leaves
PARTRIDGE-BERRY *(Mitchella repens)*, evergreen creeper, red
    berries
SHOOTING-STAR *(Dodecatheon meadia)*, pink, lavender, white
SKUNK-CABBAGE *(Symplocarpus foetidus)*, brown flowers, very
    early
SOLOMON'S-SEAL, GREAT *(Polygonatum commutatum)*, yellow bells,
    then blue berries
TRILLIUM *(Trillium grandiflorum* and other species), white,
    maroon, yellow
VIRGINIA BLUEBELLS *(Mertensia virginica)*, blue bells
WILD LILY-OF-THE-VALLEY *(Maianthemum canadense)*, short white
    spikes

WILD FLOWERS IN SUN—There are many wild plants for sun, but
many are often more familiar as cultivated plants in flower gardens. For instance, the bright orange butterfly weed is showy
enough to compete with any man-made hybrid.

A sunny wild-flower garden can sometimes resemble a rat's
nest, but in the right situations, such as sun-drenched banks of
indifferent soil, along a drive of a country place, and around
seaside and lakeshore properties, there are many places appropriate for sowing wild-flower seeds or naturalizing purchased or
collected plants.

MEADOW WILD-FLOWER GARDENS—Anyone who has ever enjoyed the sight of a country field dotted with wild flowering plants
through the often tall grass can understand why the idea of creating a meadow wild-flower scene has such appeal today. And
undoubtedly, the search for alternatives to the high dollars and
high maintenance of lawn care has spurred interest in a solution
that eliminates frequent mowing and heavy fertilizer and weed
killer applications.

Seed mixtures are being formulated for just about every cli-

mate and exposure that exist over the country. The mixtures
contain balanced amounts of annuals, biennials, and perennials,
which means that a year or so will be required before most flowers bloom. However, you can also buy single amounts of one kind
of flower. Usually nonspreading grasses, such as fescues, are
suggested for mixing with the flower seeds, especially on slopes,
where erosion can occur. Not all the wild flowers are natives:
many from around the world are included.

From a landscaping point of view, the ideal meadow wild-
flower gardens are established on large fields and extensive lawn
areas of estates and country places, as they are more attractive
when viewed as part of a vista and may not stand up to the close
scrutiny directed at suburban lots. However, there is no reason
why owners of smaller properties can't experiment with miniature wild-flower meadows. One way to do this is to carve informal
strips or islands out of a lawn area. In fact, this method has been
used as a way to gradually convert large meadows on estates into
wild-flower preserves.

Whatever the situation, don't expect a miracle if you fling the
seeds over a lawn or pasture of strong-growing grasses. Few wild-
flower seedlings will survive with such competition. Instead,
close-mow any existing vegetation and then cultivate the soil.
Sow the seeds at the right time of the year—early spring or fall—
or as directed by the packager. Weeds will appear, but with anywhere from fifteen to twenty-four kinds of wild flowers in a mixture (as claimed by one formulator), separating weeds from legitimate seedlings would be tedious and impossible. The wild
flowers have been chosen for their ability to overcome most
weeds if sown on a prepared seedbed. Mowing at least once a
year is recommended for most mixtures, but the good news is to
forget about fertilizers!

A WILDFLOWER SAMPLER FOR SUN

ASTER, NEW ENGLAND (*Aster novae-angliae*), purple, very tall,
late

BLANKET FLOWER *(Gaillardia aristata)*, yellow, burgundy
COREOPSIS, LANCE-LEAVED *(Coreopsis lanceolata)*, golden yellow, tall
BEARBERRY *(Arctostaphylos uva-ursi)*, creeper, sandy, acid soil
BLACK-EYED SUSAN *(Rudbeckia hirta)*, yellow
BUTTERFLY WEED *(Asclepias tuberosa)*, orange, yellow
CULVER'S ROOT *(Veronicastrum virginicum)*, white, very tall
GENTIAN, CLOSED or BOTTLE *(Gentiana andrewsii)*, blue, late
GOLDENROD *(Solidago* species), yellow, late
HAREBELL *(Campanula rotundifolia)*, blue
LUPINE *(Lupinus perennis)*, blue to pink
PUSSYTOES *(Antennaria plantaginifolia)*, white, woolly

WINDOW BOXES. See Pots and Other Containers.
WOODLAND GARDEN. See Wild Flowers.

Z

ZONES, CLIMATE. The U.S. Department of Agriculture has produced a map (U.S.D.A. Plant Hardiness Zone Map, Miscellaneous Publication No. 814) on which the country is divided into ten zones according to climate. (The Arnold Arboretum, Jamaica Plain, Massachusetts, has developed a similar map.) Knowing the zone number in which you garden can be helpful when you order from mail-order nurseries, as many now list the zone to which a particular plant is hardy.

While the temperature of a geographical region is the major influence on a plant's hardiness, the amount of rainfall, soil, exposure, wind, presence of air pollution, and general care can also affect a plant's survival. Climates can vary in a zone and even on a property, where a microclimate may make it possible to grow a plant successfully beyond its hardiness limit. But it does not follow that a plant that requires a rest in winter—a period of dormancy during cold weather—can be established in mild regions where this chilling is absent.

Within a plant genus, the hardiness of its various species (see Nomenclature) can differ. An example is the viburnum, whose genus has species that are quite tender as well as others that are exceptionally hardy. Laurustinus, an evergreen viburnum *(Viburnum tinus)* from the Mediterranean region, has been assigned to Zone 7, where the range of average minimum temperatures is 0° to 10° F. Another viburnum, commonly known as highbush-cranberry *(V. trilobum)*, can be grown considerably farther north—to Zone 2, where the range of average annual minimum temperatures is −50° to −40° F. However, the highbush-cranberry can also survive throughout the North in the various cold zones below Zone 2.

Here are examples of a few other well-known shrubs and the zones in which they should perform well, the first zone number representing the coldest temperatures, the second the warmest:

AZALEA, ROYAL *(Rhododendron schlippenbachii)*. Zone 4 (−30° to −20° F) to Zone 8 (10° to −20° F).

BURNING BUSH *(Euonymus alatus)*. Zone 3 (−40° to −30° F) to Zone 9 (20° to −30° F).

BUTTERFLY BUSH *(Buddleia davidii)*. Zone 5 (−20° to −10° F) to Zone 9 (20° to −30° F).

DOGWOOD, RED-TWIG or TARTARIAN *(Cornus alba)*. Zone 2 (−50° to −40° F) to Zone 8 (10° to −20° F).

MOUNTAIN-LAUREL *(Kalmia latifolia)*. Zone 4 (−30° to −20° F) to Zone 8 (10° to −20° F).

SHADBLOW *(Amelanchier laevis)*. Zone 4 (−30° to −20° F) to Zone 8 (10° to −20° F).

PLANT HARDINESS ZONES

Zone 1 Below −50° F	Zone 6 −10° to 0° F
Zone 2 −50° to −40° F	Zone 7 0° to 10° F
Zone 3 −40° to −30° F	Zone 8 10° to 20° F
Zone 4 −30° to −20° F	Zone 9 20° to 30° F
Zone 5 −20° to −10° F	Zone 10 30° to 40° F

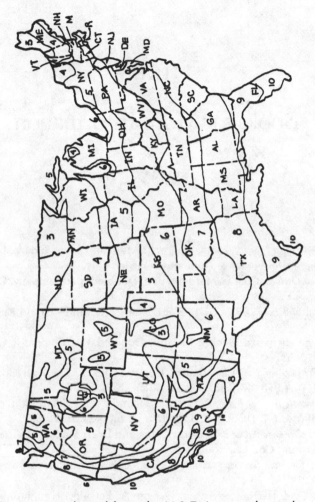

The above map, adapted from the U.S.D.A. map, shows the various hardiness zones, based on the annual minimum temperature for each zone.

THREE

Books for More Information

All About House Plants, Montague Free, revised and expanded by Marjorie J. Dietz. Doubleday & Company, Garden City, N.Y.

All About Orchids, Charles Marden Fitch. Doubleday & Company, Garden City, N.Y.

The Beautiful Food Garden, Kate Rogers Gessert. Van Nostrand Reinhold Co., New York.

Bonsai for Americans, George F. Hull. Doubleday & Company, Garden City, N.Y.

Color Schemes for the Flower Garden, Gertrude Jekyll. The Ayer Co., Inc., P.O. Box 958, 47 Pelham Rd., Salem, N.H. 03079.

The Complete Book of Bulbs, F. F. Rockwell and Esther C. Grayson, revised by Marjorie J. Dietz. J. P. Lippincott Co., New York.

The Complete Greenhouse Book, Peter Clegg and Derry Watkins. Garden Way Publishing Co., Charlotte, Vt. 05445.

Conifers for Your Garden, Adrian Bloom. Charles Scribner's Sons. New York.

A Field Guide to Trees and Shrubs, George A. Petrides. Houghton Mifflin Co., Boston, Mass.

A Field Guide to Wild Flowers, Roger Tory Peterson and Margaret McKenny. Houghton Mifflin Co., Boston, Mass.

The Garden Book, Peter Brookes. Crown Publishers, New York.

Garden Construction, Ogden Tanner. Time-Life Books, Inc., Alexandria, Va.

A Gardener's Guide to Plant Names, B. J. Healey. Charles Scribner's Sons, New York.

Gardening by the Sea from Coast to Coast, Daniel J. Foley. Parnassus Imprints, Box 335, Orleans, Mass. 02653.

Gardening for All Seasons—Complete Guide to Producing Food at Home 12 Months a Year, New Alchemy Institute Staff. Brick House Publishing Co., Andover, Mass. 01810.

Gardens in Glass Containers, Robert C. Baur. Hearthside Press, Inc., New York.

Herb Gardening at Its Best, Sal Gilbertie with Larry Sheehan. Atheneum/ SMI, New York.

Homeowners Complete Outdoor Building Book, John Burton-Brimer. Popular Science & Harper and Row, New York.

The Indoor Gardener's How-to-Build-It Book, Jack Kramer. Simon and Schuster, New York.

Japanese Gardens Today, Tatsuo and Kiyoko Ishimoto. Crown Publishers, Inc., New York.

Landscape Gardening, James Underwood Crockett. Time-Life Books, Alexandria, Va.

Natural Landscaping: Designing with Native Plant Communities, John Diekelman and Robert Schuster. McGraw Hill Book Co., New York.

Perennials, James Underwood Crockett. Time-Life Books, Alexandria, Va.

Perennials for Your Garden, Alan Bloom. Charles Scribner's Sons, New York.

Peter Malins' Rose Book, Peter Malins and M. M. Graff. Dodd, Mead and Co., New York.

Plant Propagation in Pictures, Montague Free, revised by Marjorie J. Dietz. Doubleday & Company, Garden City, N.Y.

Pruning Simplified, Lewis Hill. Rodale Press, Emmaus, Pa.

Rock Gardening, H. Lincoln Foster. Houghton Mifflin Co., Boston, Mass.

10,000 Garden Questions Answered by 20 Experts, edited by Marjorie J. Dietz. Doubleday & Company, Garden City, N.Y.

The Terrace Gardener's Handbook, Linda Yang. Doubleday & Company, Garden City, N.Y.

Theme Gardens, Barbara Damrosch. Workman Publishing Co., New York.

Wood and Garden, Gertrude Jekyll. The Ayer Co., Inc., P.O. Box 958, 47 Pelham Rd., Salem, N.H. 03079.

Wyman's Gardening Encyclopedia, Donald Wyman. Macmillan Co., New York.

FOUR

Sources for Seeds, Plants, and Supplies

W. F. ALLEN CO.
P.O. Box 1577
Salisbury, Md. 21801-1577
Fruits.

APPLEWOOD SEED CO.
5380 Vivian St.
Arvada, Colo. 80002
Wild flower, herb, and everlastings seeds.

ARTHUR EAMES ALLGROVE
P.O. Box 459
North Wilmington, Mass. 01887
Wild flowers, partridge-berry kits, terrarium supplies. Catalogue 50 cents.

BLUESTONE PERENNIALS
7211 Middle Ridge Rd.
Madison, Ohio 44057
Wide selection of young perennials.

BOUNTIFUL GARDENS
5798 Ridgewood Rd.
Willits, Calif. 95490
Seeds and supplies. Catalogue $1.

W. ATLEE BURPEE CO.
Warminster, Pa. 18974
Seeds, plants, and supplies.

CARROLL GARDENS
Box 310, Westminster, Md. 21157
Perennials, herbs, shrubs. Catalogue $1.50.

COMSTOCK, FERRE & CO.
Wethersfield, Conn. 06109
Seeds, including many herbs.

DAVIDSON'S QUALITY TOOLS
P.O. Box 195
Wellesley, Mass. 02181
Tools.

DEAN FOSTER NURSERIES
Hartford, Mich. 49057
Fruits.

DEGIORGI CO., INC.
Council Bluffs, Iowa 51502
Seeds. Catalogue $1.

DE JAGER & SONS
188 Asbury St.
South Hamilton, Mass. 01982
Bulbs.

EMLONG NURSERIES, INC.
2671 West Marquette Woods Rd.
Stevensville, Mich. 49127
Fruits, roses, and others.

EPICURE SEEDS LTD.
P.O. Box 450
Brewster, N.Y. 10509
Imported vegetable seeds.

HENRY FIELD SEED & NURSERY CO.
407 Sycamore St.
Shenandoah, Iowa 51602
Seeds and plants. Supplies.

GARDENS FOR ALL
180 Flyn Ave.
Burlington, Vt. 05401
Tools, growing supplies.

GIRARD NURSERIES
P.O. Box 42
Geneva, Ohio 44041
Trees and shrubs, evergreens, azaleas, dwarf conifers.

GURNEY SEED & NURSERY CO.
Yankton, S. Dak. 57079
Seeds. Nursery stock. Supplies and aids.

HARRIS SEEDS
3670 Buffalo Rd.
Rochester, N.Y. 14624
Seeds and supplies.

CHARLES C. HART SEED CO.
Main & Hart Sts.
Wethersfield, Conn. 06109
Seeds.

H. G. HASTINGS CO.
P.O. Box 4274
Atlanta, Ga. 30302
Seeds, nursery stock, supplies. Regional growing information.

HERBST BROTHERS SEEDSMEN, INC.
Brewster, N.Y. 10509
Seeds. Supplies.

HOLBROOK FARM & NURSERY
Route 2, Box 223, 4015
Fletcher, N.C. 28732.
Perennials and wild flowers. Catalogue $2.

JACKSON & PERKINS CO.
P.O. Box 1028
Medford, Ore. 97501
Roses.

JOHNNY'S SELECTED SEEDS
Box 650
Albion, Maine 04910
Seeds.

KARTUZ GREENHOUSES
1408 Sunset Dr.
Vista, Calif. 92083
House plants. Catalogue $1.

KELLY BROS. NURSERIES, INC.
425 Maple St.
Dansville, N.Y. 14437
General nursery stock.

KILGORE SEED CO.
1400 W. First St.
Sanford, Fla. 32771
Seeds for Gulf Coast regions.

LAMB NURSERIES
E. 101 Sharp Ave.
Spokane, Wash. 99202
Perennials, herbs.

A. M. LEONARD, INC.
6665 Spiker Rd.
Piqua, Ohio 45356
Tools and supplies.

LILYPONS WATER GARDENS
Lilypons, Md. 21717
Complete supplies for water gardens. Catalogue $3.50.

LOGEE'S GREENHOUSES
55 North St.
Danielson, Conn. 06239
Extensive house plant listings. Catalogue $2.50.

MELLINGER'S NURSERY
2310 West South Range Rd.
North Lima, Ohio 44452
House plants. Nursery stock. Supplies.

MICHIGAN BULB CO.
1950 Waldorf N.W.
Grand Rapids, Mich. 49550
House plants, bulbs, and nursery stock.

MILAEGER'S GARDENS
4838 Douglas Ave.
Racine, Wis. 53402
Perennials.

J. E. MILLER NURSERIES
Canandaigua, N.Y. 14424
Fruits.

MOORE MINIATURE ROSES
2519 E. Noble Ave.
Visalia, Calif. 93277
Miniature roses.

MUSSER FORESTS, INC.
Indiana, Pa. 15701
Evergreens, trees, and general nursery stock.

NICHOLS GARDEN NURSERY
1190 North Pacific Hwy.
Albany, Ore. 97321
Extensive listings of herbs, everlastings, vegetable seeds. Supplies.

NOR'EAST MINIATURE ROSES
58 Hammond St.
Rowley, Mass. 01969
Miniature roses.

GEORGE W. PARK SEED CO.
Greenwood, S.C. 29647
Seeds. Plants, including house plants. Indoor gardening supplies and lights.

PINE TREE GARDEN SEEDS
New Gloucester, Maine 04260
Small-size seed packets, supplies.

PLANTS OF THE SOUTHWEST
1570 Pacheco St.
Santa Fe, N. Mex. 87501
Wild flower, tree and shrub, vegetable seeds. Growing information. Catalogue $1.

ROCKNOLL NURSERY
9210 U.S. 50
Hillsboro, Ohio 45133
Rock garden plants, perennials, dwarf evergreens.

ROSES OF YESTERDAY AND TODAY
802 Brown's Valley Rd.
Watsonville, Calif. 95076
Roses old and new. Catalogue $2.

SEXTON NURSERY
23340 Doane Creek Rd.
Sheridan, Ore. 97378
Perennials, herbs, wild flowers. Catalogue $1.

SHADY OAKS NURSERY
700 19th Ave. N.E.
Waseca, Minn. 56093
Perennials, ferns, wild flowers, and shrubs for shade. Catalogue $1.

SMITH & HAWKEN
25 Corte Madera
Mill Valley, Calif. 94941
Quality garden tools, clay pots. Supplies.

SPRING HILL NURSERIES
110 West Elm St.
Tipp City, Ohio 45371
Roses and general nursery stock.

STOKES SEEDS, INC.
Box 548
Buffalo, N.Y. 14240
Seeds and supplies.

THOMPSON & MORGAN, INC.
P.O. Box 100
Farmingdale, N.J. 07727
Very extensive listings of seeds, some plants.

OTIS S. TWILLEY SEED CO., INC.
P.O. Box 65
Trevose, Pa. 19047
Seeds.

VAN BOURGONDIEN BROS.
245 Farmingdale Rd., Rt. 109
Babylon, N.Y. 11702
Bulbs, perennials.

VERMONT BEAN SEED CO.
Garden Lane
Bomoseen, Vt. 05732
Seeds, including old (heirloom) vegetable varieties.

VESEY'S SEEDS LTD.
York, Prince Edward Island
Canada COA 1PO
Seeds and supplies.

WAYSIDE GARDENS CO.
Hodges, S.C. 29695
Perennials and extensive tree, shrub, and bulb listings. Catalogue $1.

WHITE FLOWER FARM
Litchfield, Conn. 06759-0050
Perennials, general nursery stock. Catalogue $5.

Index

(Numerals in **boldface** indicate illustrations)